CW00688126

STAR TREK®

EPIC EPISODES

TITAN

WWW.TITAN-COMICS.COM

THANK YOU

Titan would like to thank the casts and crews of *Star Trek* and *Star Trek: The Next Generation*, CBS Television, Paramount Pictures, and John Van Citters, Marian Cordry and Risa Kessler at CBS Consumer Products for their invaluable assistance in putting this volume together.

Star Trek: Epic Episodes
ISBN: 9781785868795
Published by Titan
A division of Titan Publishing
Group Ltd.,
144 Southwark Street,
London
SE1 0UP

Collecting the best articles and interviews from *Star Trek* Magazine.

A CIP catalogue record for this title is available from the British Library.

First Edition November 2018
10 9 8 7 6 5 4 3 2 1

Printed in China.

Editor Nick Jones
Senior Editor Martin Eden
Art Director Oz Browne
Publishing Manager Darryl Tothill
Publishing Director Chris Teather
Operations Director Leigh Baulch
Executive Director Vivian Cheung
Publisher Nick Landau

Contributors:
David Bassom, Paul F. Cockburn, Keith R. A. DeCandido, Kevin Dilmore, Frank Garcia, David R. George III, Pat Jankiewicz, Nick Joy, Andy Lane, Rich Matthews, William S. McCullars, David A. McIntee, Joe Nazzaro, Larry Nemecek, Mark Newbold, Marco Palmieri, Anthony Pascale, Scott Pearson, Brian J. Robb, Dave Rossi, Ian Spelling, Timothy J. Tuohy, Dayton Ward, Toby Weidmann.

Please note:
The interviews collected in this volume were originally printed in *Star Trek Magazine*, some of which date back almost 20 years. In order to maintain the originality of the material, we have not modified the interviews unless absolutely necessary.

STAR TREK®

EPIC EPISODES

EPIC EPISODES

FEATURES

INTERVIEWS

THESE ARE THE VOYAGES...

"The Cage." "The City on the Edge of Forever." "The Best of Both Worlds." In the annals of *Star Trek* there are certain episodes that seem to reach beyond the confines of the small screen, taking on near-mythic status. Whether they be standalone installments or two-parters, these episodes live in the imagination as fully realized epics.

This special collection of articles and interviews taken from the pages of *Star Trek Magazine* is devoted to some of the most epic episodes from the original series and *Star Trek: The Next Generation*.

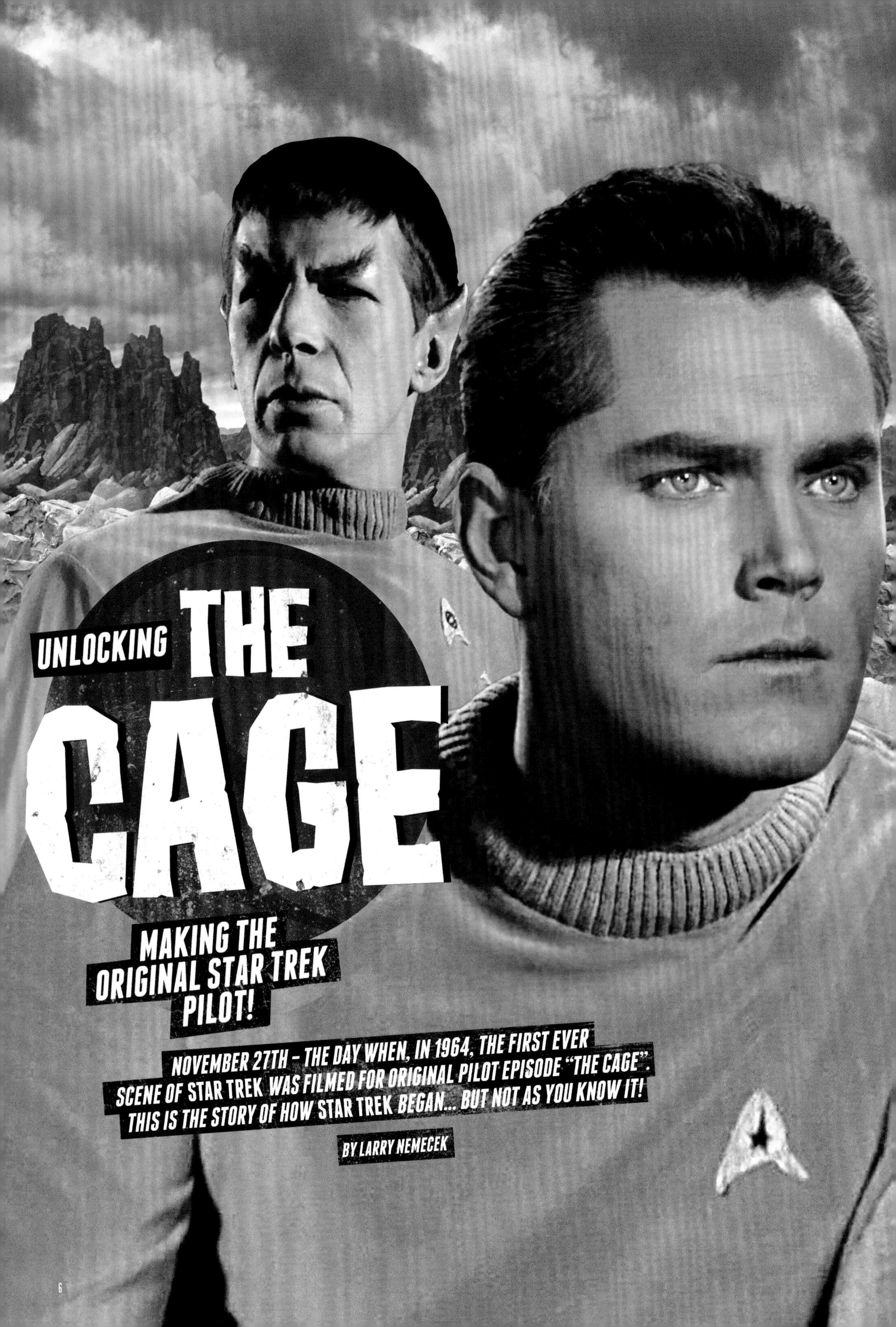

UNLOCKING THE CAGE

MAKING THE ORIGINAL STAR TREK PILOT!

NOVEMBER 27TH – THE DAY WHEN, IN 1964, THE FIRST EVER SCENE OF *STAR TREK* WAS FILMED FOR ORIGINAL PILOT EPISODE "THE CAGE". THIS IS THE STORY OF HOW *STAR TREK* BEGAN… BUT NOT AS YOU KNOW IT!

BY LARRY NEMECEK

As diehard fans will know, not one but *two* pilot episodes were made to try and sell *Star Trek* to TV executives. Ultimately, it was Kirk & co's exploits in 1965's "Where No Man Has Gone Before" that actually convinced NBC to carry the series. And yet it was 1964's "The Cage" that presented creator Gene Roddenberry's first take on *Trek* – similar to what came later, but different... No Kirk, Shatner, redshirts, phasers or tricorders... but you could still make out Spock, the *Enterprise*, transporters, and the bridge – even if all were dressed in more somber colors.

to the military, and this series told one-hour stories about the peacetime U.S. Marine Corps. Formerly one of TV's most prolific freelance writers, and the top contributor to Western series *Have Gun, Will Travel*, Roddenberry had graduated to running his own shows – and had every intention of making them smart and sophisticated. But every producer must answer to his network, and when Roddenberry pushed the envelope with a *Lieutenant* script about racism, NBC refused to air the episode. Race was still a TV taboo in the early 1960s, and the resulting bad blood spelled the end of the show.

The *Enterprise* sported more muted decor

Some might say "The Cage" is a purer *Star Trek* than what we came to know. After all, this *was* Roddenberry's original concept: star-spanning storytelling with uncensored social commentary. And was it truly such a "failure" when, expense be damned, NBC execs gave the series an unheard-of second try?

The episode remained unaired until 1986, but 60s fans could at least have a glimpse of "The Cage," thanks to its use as "flashback" filler in Season One's "The Menagerie" two-parter. Still, you had to read Stephen Poe's "The Making of *Star Trek*" to discover the full plotline of "The Cage."

CONCEPT

In the beginning, *Star Trek* started and ended with Gene Roddenberry. So what was it that led the one-time pilot and LAPD officer to the 23rd Century? Call it career motivation and censorship camouflage.

Roddenberry sold his first TV series, *The Lieutenant*, to NBC in 1963. He and the rest of his World War II generation were no strangers

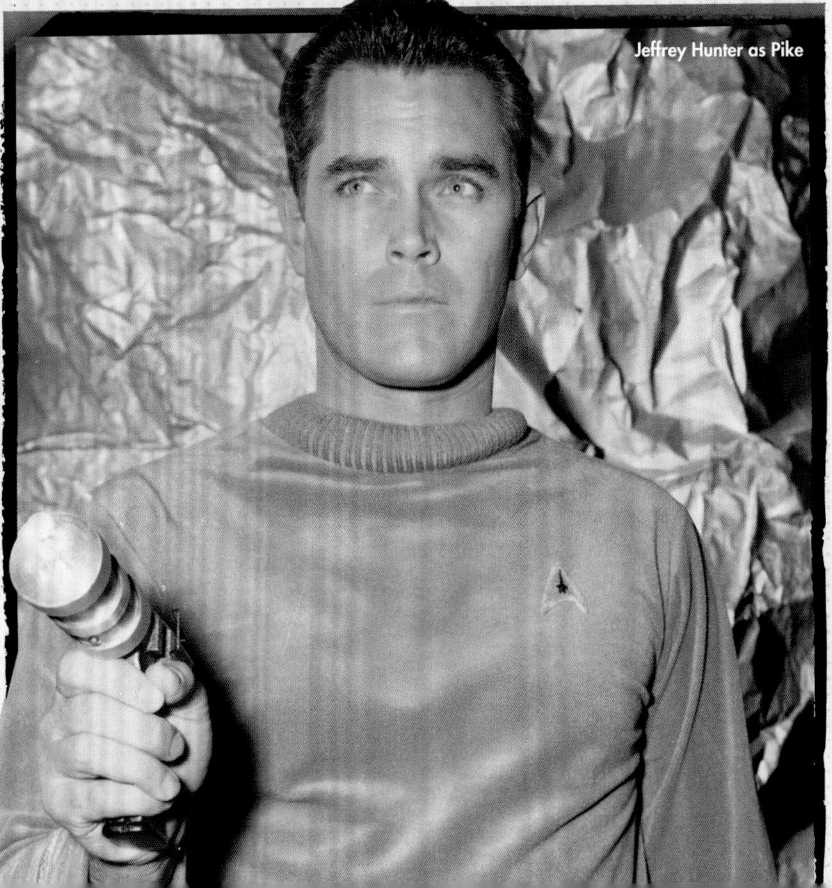

Jeffrey Hunter as Pike

As a fan of Jonathan Swift and *Gulliver's Travels*, Roddenberry emerged from that fracas to believe that, like Swift, he could employ allegory amid sci-fi settings to sneak adult topics *past* the censors – to an audience he knew were more intelligent than they were credited to be.

"Although *Star Trek* had to entertain or go off the air, we believed our format was unique enough to allow us to challenge and stimulate the audience," Roddenberry said in 1968. "Unless it also 'said something' and we challenged our viewers to think and react, then it wasn't worth all we had put into the show."

Roddenberry wanted a family of characters in a "home" setting – and that's why the movie *Forbidden Planet*, with its crew, space cruiser, and background mission, had an impact on *Star Trek*: Roddenberry and his contemporaries felt at home with stories set around a military service, and it made sense as a background for his show. It's also why, to use classic Hollywood "pitch-ese," amid the great era of the TV Western Roddenberry came up with the marketing line, "*Wagon Train* to the Stars" (see boxout on p10).

In 1964, with his *Star Trek* blueprint in place – adult tales and issues, told via science fiction to hide it from the gatekeepers, and organized around a military motif – Roddenberry set about outlining his vision to the TV network in a now-famous 16-page pitch memo. With 25 story ideas, he set out his intentions for the show, while the limit of visiting only Earth-like cultures meant it could be done without breaking the bank.

RODDENBERRY'S INITIAL STORY PITCH:

"THE DESPERATION OF OUR SERIES LEAD, CAGED AND ON EXHIBITION LIKE AN ANIMAL, THEN OFFERED A MATE."

That suited Desilu Productions just fine. It was newly hired Desilu junior exec Herb Solow who was tasked with helping the studio move beyond its usual sitcoms to sell one-hour dramas: *Trek* and *Mission: Impossible* were the result. In fact, we now know that without Solow's deal-making at NBC, "The Cage" might never have been made: "I'm not leaving this room," he told old friends Grant Tinker and Jerry Stanley of NBC, "until we have a deal." Considering Roddenberry's recent history with NBC, it's amazing the Peacock Network would listen to him at all.

The idea for "The Cage" came from "The Next Cage," the first of 25 "story springboards" in Roddenberry's March memo. It read simply: "The desperation of our series lead, caged and on exhibition like an animal, then offered a mate." Roddenberry had to offer three story choices for NBC: his others were "Visit to Paradise," a critique of controlled societies that later became "The Return of the Archons," and "The Women," later the root of "Mudd's Women," pitched in the memo as, "Hanky-panky aboard, with a cargo of women destined for a far-off colony."

BY THE NUMBERS

SHOOT DATES: Fri, Nov. 27 - Fri., Dec. 18, 1964 (5 days over scheduled 11-day shoot)

STUDIOS: Stages 14-15-16, Desilu Culver, Culver City

TOTAL PILOT BUDGET: $451,503 ($3.47 million in 2014 dollars)

TOTAL PILOT ACTUAL COST: $615,751 ($4.73 million in 2014 dollars)

Star Trek would be about more than storytelling, of course: it would have to actually be produced, and Roddenberry's *The Lieutenant* still had a part to play. "The Cage" director Bob Butler, casting agent Joe D'Agosta (moonlighting for Desilu's *Trek*), and one-time guest star Leonard Nimoy all made the transition from navy corps to space exploration.

Way-out anthology show *The Outer Limits* also provided some of the *Star Trek* personnel. The sci-fi show lasted only a year, but the likes of sculptor-artist Wah Chang, make-up designer Fred Phillips, and pilot post-producer Byron Haskin all wound up bringing Roddenberry's ideas to life every week, working miracles

Pike and his Number One, Majel Barrett

Young Spock favored a tousled look

An animated Pike

with 1960s budgets and technologies. From Desilu itself came Matt Jefferies, *Star Trek*'s art director-designer and, like Roddenberry, a B-17 bomber vet. And with the dancing Vina to dress, costume designer Bill Theiss and his famed "hang by a thread" theory of female gown design also began. Most of all, the *Outer Limits* link made "The Cage" the first collaboration between Roddenberry and the guy who made the show work from Day One: unsung but amazing line producer Bob Justman. In 1996, Justman and Solow co-wrote *Inside Star Trek*, revealing many of *Trek*'s secrets, with "R.J." displaying typical wry humor and, thankfully, huge attention to detail and record-keeping.

CHARACTERS

With a space service as structure, ideas for a character line-up of captain, "exec," ship's doctor, yeomen, bridge officers and specialists soon followed.

A heroic male captain was a given (this was the 1960s after all), but it was the hunt for his *name* that proved most arduous. *Star Trek*'s first draft had Captain Robert M. April in command, before it shifted to Captain Pike – with a Captain Winter along the way. April was eventually resurrected by *Star Trek: The Animated Series* as the canonical first captain of the *Enterprise*, but *Trek* canon has no such love for Captain Winter.

Roddenberry made a major statement with his inclusion of "Number One," a strong female second-in-command, but his original ideal of a 50/50 gender split in his crew was squashed by NBC to 70/30 on the male side. As Roddenberry recalled for the 1977 "Inside *Star Trek*" live recording, the suits pleaded that true sex equality "would look like there's a lot of foolin' around goin' on up there!" (Note too, at least in this first incarnation of the "space service," there are no miniskirts.)

With Number One originally the captain's number one, Spock would be second officer – originally described in the series bible as "half-Martian." Aside from scientific sanity and a yen for expansiveness, the biggest reason Spock's background eventually became "Vulcanian" was his make-up: the assumed reddish hue of a Martian just read as dark and gray on black-and-white TV. It was discovered that a yellowish tone for the newly created species worked much better in both formats.

SOLD AS UNSEEN

Because "The Cage" was primeval *Star Trek* in look, feel and faces, it was seen as useless for primetime or even the rerun era. What's more, no station wanted to interrupt its color *Star Trek* reruns for a lower quality, black-and-white film: The color neg had been lost, and the only color print at budget-conscious Desilu had been the one cut up to supply the flashback scenes for "The Menagerie."

So, when Gene trotted out a viewing of "The Cage" as part of his college tours of the 1970s, the first wave of militant Trekkers only got to see the studio's B&W copy – the only intact version then known to exist. Fast forward a decade into the home-video era, four *Star Trek* movies and a whole genre evolution later, and it's easy to see why Paramount suddenly had an interest in making this "lost episode" available... even if it meant stitching together the color *and* black and white scenes to make "The Cage" whole again.

CASTING

The original "wish list" for Captain Pike included Peter Graves, Rod Taylor, George Segal, Efrem Zimbalist Jr., and William Shatner; NBC left their shortlist at Patrick O'Neal, James Coburn and the eventual choice, Jeffrey Hunter, the handsome one-time movie star of *The Searchers* and *King of Kings*, who'd found less success on TV. Thanks to an unpleasant experience on short-lived Western series *Temple Houston*, Hunter almost didn't consider TV or *Star Trek* at all. Hunter's movie comeback was ultimately cut short when he suffered a fall on a film set, followed by a fatal stroke on May 27, 1969.

Roddenberry had been considering Leonard Nimoy for the role of Spock ever since they met on an episode of *The Lieutenant*. However, Desilu and NBC higher-ups wanted a familiar face, and Nimoy was not approved until the role had been turned down by both DeForest Kelley (yes, really – because of the ears) and Martin Landau (who thought the role "limited").

Nimoy himself was sold on the potential of the role until the reality of the pointed-ear look set in weeks before filming. Smarting from crew teases of "pixie" and "jackrabbit," the actor met with Roddenberry on the eve of filming, saying he didn't want the part. An argument ensued, as Roddenberry recalled: "Finally, the only thing I could think of to say to him was, 'Leonard, believe me. I make this pledge to you. If by the thirteenth show you still don't like the ears, I will personally write a script in which you'll get an ear job and go back to normal.' He looked at me for a minute and then practically fell down on the floor laughing. Suddenly the ears had been put back in proper perspective and that was the end of that."

Dr. Boyce (John Hoyt) offers Pike more sage advice

"I'M NOT LEAVING THIS ROOM UNTIL WE HAVE A DEAL."
HERB SOLOW TO NBC'S EXECS

There was a reason DeForest Kelley was on Roddenberry's radar, too: from the beginning, the producer had wanted him as his ship's doctor but, as with Nimoy, he faced resistance: the TV suits could only see Kelley as the parade of villains he'd played in many Westerns over the years. They also saw Bones' mentor dynamic with Pike as requiring an older Doc. The man who became Dr. Boyce, John Hoyt, had played his share of cowboys – and was seen as reliable. But once the shoot was done he wanted out, and Roddenberry would again be overruled for his doctor choice, when grandfatherly Paul Fix was hired as Dr. Piper. Not until *Star Trek* went to series did Roddenberry get his wish – by which time his other pilot show, *Police Story*, had featured Kelley as a forensic lab doc... and the naysayers finally "got it."

Another actor considered for the role of Dr. Boyce had been Malachi Throne, now known as Commodore Mendez from "The Menagerie." When Throne instead asked to play Spock, Roddenberry countered by offering the voice of The Keeper Talosian. The Keeper's voice would be modified to a higher pitch after

THE WESTERN CONNECTION

"*Wagon Train* to the Stars" – what does Roddenberry's original 1964 *Star Trek* pitch line really mean?

After a peak of 25 series in 1959, 10.5 of the 25 hours of primetime TV were still Westerns in spring 1964. But that's a simplistic point: in his attempt to sell his pitch, why did Gene not dub *Star Trek* "*Bonanza* to the Stars", or "*Gunsmoke* to the Stars"? The answer reveals more awareness of what he was pitching to any network, to wit: those two Western classics featured a cast family who also mostly *stayed put*, on a familiar home base: Dodge City, and the Ponderosa ranch. *Wagon Train* had a regular cast, but their "home base" was the titular wagon train: which, by definition, was always on the move. In other words, the family of characters with wagonmaster Ward Bond on *Wagon Train* journeyed to a new place each week, and encountered guest characters when they did – sometimes even previously unseen characters from within their own party.

Also, the best of adult American science fiction on prime-time network TV had, until 1964, been anthologies: each episode of both *The Twilight Zone* and *The Outer Limits* featured a new cast-of-the-week, not a known group in a familiar setting. And most of those settings were grounded in the present, not 300 years in the future – which made props hard to find down at the set dressing rental warehouse. Having a home cast *and* a home base in a sci-fi series would be truly groundbreaking – *if* Roddenberry and his studio could pull it off.

Throne wound up back onscreen as Mendez, spliced in amongst his Keeper scenes.

Majel Barrett had also met Roddenberry doing an episode of *The Lieutenant*. She came into his life as his first marriage was failing, and Roddenberry wanted his romantic interest to play his groundbreaking Number One as well – even as the network remained uneasy about the arrangement. When character changes were demanded by NBC after "The Cage," Roddenberry opted to "fight to keep Spock and marry the woman, and not the other way around," as he quipped.

With the principal cast in place, the team needed to also populate the planet which the crew would be exploring in "The Cage". Director Bob Butler decided to cast small women as the Talosians with overdubbed male voices. That great "throbbing vein" skull seen during Talosians' telepathic exchanges was a simple effect: a manually operated squeeze bulb, attached via tubing that ran off camera out from under the Talosians' gowns. It was none other than Bob Justman who pumped the squeeze bulb in time to the "telepathic" dialogue read live by script supervisor George Rutter.

Later known to fans as the Horta, and the Mugato in a suit he created, Hungarian creature-maker Janos Prohaska is onscreen here, too: During the Talosian zoo intro, he's the stuntman inside the "anthropoid ape" (originally an "anthropoid spider") and the barely seen

Laurel Goodwin (left) as Yeoman J.M. Colt

"humanoid bird" – both suits among Wah Chang's earliest *Star Trek* creations. Cut from the final print, however, was another genre "insider". Later known as the robot "Twiki" on *Buck Rogers*, the diminutive Felix Silla was filmed as a far-off Talosian, after Justman had the idea to cast smaller people to create a forced-perspective effect.

Fans today will notice that the main cast were all very much Caucasian in "The Cage," and not as diverse as *Star Trek*'s eventual main cast. We may see an Asian and an African-American extra in the secondary faces, but even they drew fearful grumbles from some in NBC's sales division. Fortunately, within a year, the network brass were pushing for more obvious diversity on its shows – merging perfectly with Roddenberry's plans.

CANON

Despite his belief in the product, Roddenberry's studio ally Herb Solow was not beyond pulling up his producer, and spending on "The Cage" was growing as filming stretched from summer into fall. Even on this sample episode, a lot of those bucks went into what *Star Trek Lives!* authors Sondra Marshak and Myrna Culbreath later called the "Believability Factor." Some would call it "continuity," or "respecting the audience". There was also an emphasis on thoughtful projections of future tech, and keeping details like doors and

"WE BELIEVED OUR FORMAT WAS UNIQUE ENOUGH TO ALLOW US TO CHALLENGE AND STIMULATE THE AUDIENCE."

GENE RODDENBERRY

controls the same from week to week. Today, we see it as the extra spice in the *Trek* recipe – and why *Trek* has that beast called "canon" that inspires so much loyalty and debate. "To the studio, this approach seemed to be an enormous waste of time and money," Roddenberry said in 1968, "whereas we felt that the audience isn't dumb, and therefore if it was designed right, it would 'smell right' to [the audience]. During these months, I was under enormous pressure from the studio to quit spending money on this sort of thing. They kept saying, 'Back off, you've got something that works, what are you, some kind of scientist? You're a writer. Write the script. You've got some chairs and some blinking lights. Put in some people and let's go.' "

And there was another *Star Trek* tradition that dates back to "The Cage." The original pilot episode had its own science advisor: Harvey P. Lynn, of the original science research think-tank, the RAND Corporation.

Now, fans may wince every time they hear Pike's crew talk about their "laser" weapons – even with adjustable settings – and the creators did try to shoehorn lasers into canon just before "phasers". Lynn had advised going to a more "futuristic" acronym like "maser," an idea that was bypassed... for the time being. Even back then, in one early draft, Lynn pointed to the dialogue line "disappeared in that quadrant," and noted that "quadrant' signifies 'one-fourth of something' – how about substituting it with the word 'region'?" Most of all, we can thank Lynn for the notion of a hangar bay.

CAMERAS!

As it happened, Day 1 of shooting began on November 27 (the Friday after Thanksgiving), with Boyce's bartending visit with Pike. Filming continued all the way through two days of location shooting for the outdoor Rigel VII fortress on Desilu-Culver's onetime "40 Acres" backlot. Work eventually wrapped on December 18, five days behind schedule, with Vina's picnic illusion on Stage 16. The original shooting script gave the picnicking couple *two* horses, not one: alongside Tango was to have been a mare, "Mary Jane," but she fell victim to trims on the escalating budget.

"The Cage" got behind schedule right off the bat thanks to a battle with nature – and the ageing stages at Desilu-Culver, the old RKO Studios. The non-bridge ship sets had been erected on Stage 16, built in the silent movie days for Cecil B. DeMille epics – and by 1964, long disuse had left them as pigeon roosts. The bustle and lighting led the birds to coo so loudly during dialogue that filming had to stop until they could be cleared out by scattering birdseed outside.

Next-door, Stage 15, home of the bridge, apparently had the noisiest ageing pipes and toilets in Hollywood – it took a live guard being posted to keep people from flushing during takes, after a red light was ignored. Hours of delays were caused by the plumbing – and that's without mentioning the time lost to bees in the rafters!

With filming done and the holidays over, "The Cage" had a little over a month for post-production as 1965 dawned: editing, dubbing, effects, and, of course, music. Even in the mid-1960s, the "wishlist" composers for "The Cage" included now household names like Jerry Goldsmith and John Williams, but it was low-profile composer Alexander Courage who was hired to deliver the iconic *Star Trek* theme music. Courage even found the right kind of noise for the passing starship in the opening titles, by simply taking a microphone and making several "whooshing" noises – the basis of what we've heard as motion in the "noisy" vacuum of space ever since.

CAVEAT !

Wildly inventive and yet so over-budget it set its own studio on edge, "The Cage" was finally screened for NBC in February, 1965. Solow swore it was the best screening he ever gave for execs: almost to a man, they sat stunned, impressed with lowly Desilu's work, and wondering if they'd just watched a mid-budget feature... Before promptly rejecting it. "Too cerebral for TV," they said, but added a simple yet historic request: Try again. NBC was still in last place among the three major networks at the time... they still wanted diversity and color... and Solow still knew the guys there. Roddenberry picked his battles, found a new captain with swagger and humor, threw in a fistfight, overspent again on this rare second-chance pilot – and did indeed take TV science fiction "Where No Man Had Gone Before." But that's a tale for another time.

Pike and Vina (Susan Oliver)

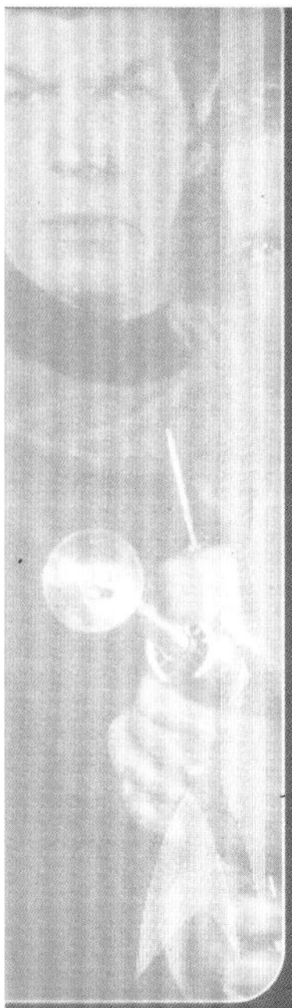

FASCINATING!

Although Captain Kirk was the main protagonist, perhaps the standout character of *Star Trek: The Original Series* was Commander Spock, the cool, logical alien from the planet Vulcan. Present right from the get-go, Leonard Nimoy's portrayal of the *Starship Enterprise*'s level-headed science officer was a keystone in the absorbing triumvirate of Kirk, Spock and McCoy that made the show such a hit. Toby Weidmann discovers what the star himself thinks about the series' success…

"**Unbeatable! Unmatchable! Unique!**" exclaims Mister Spock's alter ego, Leonard Nimoy, explaining the dynamic he shared on screen and off with two of *Star Trek*'s other key draws, Captain James T. Kirk and Doctor Leonard 'Bones' McCoy, played by William Shatner and DeForest Kelley respectively. "It was quite marvellous," he continues. "It was just a very successful chemistry."

After an acting career that has spanned more than 50 years, the actor behind perhaps *Star Trek*'s most iconic character has settled for a more sedate pace of life of late, relaxing with his wife, Susan, enjoying working on his distinctive photography and sorting through his files and memorabilia at home. However, his association with *Star Trek* is not completely exhausted – Nimoy still regularly attends *Star Trek* conventions around the world and has recently recorded an

TWINKLE, TWINKLE, MAJOR STAR

If you've been wondering how William Shatner is of late, well, the answer is: as busy as ever. The charismatic actor who put the twinkle into Captain James T. Kirk's eye has a number of projects on the go, including appearing in new TV and film productions, writing another Kirk novel and – yes, you read right – producing a new music album. With news that Shatner may still guest star in *Star Trek: Enterprise*, Ian Spelling catches up with *Star Trek*'s shining light to hear more…

William Shatner is, was and, from the look of it, will always be the busiest man in the *Star Trek* universe, or any universe for that matter. Every time one turns around – be it in a bookstore, a movie theatre, at a convention, on television, at a charity horse show, the list goes on – Shatner is there, either in person or represented by something of his own making. An interview with Shatner these days isn't so much a look back at *Star Trek* days gone by, but rather a personally guided all-new interview for the special features of the forthcoming *Star Trek: The Original Series* DVD release.

For many of *Star Trek*'s older fans, the release of this classic 1960s series on the format is long overdue, but hopefully the addition of exclusive material will make it worth the wait. For Nimoy, revisiting the show has been a leisure of love: although he didn't watch every episode again for the DVD project, Nimoy notes that he had seen them all fairly recently. "In the last few years I reviewed all of the episodes," he says. "We did some commentary for the [US] Sci Fi Channel on each of the episodes and I sat down and watched every one of them afresh. I've been going through some archive material at home as well."

So, what was it like seeing them all again? "I was impressed with the stories that work," he admits. "Not all of them do, but by and large the success of the series was based on the fact that we had interesting stories to tell. We were also budgeted in such a way that we couldn't afford a lot of very complicated special effects, so we were heavily dependent on performance and story. The ones that had strong stories still have strong stories. A good story holds up for a long time."

Indeed, it's been almost 40 years since *ST:TOS* originally appeared on US television screens, and yet Mr Spock is still the character that the Boston-born actor is most identified with. This is despite a career outside of *Star Trek* that includes acting alongside the likes of Ingrid Bergman, Slim Pickens, Yul Brynner, Peter Falk, Henry Fonda and Donald Sutherland, among others. It's also been more than 13 years since he last portrayed the Vulcan, as Ambassador Spock in the two-part *Star Trek: The Next Generation* episode, *Unification* (which incidentally also marked the final appearance of Spock's father, Sarek, played by Mark Lenard). But, there's no doubt that Spock, and the series that spawned him, had a massive impact on not only a generation but also the science fiction genre as well.

However, after all this time, surely Nimoy finds it weird discussing the character and show to packed crowds at conventions, particularly as many of the younger attendees had not even born when the show originally aired. "I don't find it any more weird than a lot of other weird things that go on in this world, you know? I find other things far weirder quite frankly. It's part of our culture, it's certainly part of our television history, part of our motion picture history and I understand it, so I don't find it weird at all. I found it weird in the 1970s, 30 years ago, when the show was growing enormously popular in its revival in syndication. That was surprising to me. But since then, nothing about it surprises me."

Considering what a massive franchise *Star Trek* is now, it's easy to forget that the show was actually cancelled at the end of its third season following disappointing viewing figures and budget cuts. Back in the 1970s, it was syndication and the convention circuit that kept *Star Trek* alive. Its subsequent success – 10 films and four spin-off shows later – could hardly be imagined in June 1969, when the final episode *Turnabout Intruder* aired.

Above: The very different Spock from *The Cage*
Below: The director on location in San Francisco for *Star Trek IV: The Voyage Home* – nice dressing gown!

"The success of the series was based on the fact that we had interesting stories to tell... We were heavily dependent on performance and story and I think they hold up very well."

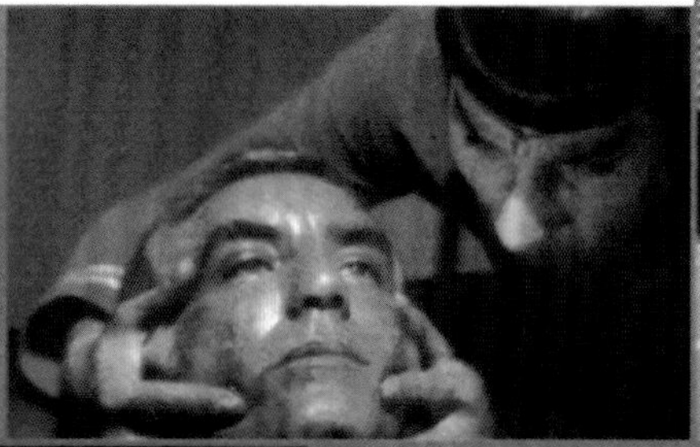

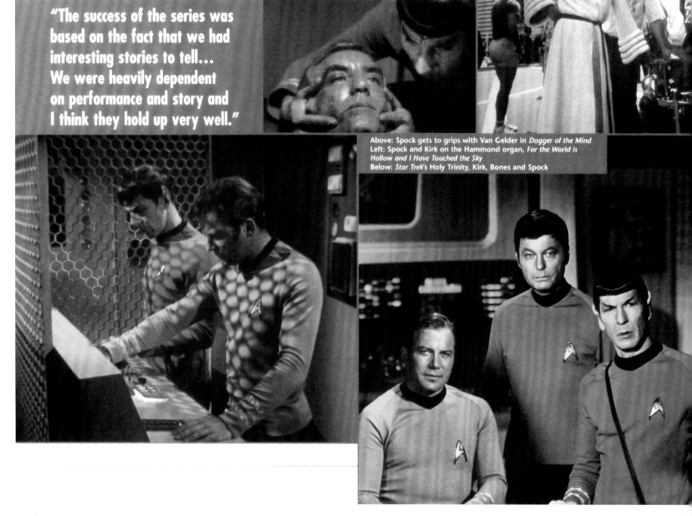

Above: Spock gets to grips with Van Gelder in *Dagger of the Mind*
Left: Spock and Kirk on the Hammond organ, *For the World is Hollow and I Have Touched the Sky*
Below: *Star Trek*'s Holy Trinity, Kirk, Bones and Spock

glimpse into his plethora of projects, some of which are *Star Trek*-related.

A few months ago, Shatner published his latest novel, *Captain's Blood*, written in collaboration with Judith and Garfield Reeves-Stevens. In the story, set after the events of *Star Trek Nemesis*, Spock, who has been attempting to reunify the Romulans and the Vulcans, is assassinated during a peace rally. And thus it's up to Kirk to find the killer, a task he undertakes with some assistance from Will Riker, Jean-Luc Picard, Dr McCoy and Scotty, among others. Also by Kirk's side for much of the adventure is Joseph, his five-year-old son.

"*I'm Working on That* was out about a year ago and *Captain's Blood* is out now," the ever-tireless Shatner begins. "That's a pretty good pace. *Captain's Blood* is part of a trilogy that's based around the different kinds of love that exist in the world. This particular book is about filial love, if you will. As I say in my dedication, love is the difference between the cold universe and the warm planet Earth. Everybody discovers, from time in memoriam, that love is all that matters, that fame and riches and the good life are depressing without love. I suppose health enters into that, too, and that might be a good theme for another book, because without feeling physically good, it's difficult to love. If you're not healthy, all of your time and impetus is devoted just to surviving."

Fortunately, Shatner himself is hale, hearty and healthy, as are several of the other original *Star Trek* stars. However, DeForest Kelley died in 1999 and James Doohan has been battling Parkinson's disease. Though he's stated in the past that everything in his life impacts on his *Star Trek* stories, he hastens to add that such things don't necessarily colour the familiar characters.

"It doesn't enter into it," Shatner notes. "The characters are almost autonomous and immortal in their own way. They exist on a plane that doesn't belong to the actors, especially with most of us having been away from the films and shows all these years. So the actors almost don't exist anymore, including myself. The actors have aged and the characters remain fixed in time, almost."

Almost, indeed. On the written page, in *Captain's Blood*, a certain green-blooded Vulcan is referred to as Uncle Spock. "I don't think I ever imagined that I'd write those very words, no, probably not," Shatner acknowledges with a chuckle. "But as you reach further and further for more and more shock in these books, you get to Uncle Spock. It's almost up there with killing Kirk, though I didn't write that."

Next up on the book front will be *Captain's Glory*. Shatner explains that he'll team up again with the Reeves-Stevens on the upcoming tale. "*Captain's Glory* is a two-page outline in my files right now," he says. "We'll start work on that soon. We thought that we could do the ideas we had in *Captain's Blood*, as one novel, but the ideas got so large that we decided that the second half of *Captain's Blood* would make *Captain's Glory*. We'll get working on that one soon."

Meanwhile, there's much more to discuss. Anyone turning on a TV in the US these days is liable to catch Shatner and his old pal Nimoy sparking anew in a series of commercials for Priceline, the online discount travel site with which Shatner has been associated with for several years. Pairing the two, Shatner admits, was Priceline's idea, not his.

"They came up with the notion, then I got Leonard involved, and we went from there," Shatner says. "The first one was the mystery of 'Who could possibly replace me as the Priceline spokesperson?'

PHOTO BY ALBERT L. ORTEGA

Before and after: William Shatner, Sally Kellerman and Gary Lockwood, as seen in *Where No Man Has Gone Before* (top) take the stage at a Creation Convention

"The *Star Trek* characters are almost immortal in their own way. They exist on a plane that doesn't belong to the actors... The actors have aged and the characters remain fixed in time, almost."

"I knew that Spock was an interesting character," Nimoy recounts, "a character with an interesting internal life. He was a unique presence on the show and I was excited by the opportunity for performance, but I had no way of knowing whether *Star Trek* would be a success, nobody did. There was no way of knowing what the audience reaction would be. I was interested in it from the point of view of the acting challenges it presented."

For Nimoy, 'challenge' is the key word: in our last interview with the star (*STM* Issue #111), he said about his photography that, "it's the things that scare you that you have to approach and explore in order to create art." This almost sounds like a motto, but is it an edict he has applied to all of his projects, not just photography? "I think that's true," he ponders. "It's the thing that's fresh and unique and unknowable that's challenging and sometimes a breakthrough into work that you wouldn't have done otherwise. If you keep doing the same thing over and over again, playing it safe, you might be successful at it, but you might not be terribly creatively challenged."

Fortunately, Nimoy's professional life has been diverse to say the least. As well as acting, he has directed the likes of hit comedy *Three Men and a Baby* and lent his oh-so recognisable voice to the likes of such favourites as *The Simpsons*.

One particularly memorable venture into the animated world was Nimoy's performance as himself for the hilarious *Futurama Star Trek* homage, entitled *Where No Fan Has Gone Before*, in which he joined forces with his former co-stars, William Shatner, Nichelle Nichols (Uhura), George Takei (Sulu) and Walter Koenig (Chekov) to poke good-natured fun at both themselves and *ST:TOS*.

"I think the [*Simpsons-Futurama* teams] are very, very creative, fresh, irreverent and adventurous," Nimoy notes. "I enjoy working for them. They are very talented people and it's a fun thing to do."

As for his photography, Nimoy has devoted some time to it over recent years. Soulful black and white images of the nude female form, adorned with religious iconography, formed the basis of his most recent endeavour, *Shekhina*, which was met with critical praise from many quarters and furore in some divisions of the Jewish community. However, the project proved so successful that it provoked a dance version, which was premiered in New York in February of this year by the Elisa Monte Dance Company, which Nimoy describes as, "quite wonderful, very well-received and is now in their repertoire. They travel all around the world and do pieces from their repertoire, so it will be performed again."

With such a mixture of skills at his disposal, does he have an area that he loves more than others? Is his photographic work more enjoyable than directing, for instance? "It's a question of the particular project. If a project is going well, I'm perfectly happy being the actor or the director. If it's not going well, I'd rather not be either – I'd just rather not *be* there," he laughs. "Believe me, after a number of years of work, you can tell if you are doing a project that's going well or not and there have been times when I was directing when I've thought, 'I'm in hell.' Other times when I've been directing, I've thought this is the greatest thing that's ever happened to me."

"I knew Spock was an interesting character, a character with an interesting internal life. He was an unique presence on the show and I was excited by the opportunity for performance."

"I've had some fantastic experiences during my career," he continues. "The making of the *Star Trek* series was a thrilling experience for me. The directing of *Star Trek III* and *IV* were especially thrilling. I've had some other kinds of experiences that are memorable and I'll never forget; working with Ingrid Bergman in her final performance in a television movie called *A Woman Called Gorda*, where I played her husband, is one. Another was when I was at a party one night in New York, some years ago – there were a lot of people there who were appearing in Paramount films – and someone came up behind me and put their hands on my shoulders and whispered in my ear,

Above: Kirk was happy to pose for Spock's interpretation of The Thinker, *The Deadly Years*
Below: *Mirror, Mirror* on the wall...

Above: Saurian brandy is a tipple not to be trifled with, *The Enemy Within*
Left: The missus, *Amok Time*

We had a lot of fun. We'd done conventions together, which are really a performance of sorts, and we sat down to do *Mind Meld*. The commercials are an extension of that in a way. They play on the friendship, the chemistry and the characters."

Speaking of *Mind Meld*, the first one sold well enough to warrant a follow-up, and Shatner hopes to deliver the goods eventually. But he's not certain if it will ever come together. "I don't know," he explains. "I wanted to get Patrick [Stewart] in on it. I want to get Kate Mulgrew in on it. Kate is perfectly willing, but I think in terms of marketing that we need to get Patrick first. We've worked together and can talk about that. And there was a funny thing happened not too long ago – Patrick had a dinner party at his house and invited me. [*X-Men* director] Bryan Singer was there, too, and he's a big Kirk fan. So I met Bryan and, at some point in the evening, the three of us were all upstairs in Patrick's game room playing a *Star Trek* pinball machine together! That's a true story."

Meanwhile, the possibility of an appearance as Kirk – or perhaps Kirk's own grandfather – on *Star Trek: Enterprise* remains a possibility, particularly now that UPN has elected to pick up the struggling series for a fourth season. "When Rick Berman broached the subject I said, 'It's possible if you have the time and you have the money,'" Shatner recalls. "He said, 'Well, I've got the money.' So we'll see. I don't know if he's still got the money and I'm going to be pretty busy, but I have a couple of ideas about how to make it work."

So what is Shatner busy with? Well, plenty, of course. Just before press time, ABC announced that Shatner would join actor James Spader in a spin-off of the long-running and just-cancelled legal drama, *The Practice*. Shatner memorably portrayed a blustery lawyer in half a dozen episodes of the show, and series creator David E. Kelly subsequently built the spin-off, *The Practice: Fleet Street* around Spader's Alan Shore and Shatner's Denny Crane characters. Beyond the series, there are several films finished or in the works, as well as – yes, it's true – a new album.

"I don't know if *Free Enterprise 2* exists," Shatner says, referring to a proposed sequel to the cult indie comedy that cast Shatner as a wild and crazy version of himself. "They talked to me a long time ago about it. I suggested certain avenues to go in with the story. And I haven't heard back. In lieu of that, I've got *Dodgeball: A True Underdog Story* coming out. That's a comedy with Ben Stiller and Vince Vaughn and I play a less than minor part, a character named the Chancellor. I was just doing a favour for a friend of mine. And I am in the sequel to *Miss Congeniality*. Everybody is coming back for that, including Sandra Bullock.

"The album, I think, is going to be one of the better things I've done. It's a rock-talk album, if you will. I'm doing it with Ben Folds. It's an eclectic album. Ben produced. He wrote a lot of music and I wrote a lot of lyrics. We've got some wonderful artists aiding and abetting us. It's a very meaningful album for me. I was invited to do an album by the people who owned Rhino Records at one time. They've got a new record company out called Shout Factory. They said, 'Would you like to do an album.' I was then faced with my own question of, 'Yes, I'd like to do an album, but what am I going to do?' What I did was write from my heart some truths that are within me. So some of the songs are

"When Rick Berman broached the subject [of Kirk appearing on *ST:ENT*], I said, 'It's possible if you have the time and the money.' He said, 'Well, I've got the money.' So we'll see... I have a couple of ideas about how to make it work."

Above: The usual suspects, *The Omega Glory*
Below: The gang's back, *Star Trek: The Motion Picture*

Star Trek V: The Final Frontier's director sets up a shot

Face of the enemy, *Turnabout Intruder*

© LEONARD NIMOY

These images are just two examples of Mr Nimoy's stunning photographic work

'I recognise you, you've had your ears fixed.' I turned round and it was John Wayne. That was a great moment... I'm having a good time with my life. Bill Shatner and I are good friends. We've done a Priceline commercial together. It's a very successful commercial and we're now contracted to do some more... We meet up periodically. I travel a lot, he travels a lot, so it's difficult for us to find time, but when we get a chance in Los Angeles, we do get together."

So, although Leonard Nimoy continues to look back fondly on *Star Trek*, he prefers to seize today than spend too much time in the past. Right now, he's doing a bit of both – continuing to sort through the memorabilia he has collected over the years, which includes plenty of *Star Trek* material, at his home and enjoying the moment at the same time, too. "I'm still going through it," he notes with a sigh. "It's very time-consuming. I'm doing it for the sake of my family, to see what they may find of interest and would like to have. I'm sorting out, cleaning out and fresh filing a lot of memorabilia from the last 35-40 years and we'll see what comes of it. A lot of old memories came back, things that I had forgotten about and it's fun.

"It's a nostalgic trip down memory lane, but I don't like to spend too much time there. I'd rather deal with today." ■

To see more of Leonard Nimoy's photography, visit *www.leonardnimoyphotography.com/*

FIVE THINGS YOU MAY NOT KNOW ABOUT LEONARD NIMOY

Leonard Nimoy was born to parents Dora and Max, Jewish immigrants from the Ukraine who settled in the US. His father earned a living cutting hair, owning his own barbershop.

Leonard Nimoy's big break came in the film *Kid Monk Baroni*, in which he played the title character – a boxer with a deformed face. However, he had appeared in a few things before that – one of his first TV screen appearances was in the cop show *Dragnet* in 1951, where he played the character Julius Carver in the episode entitled *The Big Boys*.

Leonard Nimoy not only directed but also starred in the Bangles' promo video 'Going Down to Liverpool'.

Leonard Nimoy is an accomplished singer and has released several singles and albums, including *Mr Spock's Music from Outer Space, The Two Sides of Leonard Nimoy, The Green Hills of Earth, Outer Space, Inner Mind* and *Space Odyssey*. Sadly, a compilation album, *Spaced Out: The Best of Leonard Nimoy & Bill Shatner*, is the only one currently available in UK shops.

In September 2000, Leonard Nimoy was awarded an Honorary Doctorate of Humane Letters from Antioch University for his work in Holocaust remembrance, the arts and the environment.

PHOTO BY ALBERT L. ORTEGA

Leonard Nimoy enjoys himself at a recent Creation convention appearance

"It's the thing that's fresh and unique and unknowable that's challenging, and sometimes a breakthrough into work that you would not have done otherwise."

light-hearted and some of them are very deep, but everything, for better or worse, carries a sense of me. I think that we're looking at a late summer release, and Ben and I are talking about going to a select eight or 10 cities on tour."

Shatner's assistant then buzzes through; there's an important phone call he must take regarding his upcoming annual Hollywood Charity Horse Show, which was held in May and benefited a number of children's causes. Shatner excuses himself for a moment, returns to explain that he really must deal with this matter, and offers to answer one more question before he bids farewell for now. And that question is this: given the less-than-stellar response to musical output of just about any actor from any *Star Trek* show and, particularly taking into account the battery of photon torpedoes fired at Shatner's album *The Transformed Man*, isn't he taking a heck of a gamble?

"The new album is going to be one of the better things I've done. It's a rock-talk album. I'm doing it with Ben Folds. He wrote a lot of music and I wrote a lot of lyrics. We've got some wonderful artists aiding and abetting us. It's a very meaningful album for me."

"It is a dangerous road for me to tread again as a result of that ribbing," he concurs. "I asked for it and I accepted it. Although I have to say that that original album, *The Transformed Man*, had a serious thought behind it. Were one to actually play the album, as some people did, they would have seen what was behind the performance of some of those songs. One or two of those songs taken alone, I can understand why people might find them funny, but if you were to listen to the whole album you'd understand what I was doing. So a couple of the cuts did get made fun of, including by Rhino Records, which is ironic.

"The danger for me now is to judge the reaction of what people will say and do about some of the songs on the new album," William Shatner notes. "I think that they're sufficiently good and sufficiently well done that the ribbing will cease fairly soon."

Keep up to date with William Shatner on his official website: *www.williamshatner.com*

This picture epitomises the two characters, *Spectre of the Gun*

Hanging around in Yosemite National Park, *ST:V*

FIVE THINGS YOU MAY NOT KNOW ABOUT WILLIAM SHATNER

William Shatner was born in Montreal, Quebec, Canada, to parents Ann and Joseph. He has a Batchelor of Arts degree from Montreal's McGill University.

The mask used by supernatural serial killer Michael Myers in the *Halloween* films was an adapted version of a Captain Kirk mask from the 1960s.

For 13 years, William Shatner has spearheaded the Hollywood Charity Horse Show, which features some of the best western reining riders in the country while raising money for charity. This year's event was held on 1 May and featured a guest appearance by Country and Western singer Brad Paisley. Find out more at *www.hollywoodcharityhorseshow.org/index.htm*

In 2003, viewers of digital TV channel Music Choice voted William Shatner's version of *Lucy in the Sky with Diamonds* the worst Beatles cover of all time.

William Shatner's young daughters, Melanie and Lisabeth, made uncredited appearances in the *ST:TOS* episode *Miri*. They were joined by Dawn and Darlene Roddenberry, the daughters of another well-known *Star Trek* personality.

"When the Network finally saw 'The Cage,' some of their executives were outraged, and I can't say I really blame them," Gene Roddenberry would insist, decades later, when introducing the first commercial release of *Star Trek*'s pilot episode on videotape. "For the considerable amount of money they'd put up, they certainly did not get a 'Western' space opera. In fact, nothing even faintly like it.

"But... the Network's very top program executive was impressed by the fact that this film made him feel as if he'd actually been flying in a spaceship. Doing something almost unprecedented, the Network ordered a second pilot. And this one had better be [a] familiar, action adventure – or else! So the second *Star Trek* pilot was made, and was accepted, and the rest turned into our shared history."

But why did that second pilot, "Where No Man Has Gone Before," succeed where "The Cage" had not? To understand this, we'll need to grab the controls of a starship, and slingshot ourselves around the sun at warp speed in order to travel back half a century, to 1965. Or alternatively, we can just check with the people who were actually there!

PITCHING THE SPACE WAGON

When pitching his *Star Trek* idea – not least, originally, to Desilu Studios' Vice President of Production, Herbert F. Solow – Gene Roddenberry had repeatedly described the new show as a "*Wagon Train* to the stars", comparing his proposed interstellar concept to the then-popular show set during the 19th Century migration across the American West. *Star Trek* would simply be dressed up with spaceships instead of horse-pulled wagons, ray guns instead of pistols, and aliens instead of Native Americans.

SECOND CHANCES

WHERE NO SHOW HAD GONE BEFORE

Had *Star Trek* failed to break free from "The Cage," chances are Gene Roddenberry's brainchild would now be a mere footnote in sci-fi history. Instead, the concept was given a rare second chance to impress network executives. Fifty years after it was filmed, Paul F. Cockburn asks what worked for the unprecedented second pilot, "Where No Man Has Gone Before."

With "The Cage," however, Roddenberry would later accept that he'd delivered, "a very different kind of story – one that dealt with the strange dangers of illusion, the enormous power of imagination, with whole worlds that could come from inside people's heads. And if that wasn't enough, back in those days before the phrase 'women's lib' was ever heard, I put a woman in second command of our starship, and my script required our actress Majel Barrett to play this woman as having a highly superior, computerized mind.

"I was 'uncooperative' in other ways too," Roddenberry would add. "For example, I had refused to cast our crew 'sensibly' – which meant, 'all whites.'"

All this fits in well with the idea of Roddenberry as the visionary writer-producer, pushing against the conservative commercial world of American network television. Yet the network for which *Star Trek* was being made was NBC, which, as Senior Vice President of Programming Mort Werner reminded his suppliers in 1966, had an employment policy that had "long dictated that there can be no discrimination because of race, creed, religion or national origin, and this applies in all of our operations."

According to Solow in the behind-the-scenes book *Inside Star Trek: The True Story*, Mort Werner was the "best programming executive at any of the three networks." When not in his office developing pilots and series for NBC, he played the piano in any cocktail lounge that would let him, and kept a Sunday-shift in a New York deli.

Werner was also the man who saved *Star Trek* from television oblivion.

He was the NBC Executive who had been impressed by the show's realism. "I've seen many science fiction, outer-space films," Solow remembered Werner telling him. "I've never felt I was aboard a spacecraft. I never believed the crew was a real crew. But you guys gave me the feeling of total belief. I loved it." But not, apparently, sufficiently enough for NBC to pick up the show as a weekly series. Subsequent histories of *Star Trek* have insisted the network's cold feet were down to "The Cage" being deemed too "cerebral," but according to Solow, there was likely another reason. In early 1960s America, there were concerns about what the "eroticism" of a certain green-skinned alien dancer implied about a potential series. The executives knew of the married Roddenberry's "roving eye," and also resented his insistence on casting his then girlfriend Majel Barrett as "Number One."

Nor had NBC come to the pilot blind; Werner had approved and selected the storyline of "The Cage" for a very specific reason: NBC had genuinely doubted that Desilu – best known for producing half-hour sitcom *I Love Lucy*, in which the only "special effect" was coloring its star Lucille Ball's hair – could make an hour-long, effects-laden adventure show like *Star Trek*.

"When we looked over the pilot stories you gave us, we chose the most complicated and most difficult one of the bunch," Solow remembered being told by Werner. "We recognize now it wasn't necessarily a story that properly showcased *Star Trek*'s series potential. So the reason the pilot didn't sell was my fault, not yours. You guys just did your job too well. And I screwed up."

So, against all precedent, Werner agreed with Solow to fund the writing of three further scripts, one of which was guaranteed to be made as a second pilot.

Providing most of the money, though, Werner had some caveats.

"We support the concept of a woman in a strong, leading role, but have serious doubts as to Majel Barrett's abilities to 'carry' the show as its co-star," Solow remembered being told. "We also think you can do better with the ship's doctor, the yeoman, and other members of the crew. We applaud the attempt at a racial mix; it's exactly what we want. Hopefully, there'll be more experienced minority actors available for next year."

One character, however, was a potential deal-breaker. "Leonard Nimoy isn't a problem, but the role he plays is!" Werner had insisted.

Only Leonard Nimoy's Spock would make the transition from first to second pilot episode

DID YOU KNOW?

Gathering together the technicians needed to make "Where No Man Has Gone Before" proved challenging, as shooting was scheduled during the busiest time of Hollywood's production year. However, the then 69-year-old cameraman Ernest Haller, though semi-retired, was hired on the spot when the producers realized that his "previous work" included shooting the classic Academy Award-winning 1939 film, *Gone With the Wind* (for which Haller won the Oscar for Best Cinematography).

Scotty (James Doohan) and Sulu (George Takei) join the *Enterprise* crew, but Paul Fix's Dr. Piper would not become a permanent fixture

The expensive *Enterprise* sets built for "The Cage" were redressed for the second pilot

"You've already heard the Sales Department reaction to the character. We can give you research numbers that support their reaction. We have to say this to you: though the Mr. Spock character is interesting and probably has potential, his inclusion in our new pilot could possibly keep *Star Trek* off the air as a series."

NBC HAD GENUINELY DOUBTED THAT DESILU COULD MAKE AN HOUR-LONG, EFFECTS-LADEN ADVENTURE SHOW LIKE *STAR TREK*.

CREW BOARDING

Subsequent decades, of course, have proved the NBC Sales Department and their figures wrong. Incredibly wrong, in fact. Once the series was being broadcast, Nimoy and his character Spock quickly became, arguably, *the* most iconic elements of *Star Trek*. When the actor sadly died in February 2015, it was headline news around the world.

Back in the mid-1960s, however, only those directly involved in getting *Star Trek* off the ground believed Spock to be a vital aspect of the show. In order to get a second pilot made, it was agreed that Spock's role in it would be minimal, in order to delay any final argument with NBC about the character until *after* they had commissioned *Star Trek* as a weekly series.

Although Roddenberry initially determined to write all the scripts demanded by NBC, Solow argued that other writers would have to be brought in, if only to ensure that three necessarily "different" scripts could be delivered in good time. Roddenberry only agreed as long as he discussed the story ideas with the writers first, could still write one of the scripts and, when deemed necessary, edit the other two.

Desilu's eventual choice of scripts came down to Roddenberry's "The Omega Glory," "Mudd's Women" by Roddenberry and Stephen Kandel, and "Where No Man Has Gone Before" by Samuel A. Peeples, a writer with science fiction experience whom Roddenberry had already consulted on several occasions while writing "The Cage."

Roddenberry, at least at the time, was the first to admit that his solo script wasn't very good. Nevertheless, it was forwarded to NBC as an example of *Star Trek*'s "parallel worlds" concept, which would enable at least some episodes to be shot on existing sets, using stock costumes. The ship-based "Mudd's Women," meantime, only required the sets already built for "The Cage." While it would later become a fondly remembered first season episode, the story's focus on an inter-galactic trader-pimp was exactly the kind of story NBC didn't want to see – at least as a pilot.

In the end, Peeples' script would be rewritten sufficiently by Roddenberry to disappoint the writer when viewing the finished episode. Nevertheless, it was the script that Desilu and NBC agreed to be the second pilot. As Roddenberry later declared in *The Star Trek*

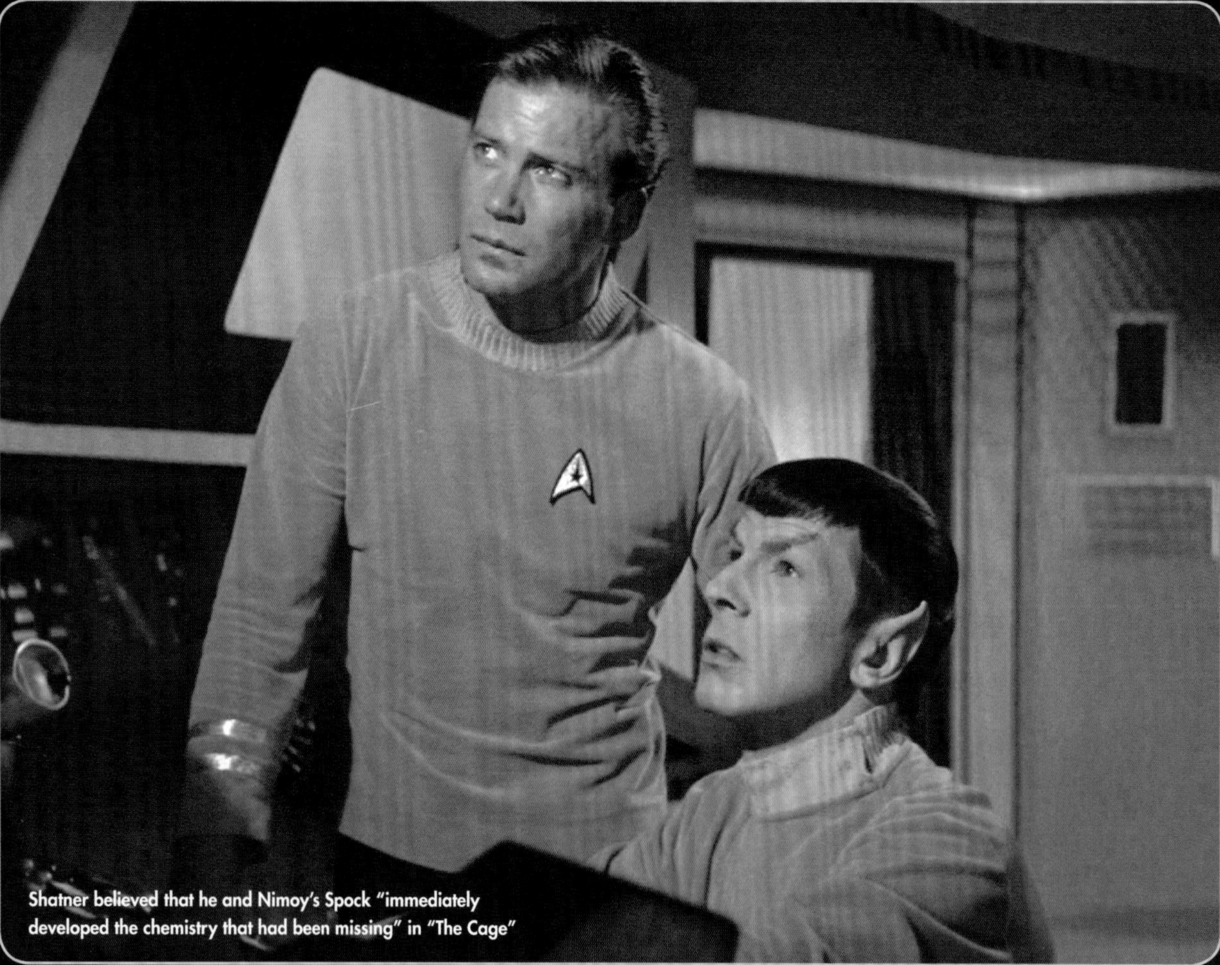

Shatner believed that he and Nimoy's Spock "immediately developed the chemistry that had been missing" in "The Cage"

IN FEBRUARY 1966, DESPITE CONTINUING DOUBTS ABOUT SPOCK, NBC ORDERED AN INITIAL RUN OF 16 EPISODES.

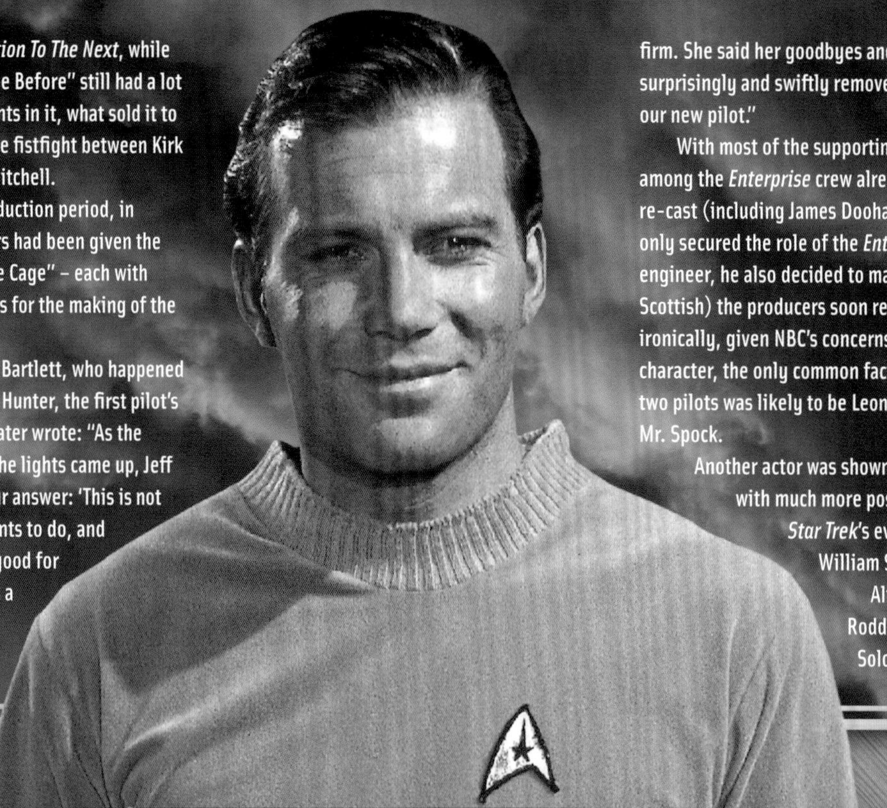

Saga: From One Generation To The Next, while "Where No Man Has Gone Before" still had a lot of science fiction elements in it, what sold it to NBC was the bare knuckle fistfight between Kirk and the god-like Gary Mitchell.

During the pre-production period, in the meantime, two actors had been given the opportunity to view "The Cage" – each with significant consequences for the making of the second pilot.

The first was Sandy Bartlett, who happened to be the wife of Jeffrey Hunter, the first pilot's leading man. As Solow later wrote: "As the end credits rolled, and the lights came up, Jeff Hunter's wife gave us our answer: 'This is not the kind of show Jeff wants to do, and besides, it wouldn't be good for his career. Jeff Hunter is a movie star.' Mrs. Hunter was very polite and firm. She said her goodbyes and left, having surprisingly and swiftly removed our star from our new pilot."

With most of the supporting characters among the *Enterprise* crew already being re-cast (including James Doohan, who not only secured the role of the *Enterprise*'s chief engineer, he also decided to make him Scottish) the producers soon realized that, ironically, given NBC's concerns about the character, the only common factor between the two pilots was likely to be Leonard Nimoy's Mr. Spock.

Another actor was shown "The Cage," with much more positive results: *Star Trek*'s eventual new lead, William Shatner.

Although neither Roddenberry's nor Solow's first choice

(both Jeff Bridges and future *Hawaii Five-O* star Jack Lord had been considered) *Star Trek*'s much-trusted co-producer Robert H. Justman was pleased, considering Shatner an "enthusiastic, good-humored, and hardworking" actor. "I knew he would bring a much-needed energy to the role, an energy we hadn't gotten from Jeff Hunter."

In his autobiography *Up Till Now*, Shatner modestly suggests that Roddenberry felt he was "the perfect choice for the lead role in a show that wasn't too intelligent for its audience and whom he didn't have to pay a lot of money."

That typical Shatner sense of humor proved key to the actor's take on the show. "After watching the pilot I told Roddenberry I thought the characters took themselves much too seriously," he wrote. "They made everything they did seem so monumental. These guys have been on this voyage for years, I told him. Sometimes a left turn is simply a left turn. It's another workday until something dramatic changes it. I see it having more humor, more fun."

WHERE NO VULCAN HAS GONE BEFORE

More importantly, Shatner believed that he and Nimoy's Spock "immediately developed the chemistry that had been missing in the pilot. Mr. Spock was half-Vulcan, an alien struggling to suppress his human emotions – his choices and decisions were all based on logic. If his commander was also serious and somber, as it had been originally written, Leonard had nothing to play against."

Once the Captain of the *Starship Enterprise* was re-imagined as a man with not just very human emotions, but also a sense of humor, the emotionless character of Spock was thrown into far greater relief.

The two men's different approaches to acting also helped. "Bill has always been a very externalized actor, he just opens his arms completely to the audience," Nimoy said many years later. "By the time this show began, I'd been a working actor for 17 years, I'd been teaching acting for five years, and my style was much more internalized; each action I took and every word I spoke seemed considered and thought-out."

Although the episode was officially scheduled for completion within seven days, co-producer Robert Justman anticipated that it would take nine to shoot "Where No Man Has Gone Before." Given how "The Cage" had gone severely over schedule and budget, some Desilu executives darkly expected it would take even longer – perhaps up to 11 days. Filming began on Monday July 19, 1965.

Work indeed soon fell behind schedule, not least thanks to the same swarm of bees in Desilu's Culver City studio building that had delayed work on "The Cage" the year before. Both Shatner and guest-star Sally Kellerman were stung, requiring time-consuming medical attention and also careful shooting around their "puffed up" faces.

Kellerman was also clearly nervous about the very form-fitting trousers she had to wear. "Every time we got ready to do a take, she'd fold her hands in front of her nether region and assume what I called her 'crotch cover' posture," remembered Justman. The solution proved two-fold: Kellerman was given a "space clipboard" prop to hold in front of her, while as many scenes as possible were shot from the waist up!

Filming on "Where No Man Has Gone Before" was ultimately completed in eight days, with one extra day for pickup shots and

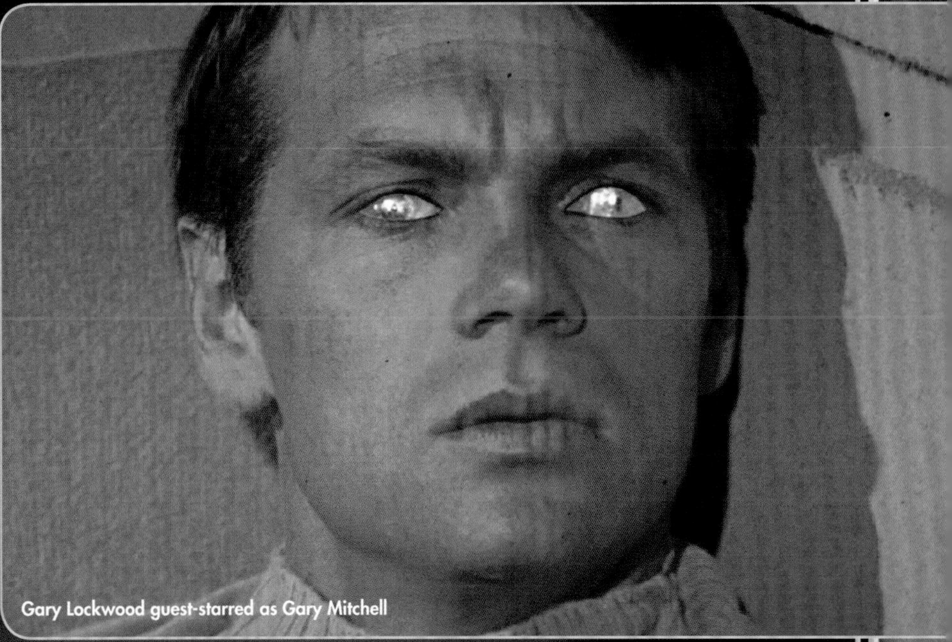

Gary Lockwood guest-starred as Gary Mitchell

Delta Vega

DID YOU KNOW?

While a slightly re-edited version of "Where No Man Has Gone Before" became the third episode of *Star Trek* broadcast in America, it would be the first to be seen in the UK. Shown on BBC1 at 5.15pm on Saturday July 12, 1969, the episode was scheduled between a *Tom and Jerry* cartoon and an early evening talk show presented by the then-popular British presenter Simon Dee.

"Where No Man Has Gone Before" script writer Sam Peeples also wrote the first animated *Star Trek* episode.

Penetrating the galactic barrier

Sally Kellerman as Dr. Elizabeth Dehner

DID YOU KNOW?

Penning the second pilot wouldn't be the only occasion Sam Peeples would be brought onboard to help relaunch *Star Trek*: Filmation's animated *Star Trek* series debuted in 1973 with his episode "Beyond the Farthest Star." However, it would prove to be third-time unlucky several years later when his screenplay "Worlds That Never Were" was rejected by Paramount, in favor of what would ultimately become *Star Trek II: The Wrath of Khan*.

"inserts" – just as Justman had originally calculated. Post-production on the pilot was not without its challenges, not least because the main production team almost immediately began working on other shows for Desilu's slate of potential pilots, including a new espionage show, *Mission: Impossible*.

All were agreed, though, that "Where No Man Has Gone Before" was an accessible science fiction action adventure story, with a cast of identifiable characters, and a heroic, energetic leading man. In February 1966, despite continuing doubts about Spock, NBC ordered an initial run of 16 episodes, alongside *Mission: Impossible*. Desilu suddenly had the "interesting" headache of making two, hour-long adventure series simultaneously.

WHAT SOLD IT TO NBC WAS THE BARE-KNUCKLE FISTFIGHT BETWEEN KIRK AND THE GOD-LIKE GARY MITCHELL.

To save money, and to give the production team some breathing space as the unremitting treadmill of weekly production began to take its toll, a slightly re-edited version of "Where No Man Has Gone Before" – adding the now iconic title sequence and Shatner's "to boldly go" narration – become the show's third broadcast episode in the fall of 1966. ("The Cage" was also drafted into service, providing the main body for the two-part story "The Menagerie.")

Four days before *Star Trek*'s television debut with "The Man Trap," on September 8, 1966, Roddenberry persuaded the organizers of *Tricon* – that year's World Science Fiction Convention, held in Cleveland, Ohio – to show "Where No Man Has Gone Before." Allan Asherman, author of *The Star Trek Compendium*, was in the audience.

"There must have been 500 people in that audience," he later wrote. "When the *Enterprise*

TREK LOVES LUCY

Lucille Ball, star of groundbreaking sitcom *I Love Lucy*, must rank among the weirdest "unsung heroes" of TV science fiction. In 1958, Desilu Studios – which she set up with first husband Desi Arnaz – produced Rod Serling's script "The Time Element," which directly led to the launch of his iconic series, *The Twilight Zone*. Six years later, the same company took a gamble on Gene Roddenberry's proposed "*Wagon Train* to the stars."

But how "hands on" was the famous redhead when it came to *Star Trek*? Answer: not very. According to Desilu's then-Executive in Charge of Production, Herbert F. Solow, Ball at one point assumed that any show called *Star Trek* could only be about movie stars entertaining American troops in the South Seas during the Second World War!

With time running out to complete the filming of the second pilot's climatic fight between Captain Kirk and Gary Mitchell, Solow and co-producer Robert Justman grabbed some brooms to help clear sand off the camera dolly tracks. Suddenly, there was a third broom in action, wielded by none other than Lucille Ball herself. Her reason? "What I won't do to get the wrap party started!"

itchell taunts Kirk with an open grave, during their final climactic
nfrontation, in "Where No Man Has Gone Before"

hit the galactic barrier, 1,000 eyes opened wide. Five hundred respiratory rates accelerated with that wonderful pleasure that comes over lovers of all things when they see their favorite subject being treated well.

"This was a science fiction television series we all wanted to see. We were extremely impressed," he added. "Roddenberry seemed to have no idea of the effect his show was having on us. He asked for the audience's opinion; we gave him a standing ovation. He smiled, and we returned the smile before we converged on him. We came close to lifting the man upon our shoulders and carrying him out of the room."

Star Trek's first contact with a mainstream television audience would prove to be somewhat more challenging but, as the years and decades have shown, those members of *Tricon* would be just the first of millions to be enthralled, entertained and inspired to go "Where No Man Has Gone Before!"

Star Trek's heroic new captain

TALOSIAN TALES

Of all *Star Trek*'s alien races and iconic villains, fans hold a special affection for the very first – those implacable, telekinetic brainiacs, the Talosians, from pilot episode "The Cage." But while Talosian leader "The Keeper" was embodied by actress Meg Wyllie, it took renowned character actor, Malachi Throne to give the exotic alien its voice.

Interviews By Pat Jankiewicz

MALACHI THRONE:
THIRD MAN THROUGH THE DOOR

With his imposing physical presence and deep, mesmerizing voice, character actor Malachi Throne (who passed away in 2013, aged 84) was as comfortable playing authority figures as he was villains, but his first *Star Trek* role was the result of turning another part down.

"That whole *Star Trek* experience, doing Gene Roddenberry's original pilot, was amazing," Throne told *Star Trek Magazine*, in an interview conducted in 2012, "I had no idea it would become what it has. There I was, my usual occasionally employed actor

self. I was called in by Gene Roddenberry, because he had seen and liked my work."

Throne recalled meeting with Roddenberry, Oscar Katz, Head of production at Desilu, and producer Robert Justman, but it was a while before Roddenberry brought up "this science fiction thing" he was working on. "So I immediately said, 'I love science fiction!', which I do," laughed Throne, "He talked about what *Star Trek* was, which at that time was only a TV pilot. I said, 'Sounds terrific, what would you like me to play?' He said, 'Well, read the script first.' I did, and when I finished it, I said, 'I want to play Spock!' Gene said, 'No, we've got Leonard [Nimoy] for that', so I said, 'So long, gentlemen, I'm late for unemployment, I don't want to lose my place in line'."

Throne's brush with *Star Trek* could have so easily ended there, but the actor soon discovered he was being considered for another major role. "Gene says, 'Is there anything else you want to do, because we want you to play the ship's doctor.'" Throne continued, "I said, 'No, no, no. [The doctor] is the third man through the door, and a friend of mine wrote a book called, 'Don't Be The Third Man Through The Door In Hollywood', because you will end up that way.' I ended up that way anyway, in spite of his warning!"

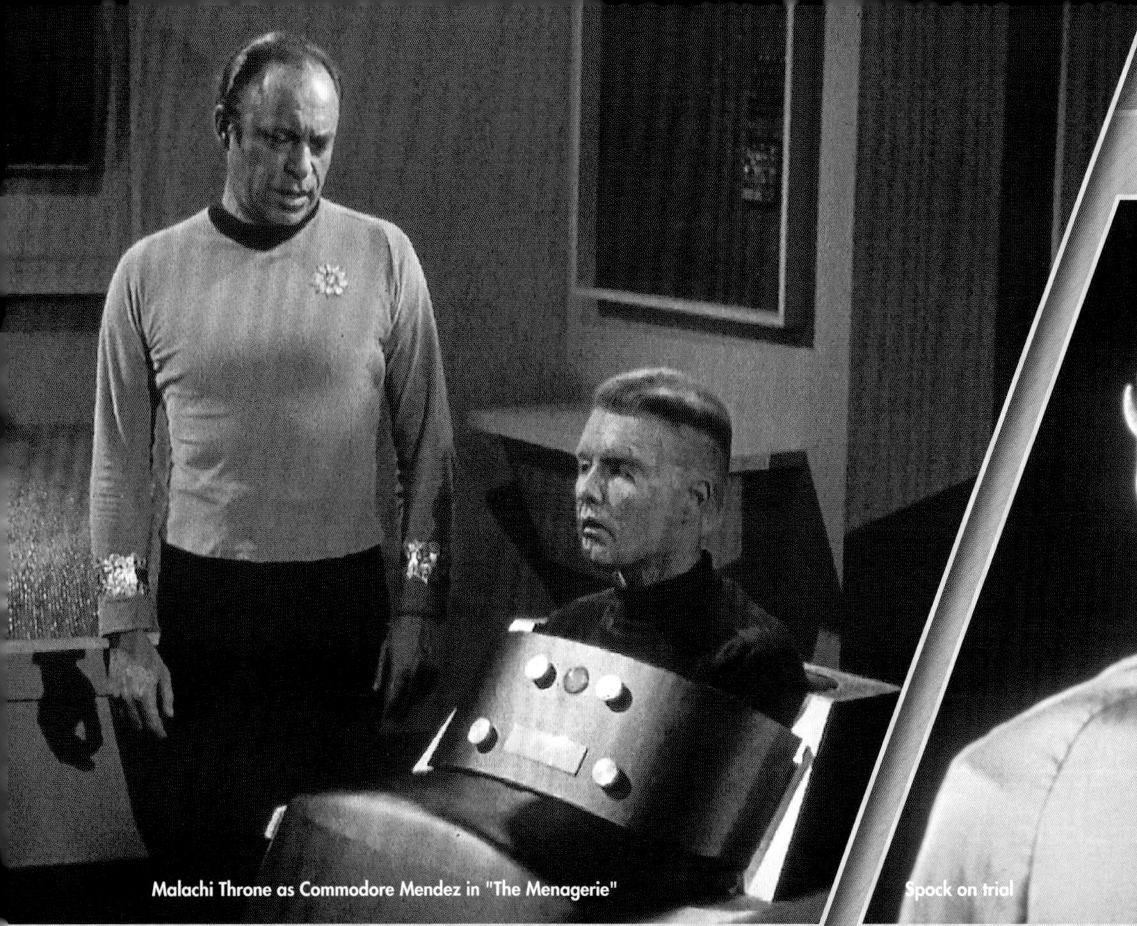

Malachi Throne as Commodore Mendez in "The Menagerie"

Spock on trial

However, having read the script, Throne's keen eye had spotted another opportunity entirely. "I said to Gene and the others, 'Well, I don't want to do that, either. I don't want to play Bones. It's not my idea to play a doctor in space. I mean, my mother would like it, but nonetheless, I don't want to do that...' I then said, 'I notice the Talosian women don't speak, but they have lines.' Gene asked, 'Can you do a woman's voice?' I said 'Yes, I can', and I auditioned for it. Gene said 'Terrific!' and I wound up doing the voices for the Talosian women in the pilot. I did The Keeper, who Meg Wyllie played, and all the other Talosians.

"Gene asked me, 'How much do you want, to do this part?' I said, 'I don't know, let me call my wife.' I called her and asked, 'How much are those chairs at Sloan's Department Store that you wanted?' She told me and I came back to Gene with the price. He said, 'Okay.' We got the chairs and I got my salary too, of course."

Noted for playing multiple bad guys throughout his career, Throne admitted to enjoying villainous roles.

"I have played a lot of villains," said Throne, "I like doing it. It's fun to be the bad guy; it's interesting. My advice to anybody playing villains: Try not to be too sibilant and wave your hands too much! Seriously, to be a great villain requires you to search for the humanity and characteristics that make you human, while still accomplishing the tasks set before you in the script. It's better than just playing him as a snarling idiot."

SWITCHING SIDES

Having laid down the vocals for the Talosians, Throne moved on to the next job, though his involvement with *Trek* was far from over. After the unaired pilot was re-tooled into the *Star Trek* we know and love, with William Shatner's Captain Kirk replacing Jeffrey Hunter's Captain Pike, the expensive original pilot was re-purposed into a two-part episode for the show's debut season. "The Menagerie" re-introduced Christopher Pike (now played by Sean Kenny) as a badly disfigured mute in

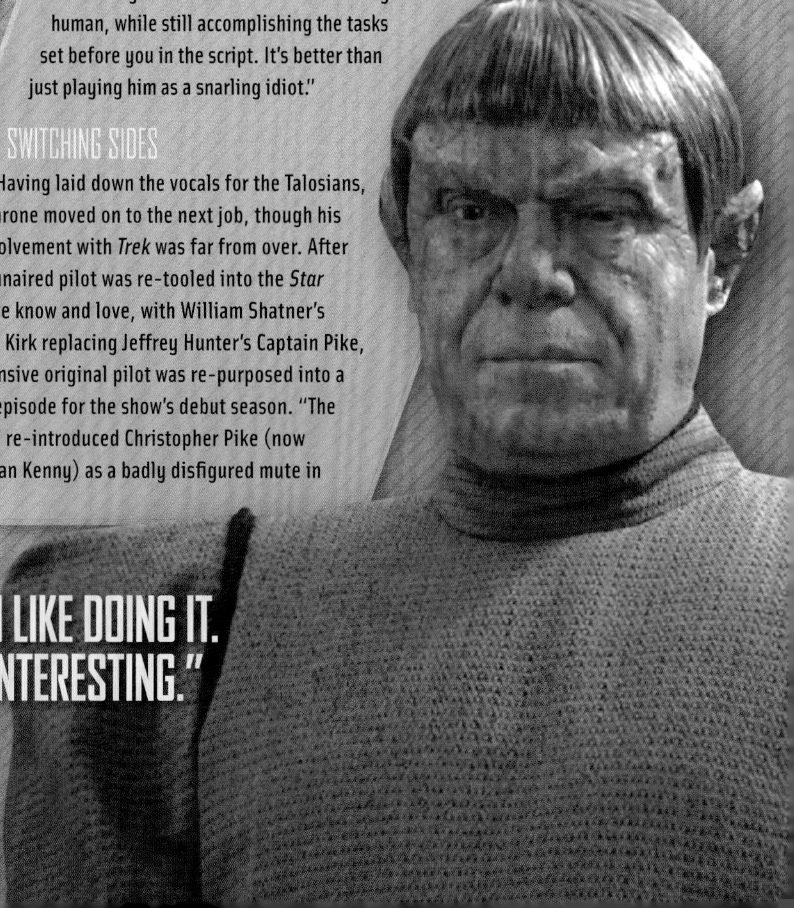

"I HAVE PLAYED A LOT OF VILLAINS. I LIKE DOING IT. IT'S FUN TO BE THE BAD GUY; IT'S INTERESTING."

a life-supporting wheelchair. When Pike's former first officer, Mr. Spock, attempts to return him to the off-limits Talos IV, Starfleet demands answers, and Throne found himself back in work – only this time he was one of the good guys (kind of...).

"It was fun to come back to *Star Trek*," Throne says of his appearance as Commodore José Mendez, the officious Starfleet officer presiding over Spock's court martial. "I saw Commodore Mendez as superior to everyone on the Starship *Enterprise*. Therefore, they are my subordinates, and they should follow my orders as such, including Captain Kirk. Because I was put in a position to hold the court martial of Spock, I therefore had to remain somewhat removed from their conviviality."

The additional courtroom sequences in Dorothy Fontana's screenplay, combined with the re-used scenes from "The Cage" pilot, meant that "The Menagerie" ended up as a two-part story, putting Throne in a unique position. "There I was, in both parts," Throne laughs, "as both the Talosian women's voices *and* as Commodore Mendez, which I found really enjoyable."

Shooting "The Menagerie" gave Throne the opportunity to work with the actors behind Jim Kirk and Mr. Spock. "Billy Shatner was a good guy," Throne remembers, "but

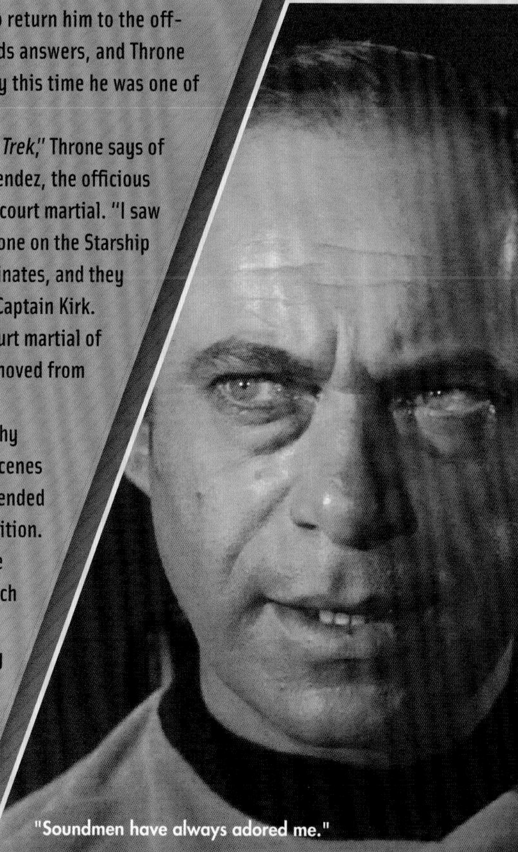

"Soundmen have always adored me."

"I SAW COMMODORE MENDEZ AS SUPERIOR TO EVERYONE ON THE STARSHIP *ENTERPRISE*. THEREFORE, THEY ARE MY SUBORDINATES, AND THEY SHOULD FOLLOW MY ORDERS."

really wrapped up with his show. Leonard [Nimoy] was always a bit distant when I worked with him on *Star Trek*, only because it was part of his understanding of the role he was playing, this alien, Spock. Leonard's demeanor in general is usually warm and friendly when you connect with him, but when you're on the set, and he's doing Spock, you don't connect that way. You have to relate to Leonard only after he takes off his make-up."

Throne had worked with Shatner earlier in their respective careers, on *The Outer Limits* episode "Cold Hands, Warm Heart." Shatner was an astronaut being seduced by a biochemistry-altering alien he'd encountered in space, while Throne portrayed his concerned physician. "Geraldine Brooks was in that with us, as well. Unlike *Star Trek*, Bill was all business on *The Outer Limits*, because it was still early in his television career. I saw him at a convention some years later, and he's always a lot of fun.

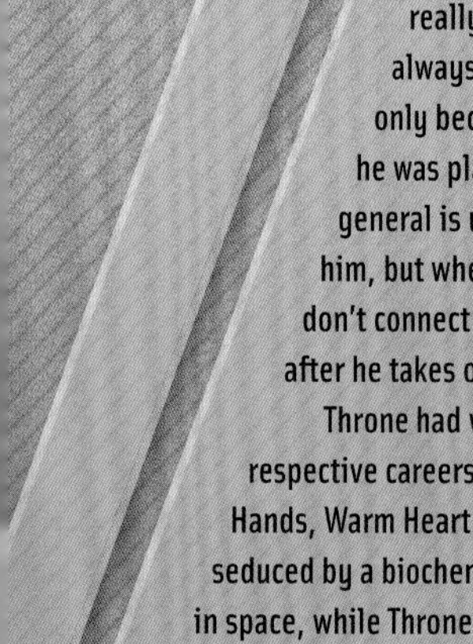

STRIKING A VOCAL CHORD

Malachi Throne always said that the key to his success was thanks to his deep, cultured voice.

"Soundmen have always adored me," Throne revealed, proudly. "My voice came courtesy of cigarettes and whiskey."

Throne lent his voice to many commercials, cartoons, and movie trailers, though perhaps his most famous came in 1977, in the original teaser trailer for a new space fantasy called *Star Wars* – "The story of a boy, a girl, and a universe!"

"George Lucas was very hands-on when I did the narration for that trailer," revealed Throne, "[He] was very generous, and I loved him for it."

Throne's resonant tones could also be heard on the science fiction-influenced hit "An Eye is Upon You", by 90s metal band Powerman 5000.

"My son, Zack, is a musician, and he brought me to these guys, who were friends of his. He took me to a session where they were cutting a record. They suggested I do the narration for it, and I said 'Okay, why not?' I never got a cent from it," he laughed. "My son did bring me a plaque when the album went Platinum."

Throne guest-starred alongside the much missed Leonard Nimoy, in *The Next Generation*'s "Unification II"

"THAT WHOLE *STAR TREK* EXPERIENCE, DOING GENE RODDENBERRY'S ORIGINAL PILOT, WAS AMAZING."

He was just superb on *Boston Legal*. What people never realized is that he had a great sense of humor, even when he was doing what he was doing as Captain Kirk. That was a bit of a put on, too. Seriously.

"*Star Trek* was a great show," Throne beams. "I even pitched Gene for writing a possible episode. Paul Carr, the first crewman to die under Captain Kirk on the show, was my tennis partner."

RETURNS AND REUNIONS

Twenty-five years later, Throne found himself back on the *Star Trek* set, as *The Next Generation* joined forces with a familiar face from the original series – and this time he would get to don those much-coveted pointy ears, albeit non-Vulcan.

"[Gene] called me and said, 'We've got a part for you.'" Throne remembered, "I said, 'Okay, what is it?' He told me it was a Romulan, two hundred years later, with Mr. Spock, [in a two-part episode called] 'Unification.' I was Senator Pardek, who is working with Spock to broker a peace treaty."

Throne enjoyed having another opportunity to work with Leonard Nimoy. "It was a lovely two-parter, and it was nice to see Leonard again." says Throne, "We were both older, and we both survived, so what the hell. I had worked with [Nimoy] the first and last time he played Spock on television."

One thing that Throne remembered vividly from the shoot were the Romulan costumes, and their capes in particular.

"As I was wearing this long cape, and walking down a rocky grotto into a deep cave to meet Spock, I tripped on the cape [during] the rehearsal," Throne explained. "On the actual shoot, I took the cape, put it over my arm and walked down the stairs, and we did the scene. The following day, the costumer comes running over to me, after having seen the dailies. He says, 'We don't do Greco-Roman in Outer Space anymore!' I nearly fell over. I could not stop laughing. '*We don't do Greco-Roman in Outer Space*...!'"

Some years later, Throne appeared as a Klingon in a *Star Trek* fan-film, much to his delight, "Now I have played a Romulan, a Klingon, a hologram, *and* a Talosian! I think I have run the gamut of *Star Trek* creatures and aliens after that. I always feel good playing an alien. Now, I will have to wait to appear on *The Next, Next Generation* or *The Next Generation After That*!"

Did he have any regrets over passing on the role that became Dr. Leonard 'Bones' McCoy? "Only the amount of money that the role accumulated over the centuries, but there are no regrets," a content Malachi Throne declared.

Difficult decisions in "The Menagerie"

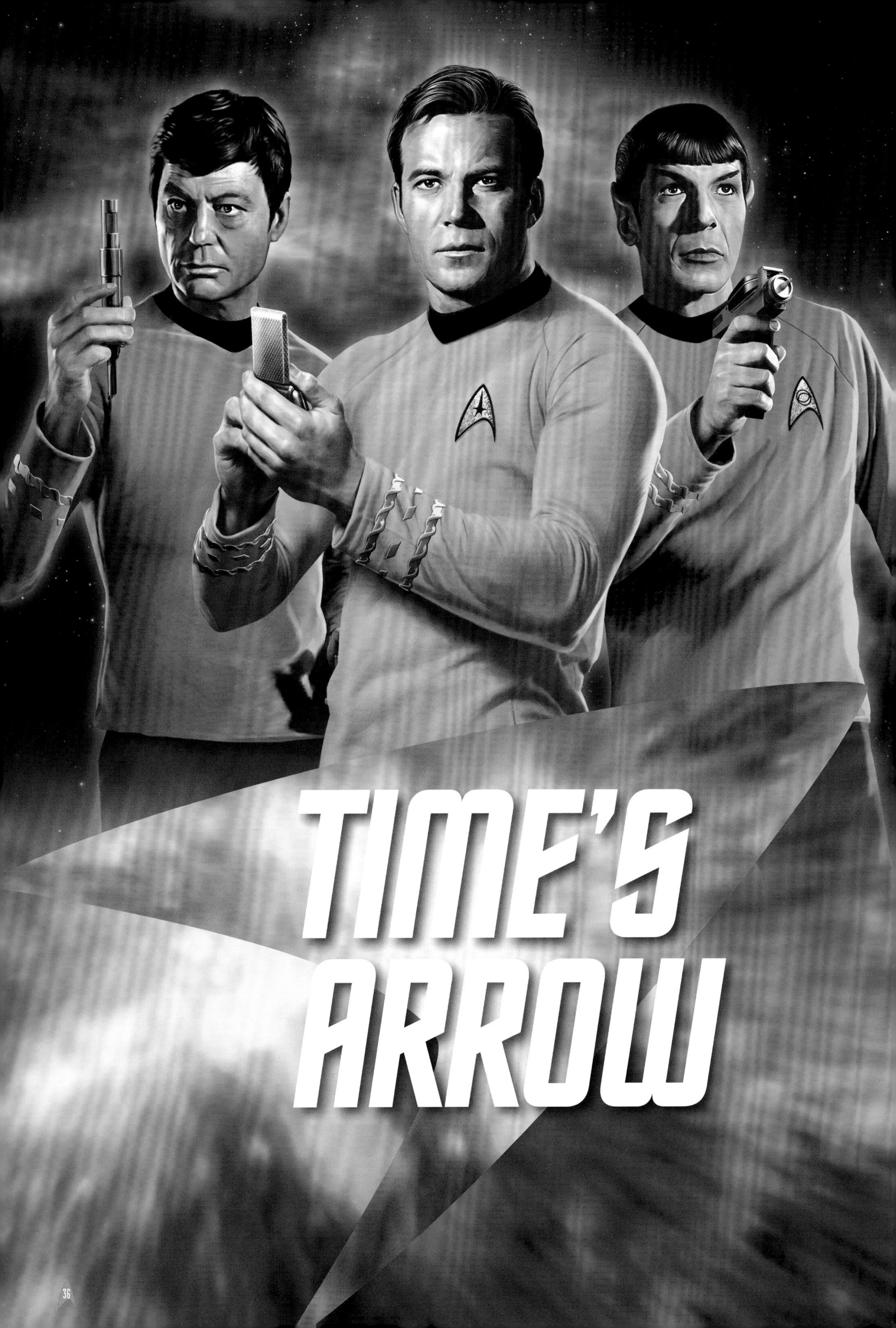
TIME'S
ARROW

THREE IS THE MAGIC NUMBER

Space may have been the final frontier, but the reason we fell in love with *Star Trek* was because of who was going boldly where no one had gone before – Kirk, Spock and McCoy: shipmates, opposites, friends...

Words: Rich Matthews

Sigmund Freud claimed that the psyche was constituted of three distinct elements – the impulsive, pleasure-seeking Id; the logical, self-regulating Ego; and the moralistic, self-judging Superego. (Do you see where we're going with this?) The psyche of *Star Trek* is likewise built around the three key figures of the libidinous, devil-may-care Captain Kirk, the emotionless rationale of Mr. Spock, and the passionate conscience of Dr. McCoy. Each is a joy, but when sparking off each other, this interstellar triptych is a wonder.

The affection that built between these men was infectious, their bonds of friendship "fascinating," the cultural divides they spanned amusing and profound. In many ways it was the perfect platonic love triangle – each pairing had a specific dynamic that stood apart from any other. Kirk and Spock's outlook and style complemented each other both as friends and in command, combining together to become a formidable team based on powerful instinct, piercing logic and genius lateral thinking. Kirk and Bones had the comfortable candidness of old drinking buddies, with an edge of avuncular disapproval from McCoy concerning Kirk's tendency to rush in where angels fear to tread, with Kirk occasionally dismissive of McCoy's "older brother" chastising. McCoy and Spock couldn't have been more different if one had been made of oily chalk and the other watery cheese (eugh), but their pointed-yet-playful interplay remains a true delight.

Spock, Kirk and McCoy – AKA *Trek*'s Holy Trinity

Occupying these iconic roles were three actors who, like their characters, all had very different styles, but William Shatner, Leonard Nimoy and DeForest Kelley clicked from their first shared moment onscreen. With the sad passing of Nimoy, we can't think of a more fitting tribute than to wax rhapsodic about the magic that he, Shatner and Kelley created, that will last long into the 23rd Century and beyond...

THREE'S A CHARM

Kirk, Spock and McCoy fulfill a tradition of dramatic archetypes, as defined by Greek

I.T. trouble for Kirk?

philosopher Aristotle – Kirk is pathos (the emotional), Spock is logos (the logical), and McCoy ethos (the ethical) – the mythic triumvirate from which all drama stems. Gene Roddenberry acknowledged this, saying that the three men personified the internal debate we all have within us – of emotion, logic and pragmatism. But this is a bit of ad-hoc retrofitting, because while Kirk and Spock's rapport was established from the get-go, McCoy's irascible contribution only started to coalesce in "The Corbomite Maneuver," and even then his relationship with Spock was far less "spiky." However, once their acerbic interplay was in full swing, the pair would always unite in support and defense of Kirk. Likewise, while McCoy often laid into Spock over moral or ethical issues that he felt the Vulcan was ignoring in favor of "damned logic," he was the first to jump to his defense if anyone else, including Kirk, criticized Spock.

"I MUST SAY I PREFER A CROWDED UNIVERSE MUCH BETTER."
KIRK, "THE THOLIAN WEB"

In "The Immunity Syndrome," just over halfway through the show's run, Kirk is put in the position of choosing between Spock and McCoy for a potentially fatal mission when the *Enterprise* is consumed by a giant single-cell organism. Spock's Vulcan strength and stoicism gets him the thankless gig, trumping Bones' medical know-how. As you would expect, when push comes to shove, Spock counsels that they should leave him and save the ship – McCoy shouts him down. Spock's reply is undeniably laced with humor: "Why, thank you, *Captain* McCoy."

THE RULE OF THREE

By season three, the writers were beginning to get more playful. While "The Empath" saw Kirk having to decide (again!) between Spock and McCoy for yet another potentially deadly mission – to be a lab rat, essentially – this time McCoy pulled the short straw. Or rather, as the Superego, he sacrificed himself so Kirk wouldn't have to choose. However, only one episode later, "The Tholian Web" saw a notable reversal of the previously standard dynamic of Spock's logic dictating that they abandon the captain in favor of the crew while McCoy carped about "not leaving

DATACORE

"THE IMMUNITY SYNDROME"

SEASON 2, EPISODE 19

The *Enterprise* encounters a huge single-cell organism that lives off pure energy. When it becomes clear to Kirk and the crew that the creature is preparing to reproduce, the future of the entire galaxy may be under threat.

FIRST AIRED:	19 JANUARY 1968
EPISODE ORDER:	47TH OF 80
WRITTEN BY:	ROBERT SABAROFF
DIRECTED BY:	JOSEPH PEVNEY

- According to Spock in this episode, Vulcan was never conquered, but when Spock declines an alcoholic beverage in "The Conscience of the King," McCoy jokes: "Now I know why they were conquered." There are many possible theories about this discrepancy, although it's entirely possible that Bones was either wrong or simply trying to rile Spock.
- This was the last episode filmed that featured Kirk's green wrap-around top, however, it aired before "Bread and Circuses," which was the final time it was seen on-screen. It was also the last episode directed by Joseph Pevney, who shares the record for directing the most episodes of the original series with Marc Daniels.
- This was the first episode to end with the Paramount logo, following the purchase of Desilu by Paramount Pictures.

Jim to die, dammit!" Here, Spock's reasoning – in what is for all intents and purposes a veritable Kobyashi Maru test (Kirk trapped on a ship out of phase with the *Enterprise*; the crew reacting violently to some unknown condition caused by the region of the space they must remain in; the Tholians weaving their deadly web around the ship) – leads him to side with rescuing Kirk, while McCoy is overwhelmed by his empathy for the crew and desire to save as many people as he can. And by this point, the show is so confident in the core of their characters, that they even have a "posthumous" Kirk lay it all out in a recorded message:

"Bones, Spock – since you are playing this tape we shall assume that I am dead, and the tactical situation is critical, and both of you are locked in mortal combat. It means, Spock, that you have control of the ship and are probably making the most difficult decisions of your career. I can offer only one small piece of advice for whatever it's worth. Use every scrap of knowledge and logic you have to save the ship, but temper your judgment with intuitive insight. I believe you have those qualities but if you can't find them in yourself, seek out McCoy. Ask his advice. And if you find it sound, take it. Bones – you've heard what I've just told Spock. Help him if you can, but remember, he is the captain and his decisions

DATACORE

"THE EMPATH"

SEASON 3, EPISODE 8

Kirk, Spock and McCoy are pulled into an alien experiment on a doomed planet.

FIRST AIRED:	6 DECEMBER 1968
EPISODE ORDER:	64TH OF 80
WRITTEN BY:	JOYCE MUSKAT
DIRECTED BY:	JOHN ERMAN

- "The Empath" was cited by DeForest Kelley as his favorite episode of the series.
- The writer of the episode, Joyce Muskat, was a fan who sold her script to the series thanks to producer Robert Justman. It was her only script sale.
- Along with "Whom Gods Destroy," "Plato's Stepchildren," and "Miri," this episode wasn't broadcast in the United Kingdom until the early 1990s. The reason given was because "they all dealt most unpleasantly with the already unpleasant subjects of madness, torture, sadism and disease." It was finally shown on 5 January 1994.

"The Empath"

must be followed without question. You might find that he is capable of human insight and human error. They are most difficult to defend, but you will find that he is deserving of the same loyalty and confidence that each of you have given me. Take care."

This actually shifts the Freudian model slightly, in favor of Kirk as the mediating ego and McCoy as the passion-governed id, but that designation isn't fair – or consistent – for Bones. No, what's more likely is that there is some shifting of roles depending on the scenario faced by the *Enterprise*, with each of the trio also possessing the same constituent parts of their psyche within their dramatic triangle. At the end of "The Tholian Web," McCoy and Spock even share a tongue-in-cheek fib about not watching Kirk's "last orders" recording. After all, Spock is meant to be devoid of emotion, but we all know the truth, that Nimoy often played him with a simmering emotion just beneath the surface. We all accepted it for the cause of drama – and we have evidence of what happened when Nimoy was instructed to play pure logic, as in *Star Trek: The Motion Picture*. Likewise, in Robert Wise's epic reintroduction of the *Enterprise* crew, McCoy is initially overplayed, all crotchety grumps and big grins ("So help me Spock, I'm actually pleased to see you!"). It only feels like true *Star Trek* when Spock loosens up and McCoy gets to expound the moral implications of V'ger's mission, the pair properly re-connecting with an invigorated Kirk. When the three components of the *Enterprise*'s psyche are in place, and interacting, they make up a Venn diagram of the perfect commander.

THE HOLY TRINITY

The high point of the Kirk/Spock/McCoy triangle fittingly came in the trilogy of interrelated stories sat within the original crew's six films. Bookended by the slightly-chilly heavy sci-fi of *The Motion Picture*, the existential holiness of *The Final Frontier*, and the spectacular allegorical cold-war swan song of *The Undiscovered Country*, *Star Treks II*, *III* and *IV* had a through line that made them feel like one continuous story – the nature of friendship. Through the story arc of *The Wrath Of Khan* we see loss, grief, anger, desperation and sacrifice all enacted on an operatic scale, with each of our three heroes integral to each other's survival. *Khan* is, on the surface, about Kirk and Spock's "best of times and worst of times" – until the final moments of Spock's life, when only Bones' huge capacity for empathy and kindness makes him the ideal human

A web of intrigue

DATACORE

"THE THOLIAN WEB"

SEASON 3, EPISODE 9

When Captain Kirk is pulled into interspace while trying to rescue the *U.S.S. Defiant*, the *Enterprise* is trapped in a web of energy by the mysterious Tholians.

FIRST AIRED:	15TH NOVEMBER 1968
EPISODE ORDER:	64TH OF 80
WRITTEN BY:	JUDY BURNS AND CHET RICHARDS
DIRECTED BY:	HERB WALLERSTEIN

- This is the only episode in the entire run where Spock uses Dr. McCoy's nickname, Bones.
- This is one of only a few episodes in which every second and third season regular all appear – Kirk, Spock, McCoy, Scotty, Sulu, Chekov, Uhura, and Nurse Chapel.
- Alongside "The Trouble With Tribbles," this was one of Nichelle Nichols' favorite episodes.

vessel for Spock's katra – or, as McCoy puts it in his inimitable way, Spock's soul. Through his absence, *The Search For Spock* shows us what life would be like for Kirk and McCoy without their "ego," their center – haunted by Spock, both men are driven to the brink of obsession and madness. They commit crimes, they endanger their crewmates, they destroy the only true romantic love of Kirk's life, the *Enterprise*, they even sacrifice his son, David. They do it because they are not complete without Spock. Just as they humanized the half-blood Vulcan, so he grounded them and brought out the best of their humanity.

Kirk is also clearly jealous of the intimacy now shared by Bones and Spock – McCoy knows Spock like no one else ever can, after having his consciousness rattling around in his skull. The only way he can get back in the game is to get Spock out of Bones' head and back in his (handily) regenerated body. But this is a major breakthrough for Kirk – he finally values a person more than his ship, more than his command (if not more than his son). And he's validated when, after Spock's mind and body are reunited, Kirk is the focus of Spock's attentions, not the ship, not Bones. "Jim. Your name is Jim" is his most profound statement of identity.

Then we enter the final chapter of this tale of brothers, as they fly back to face the music, reunited yet changed. Spock is more childlike, McCoy friendlier to his green-blooded compadre. Kirk is frustrated at this

The three components that make up the *Enterprise's* psyche

"YOU FIND IT EASIER TO UNDERSTAND THE DEATH OF ONE THAN THE DEATH OF A MILLION. YOU SPEAK ABOUT THE OBJECTIVE HARDNESS OF THE VULCAN HEART, YET HOW LITTLE ROOM THERE SEEMS TO BE IN YOURS."

SPOCK TO MCCOY, "THE IMMUNITY SYNDROME"

development – he wants the old dynamic back, but things have moved on, too much has changed. It's played for laughs (mostly), but there is a deep-rooted yearning in Kirk's interactions with Spock. True balance is only restored by a key visual reference – as the accused former crew of the late starship *Enterprise* march into the Federation courtroom to hear their fate, Spock strides from the stands to join them. Back in uniform, back in the pecking order, stood next to Kirk, balance is restored. Even more so, when Spock has spoken to his father Sarek, he and Kirk match strides to march out of the courtroom together, the gait of both men recalling their reunion on board the *Enterprise* after Kirk is beamed back to the ship from the Genesis cave inside Regula in *Wrath of Khan*. Bones is also now back in his rightful place, as emotional support, wry commentator and not-always-needed third wheel.

More lip service is of course paid to the "special relationship" in *V* and *VI*, notably Kirk's sense of betrayal when Spock nominates him as the peace envoy to the Klingons in *The Undiscovered Country*. Bones is present and correct, to call foul on a lot of Kirk's pontificating and Spock's cold logic, and truly gets to shine in the bowels of the Rura Penthe penal colony. But, if we're honest, the dynamic feels a bit forced, going through the motions. Which is fitting given what they've been through by this point. There could never be bigger highs and lows than in parts *II* to *IV*. It's all about Spock, on-screen and off, with what happens to the character becoming the catalyst for the main narrative thrust, and with Nimoy himself dictating what happened behind the camera. He wanted Spock to die in *II*. He would only come back if he got to direct *III*. He helmed *IV* to unprecedented levels of commercial and critical success for the franchise. But, without Shatner and Kelley, Kirk and Bones, where would Spock be? On Vulcan polishing his Kolinahr. So, thank Surak for space's three amigos. Live Long and Prosper, old friends.

FLASH

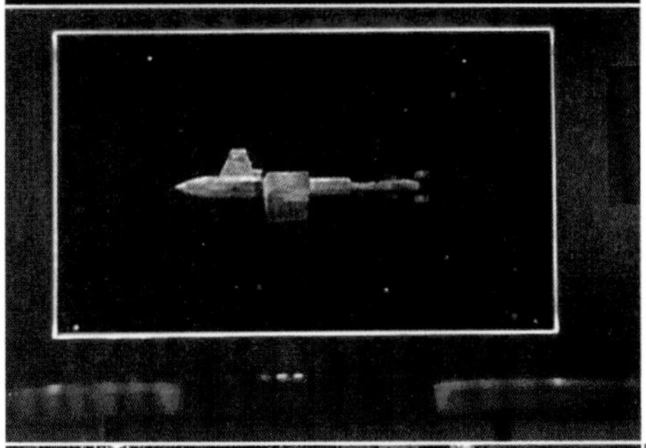

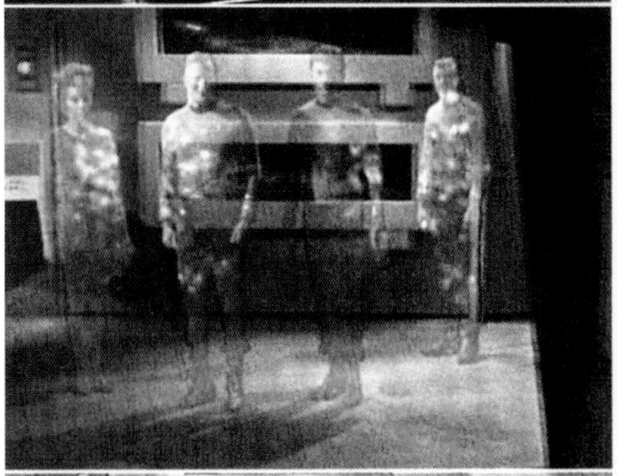

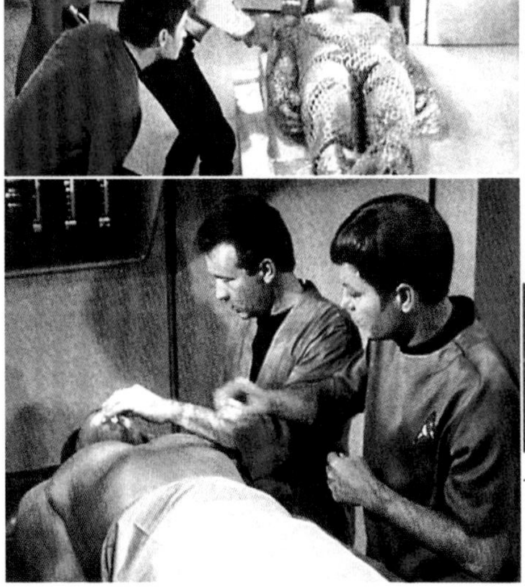

This Issue...
SPACE SEED

Frank Garcia recounts the making of classic *Star Trek* episode *Space Seed* and explores the ideas that have shaped many stories that have followed...

THE STORY

Captain Kirk and the *Enterprise* encounter a 'sleeper ship', identified as having originated from the Earth's past in the 1990s, containing 79 humans in hibernation. Their first revival is a towering man named Khan. Intrigued, Kirk and Spock search their records and discover he's Khan Noonien Singh, a genetically engineered, powerful man who was a leader in 'The Eugenics Wars'. History showed that he and his fellow 'Eugenics', young supermen, had taken political power over a quarter of the planet. But events had somehow gone wrong and they had inexplicably disappeared during a crucial time. They boarded the *S.S. Botany Bay* spacecraft, and left Earth, in search of a new world to conquer. But, as Spock remarks, "Superior ability breeds superior ambition." Khan seduces Lieutenant Marla McGivers and with her help, he and his men forcibly take control of the *Enterprise*.

Khan throws Captain Kirk into an atmospheric decompression chamber and taunts the crew. "If you join me, I will free him!" But realising what she has done, McGivers rescues Kirk. With Spock's help, Kirk gasses the entire ship, rendering most unconscious, and Khan is later defeated in a one-on-one combat with Kirk in Engineering.

Faced with a dilemma of determining the fate of the would-be-captors, Kirk decides that rather than throw them behind bars at the nearest starbase, he opts instead for an unusual sentence. Khan and his people are marooned on an unspoiled world, Ceti Alpha V, to build a life for themselves.

In the story's final scene, Spock remarks, "It would be interesting, Captain, to return to that world in 100 years and learn what crop has sprung from the seed you have planted today..."

THE PRODUCTION

Space Seed is one of the series' most memorable episodes – primarily because of the magnetic acting performance delivered by Ricardo Montalban. He infused Khan with a strong sense of intelligence, but with a megalomaniac ambition.

Thematically, the episode explored the notion of a genetically engineered human being, who had physical and mental abilities far beyond ordinary mortals. In today's world, particularly in the sports arena, we are debating and arguing about the usage of drugs or DNA-manipulation to enhance

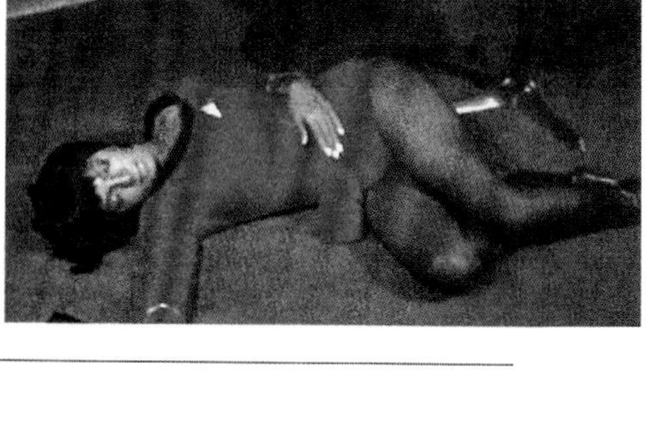

SPACE SEED MINUTAE

- Marla McGivers was played by the late Madlyn Rhue. Rhue was a popular character actress, mostly on TV shows, for over 30 years, who continued acting even after being diagnosed with multiple sclerosis in 1977, first by hiding her condition. "I was telling people I had a car accident," she once said, or an "arthritic hip." She died in December 2003.

  Although McGivers is referred to as 'lieutenant' in dialogue, she wore no rank stripe (denoting an ensign).

- One of Scotty's technical manual screens in *Space Seed* reveals the *Enterprise* to be a *Constitution*-class starship, registry number NCC-1700. According to *Star Trek* history, the Constitution-class began service in the early 23rd Century, and continued to be the backbone of Starfleet up to the 2270s.

  Stephen Whitfield's book *The Making of Star Trek*, first published in 1968, quotes memos from D.C. Fontana and Bob Justman recommending various names for starships. By then the following names had already been featured in the series: *Enterprise, Exeter, Excalibur, Lexington, Yorktown, Potemkin, Republic, Hood, Constitution, Kongo, Constellation, Farragut, Valiant*, and *Intrepid*.

- As Kirk is trying to break open Khan's glass coffin in the opening scenes of the story, his phaser falls off his belt. McCoy keeps looking down at it, as if he's wondering when they're going to yell 'cut' so they can re-shoot the scene. Apparently, the scene was never re-shot because the production couldn't afford any more glass!

- In *Star Trek II: The Wrath of Khan*, Chekov immediately recognises Khan Noonien Singh – but was not, apparently, aboard the *Enterprise* at the time of the original adventure. Asked about this during an interview for startrek.com, Koenig joked that Chekov was actually aboard the *Enterprise*. "He was working on the third deck – behind the boiler room!" he claimed.

- Watch out for an appearance by John Arndt as Fields, a regular extra, who also played an unnamed crewmen in *Miri* and *Dagger of the Mind*. He's named Fields in the episode *Balance of Terror*.

an athlete's abilities during competition. If used widely enough, genetic enhancements will blur our ability to define the best of an ordinary human against those who are covertly altering their natural abilities to exceed typical human limits.

Space Seed was written by the late Carey Wilber, a man his family describe today as " full of contradictions.

"He was by turns funny as hell," an affectionate tribute to him on the family website declares. "Passionate, irresponsible, sympathetic, crazy, eloquent, and one of the best damn writers, dialogue artists, and yarn-spinners west of the Atlantic Ocean."

Space Seed is one of The Original Series' most memorable episodes

Wilber was thrown out of Catholic school at 14 for reading Voltaire (while pretending to read his prayer missal) and turned to journalism, where he made his mark at multiple newspapers, including the *Toronto Globe* and the *New York Times*. By the early 1950s, he began writing television, a career he continued for the next 30 years, for shows as diverse as *Captain Video, Bonanza, Lost in Space, The Twilight Zone, The Time Tunnel* (a show he probably wrote more of than any other writer) and *Star Trek*.

A rare first draft copy of the *Space Seed* script, dated 7 December 1966 and credited to Carey Wilber and Gene Coon, shows the basis of the episode as it was eventually transmitted appears quite recognisable from the start – but there are minor differences.

The story structure and almost all the characters are essentially the same. An Indian helmsman, Supta, is introduced in the teaser but all his dialogue was shifted to the cast during filming. Khan Noonien Singh first introduces himself as John Ericssen, but in the course of Kirk and Spock's investigation, they realise he is really Ragnar Thorwald, and he and his surviving sleepers were, Spock explains, "products of an abortive experiment inhuman engineering. Genetically directed in conception. Born and bred, as it were, to rule."

What we know as The Eugenics Wars is referred here as a period of Earth history, "the First World Tyranny," which was a "ruthless military dictatorship."

Although dialogue and scenes are different from what has been filmed, one can recognise both the analogy and story.

In terms of personality, Ericssen/Thorwald acts very much as Ricardo Montalban played him, but here, when he breaks out of his guarded quarters and dashes to takeover Engineering, he does so not by forcing the door open and taking out the guard with his bare hands. He merely opens the door from inside and disntegrates the guard with a phaser. In this regard, Thorwald is more brutal and in the end, when he's cast out to Gamma Three, Captain Kirk appears far more generous than he should be to a killer.

The seduction of Marla McGivers is also relatively the same, but here, she's not a historian but a Systems Control Specialist, who was brought in to examine the *Botany Bay*'s environmental

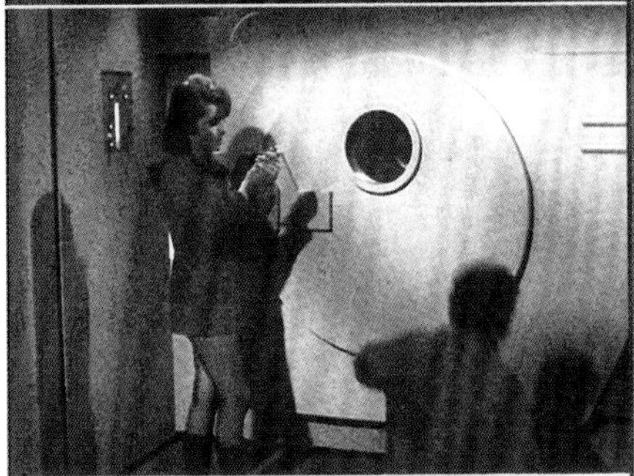

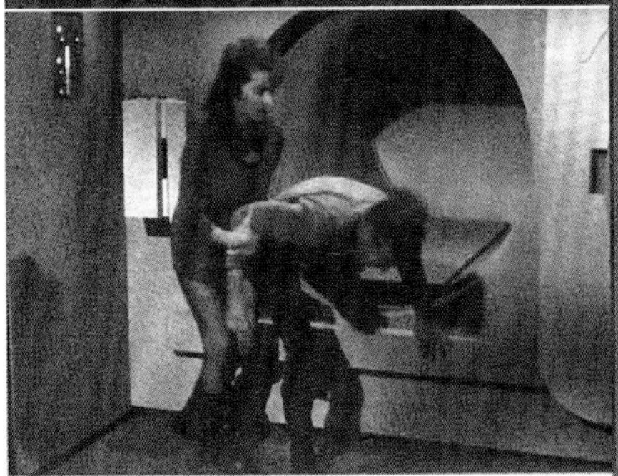

BEHIND THE SCENES: VISUAL EFFECTS

Because of the time and expense involved in designing and constructing a studio spaceship model, very few episodes of *Star Trek: The Original Series* featured new space vessels. *Space Seed* was an exception to the rule.

The *SS Botany Bay* model was designed by *Star Trek* art director Walter M. 'Matt' Jefferies. The *Botany Bay* studio model also made a cameo appearance in *The Ultimate Computer*, in which it was said to be an ore freighter which was destroyed by the M-5 computer.

Linwood Dunn's Film Effects of Hollywood filmed the special effects space scenes of the *USS Enterprise* and *Botany Bay* studio models. Dunn was a Hollywood visual effects pioneer beginning in the 1920s, with credits including *King Kong* (1933) and *Citizen Kane* (1941). Film Effects, established by Dunn in 1946, specialised in optical effects and optical printing services. Dunn died in 1998.

While it is not known who built the *Botany Bay* studio model, it was most likely built at Film Effects. Approximately 44" in length, it was a lightweight, simplistic model built of wood and it had no internal lights. Matt Jefferies added the weathering to the model.

The original *Botany Bay* studio model was publicly displayed at the US National Air and Space Museum's Star Trek Exhibition in 1992-93, and is now in a private collection.

– *William S. McCullars*

The behind-the-scenes images published here have been kindly supplied from the private collection of Cinematographer Curt McAloney. These images are digitally restored film clips which were sold by Gene Roddenberry's Star Trek memorabilia company in the 1960s and 1970s.

Curt has lovingly cleaned and restored the images, many of which were badly damaged.

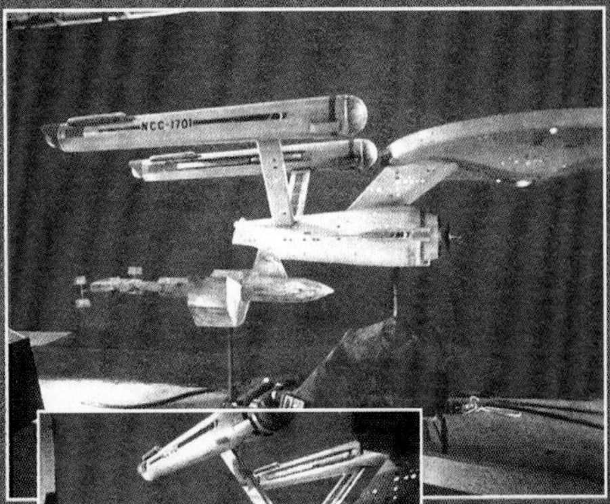

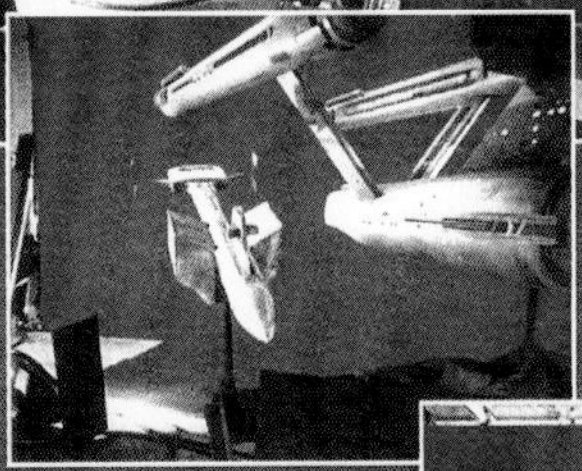

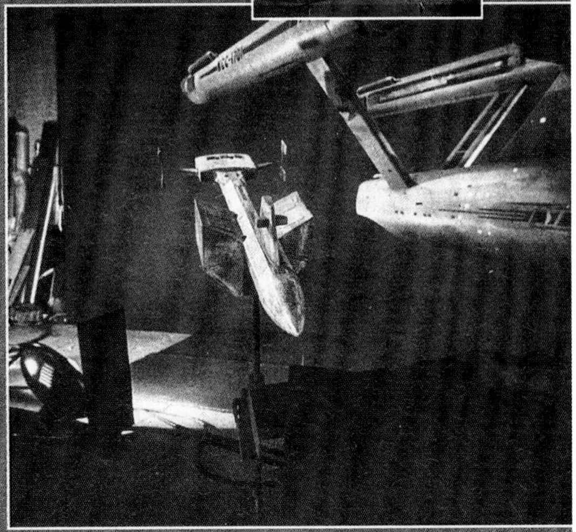

REIGNING IN HELL

Space Seed inspired a different kind of growth for novelist Greg Cox. With just one episode, there was such rich material that he was able to write three full-length novels focusing on the Khan character. In a trio of books titled *The Eugenics Wars*, Cox has crafted an elaborate prequel exploring Khan's history on Earth and revealing the exact nature of events leading up to his launch into space and into suspended animation. In these two books, he also integrates two other favourite characters from another *Star Trek: The Original Series* episode: Gary Seven and Roberta Lincoln, from *Assignment: Earth* and how they become involved in an attempt to stop Khan.

"The Eugenics Wars books were conjured up from the expository dialogue in *Space Seed*, about Khan's career back in the 20th Century," says Cox, whose novels also include other media novels for series such as *Roswell*, *Xena* and *Alias*. "The fun part of the books was trying to work Khan's story into the actual history of the 20th Century. In that respect, the books occasionally wrote themselves. Since, according to *Space Seed*, Khan was a Sikh from northern India, I did a lot of reading on Indian history, then matched up the dates to key events in Khan's life: The nuclear explosion at Rajasthan, the Bhopal chemical disaster, and so on. Trust me, there were lots of charts and timelines involved!"

"In real life, [genetic engineering] issues are a lot more ambiguous." – Author Greg Cox

However, a controversy results as a consequnce of this decision to meld "our history" with *Star Trek's* "past" history, as Cox explains. "I know some readers would have preferred that I ignore History As We Know It and just described an apocalyptic war to end all wars. That's a legitimate objection. I knew going in that there were two ways to deal with the whole '1990s' thing – ignore it or deal with it – and there were going to be objections whichever way I went."

In Book 3, *To Reign in Hell: The Exile of Khan Noonien Singh*, Cox detailed Khan's life on Ceti Alpha V, filling in all the details prior to *Star Trek II: The Wrath of Khan*, extrapolated from just a few lines of dialogue from the film.

"Since the third book takes place entirely on Ceti Alpha V, I didn't have to worry about Earth history so much," says Cox. "I was more concerned with making what Khan told Chekov in the movie play out as convincingly as possible. Why did Ceti Alpha VI blow up in the first place? How did the planet turn into a wasteland? How did Khan and his people survive all those years? And what about those eels?"

Recalling his first impressions of *Space Seed*, Greg

systems. History, however, is a hobby. She realises the severity of her betrayal after Thorwald declares that he's going to take over the ship.

The origins of the *Botany Bay* ship are also explained. "Named for the spot on the Australian coast where the first settlers landed. They were criminals, a new, raw, primitive land," says Spock.

On 30 March 2001, Ricardo Montalban, who is today confined to a wheelchair because of a spinal cord injury, appeared before fans at the Grand Slam IX convention in his first convention.

Recalling the approach in how he played Khan, Montalban remarked, "A villain doesn't know he's a villain, any more than a saint knows he's a saint. He is a man who does saintly things, and the people around him think he's a saint, and a villain does villainous things and people brand him as a villain. But he doesn't think of himself as a villain. So I played him as a man who does villainous things."

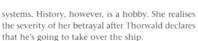

THE BIG SCREEN SEQUEL

Some 15 years later, after *Star Trek: the Motion Picture*, producer Harve Bennett was asked to take the reins of the film franchise. Previously unfamiliar with the *Star Trek* mythos, Bennett took care to screen all the episodes of the show, immediately saw the potential for a sequel to *Space Seed*, and approached Montalban to resurrect the character.

In the film, the *U.S.S. Reliant* is on a scientific mission to find a planet suitable for the "Genesis Device", an invention that can turn a lifeless planet into one that resembles the Garden of Eden (and of course, destroy a living planet, too). Khan captures the *Reliant* and immediately sets about trying to steal the device – and destroy Captain Kirk in a film whose memorable battle scenes, characterisation and direction proved such a hit with cinema-goers it assured the success of the *Star Trek* film franchise for many years to come.

"At the end of the sixth season of *Fantasy Island*, I was presented with a script for *Star Trek II*," Montalban recalled. "I read it and thought, 'the part isn't really that extensive. After being on the small screen for so long, if I'm going to go back to the big screen, it should be something with a little more size.' But then I realised that when I was not on the screen they were talking about me!" The part therefore appeared 'bigger', more substantial

Cox admits, "It wasn't one of my favourite episodes as a kid. Too much mushy stuff with Marla, and no cool monsters like the Gorn or the Salt Vampire. The ending, with Kirk giving Khan a chance to 'reign in hell,' always made an impression on me, though. The ending just cries out for a sequel. Who knew I'd get to tell that story decades later?

"Obviously, I've grown to appreciate the episode a lot more over the years," he adds, "especially after the epic events of *Star Trek II: The Wrath of Khan*. Montalban is certainly charismatic in the part. You can understand why Kirk kind of admires him."

"Oddly enough, *Space Seed* itself never mentions genetic engineering," Cox points out. "The term used is 'selective breeding', which may or may not have involved any DNA tampering. I believe it was *Star Trek II: The Wrath of Khan* that made it explicit that Khan and his followers were the product of genetic engineering.

"Certainly, the basic idea just keeps getting more and more topical. The whole time I was writing the Eugenics Wars books, I kept running into news articles on genetically-engineered crops, sex selection for babies, new breakthroughs in genetic engineering, etc. It felt like the real world was rapidly overtaking the books!

"In fact, in Book One, a scientist combines rabbit and firefly DNA to create a bunny that glows in the dark. I thought this was just a wacky idea of my own; imagine my surprise to discover that a researcher in France had already done this in real life!

"In writing the books, I felt obliged to stick to the Federation party line," Cox reveals, "that human genetic engineering is a bad thing. In real life, of course, the issues are a lot more ambiguous, with pros and cons on both sides of the issues. Science fiction provides a safe and entertaining forum to explore the possible ramifications of such technology, with the saga of Khan Noonien Singh serving as a cautionary tale about the potential dangers of trying to create "superior" human beings.

Because of *Star Trek: Enterprise*'s recent triad of episodes, exploring the 'Augments' who were also genetically-engineered supermen, Cox says he has become even more intrigued about that aspect of the *Star Trek* mythos.

"It's always fascinating when we learn more about the future history that led to the Federation; It fleshes out the universe and makes it a more convincing creation."

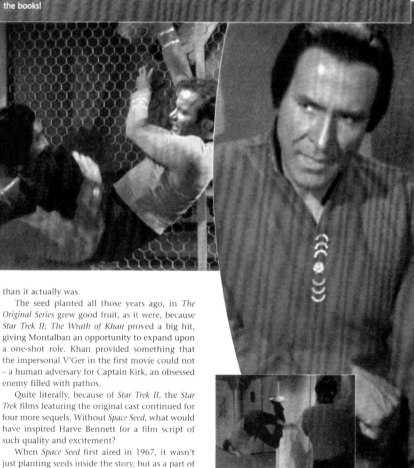

than it actually was.

The seed planted all those years ago, in *The Original Series* grew good fruit, as it were, because *Star Trek II: The Wrath of Khan* proved a big hit, giving Montalban an opportunity to expand upon a one-shot role. Khan provided something that the impersonal V'Ger in the first movie could not – a human adversary for Captain Kirk, an obsessed enemy filled with pathos.

Quite literally, because of *Star Trek II*, the *Star Trek* films featuring the original cast continued for four more sequels. Without *Space Seed*, what would have inspired Harve Bennett for a film script of such quality and excitement?

When *Space Seed* first aired in 1967, it wasn't just planting seeds inside the story, but as a part of *Star Trek* history as well. ■

EPISODE STATS

EPISODE TITLE: *Space Seed*
SERIES: *Star Trek (Original Series)*
SEASON: One
PRODUCTION NO: 22
FIRST US TRANSMISSION: 16 Febuary 1967

CAST
Credited:
William Shatner – James T. Kirk
Leonard Nimoy – Spock
DeForest Kelley – Leonard H. McCoy
James Doohan – Montgomery Scott
Nichelle Nichols – Uhura
Ricardo Montalban – Khan
Madlyn Rhue – Lt. Marla McGivers

Uncredited:
Blaisdell Makee – Spinelli
Mark Tobin – Joaquin
Kathy Ahart – Kati
Joan Johnson – Elite Female Guard
Bobby Bass – Guard
Barbara Baldavin – Angela Martine
Joan Webster – Nurse
John Arndt – Crewman #1
Jan Reddin – Crewman #2

Stunts were conducted by Gary Coombs for Kirk and Chuck Couch for Khan

CREW
Director: Marc Daniels
Teleplay By: Gene L. Coon and Carey Wilber
Story By: Carey Wilber

WEB LINKS
Carey Wilber
Link: www.tuppers.com/pop
A detailed tribute to the prolific "TV writer, raconteur and squirrel hunter" by his family. Carey died in 1998 aged 82.

Ricardo Montalbán Theatre
Link: www.nosotros.org
Nosotros was founded in 1970 by Ricardo Montalbán to improve the image of Latinos and Hispanics as they are portrayed in the entertainment industry, both in front and behind the camera. The organisation, which now has its own theatre in West Hollywood, aims to expand their employment opportunities in the industry, and to train its members to become better actors and industry professionals.

KHAN NOONIEN SINGH

Dominating the screen in both his appearances in the *Star Trek* universe, the augmented genetic superman ruled on Earth in the late 20th Century - and had his eyes on a return to power on his awakening nearly 300 years later...

Khan Noonien Singh is possibly Kirk's most infamous foe. But which Khan are we talking about? In a sense, there are two Khans.

There is the Khan of "Space Seed," the dashing, imperious, yet ruthless superman Captain Kirk first encountered in 2267 when the *Enterprise* stumbled onto the *S.S. Botany Bay,* a 20th Century sleeper ship that had fled Earth in 1996 in the wake of the infamous Eugenics Wars. A product of "selective breeding," mentally and physically superior to ordinary men and women, Khan had once ruled over more than one-quarter of the Earth's population, including much of Asia and the Middle East, before in-fighting between Khan and his fellow genetic tyrants cost him his empire. A Sikh from northern India, little is definitively known about his early years, only that he eventually seized control of several nations in 1992.

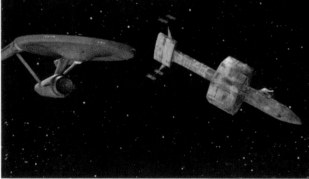

Revived by Doctor McCoy aboard the *Enterprise,* he wastes no time demonstrating that both his abilities and his ambition are undiminished by centuries spent in cryogenic suspension. His brilliant intellect allows him to master the *Enterprise*'s advanced 23rd Century systems in a matter of days, simply by reviewing the ship's technical manuals, while his sheer charisma overwhelms Lieutenant Marla McGivers, the *Enterprise*'s romantically susceptible historian. Khan seduces McGivers into betraying her captain and crew, allowing Khan and his resurrected followers to briefly take over the *Enterprise* in hopes of carving out a new empire across the galaxy. Thankfully, McGivers comes to her senses in time to help Kirk retake his ship - and place Khan and the others into custody.

STAR TREK

"Space Seed"

STAR TREK II THE WRATH OF KHAN

"To the last, I will grapple with thee... from Hell's heart, I stab at thee! For hate's sake, I spit my last breath at thee!"

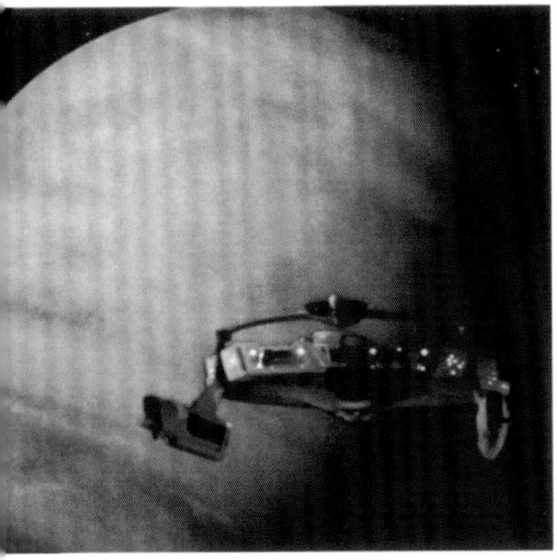

That Khan is arrogant and commanding, convinced of his own demonstrable superiority over lesser humans, but not a monster or madman. Although ruthless when necessary, he takes no pleasure in torturing Kirk and his other prisoners, and even gets frustrated when they "force" him to resort to violence by refusing to divulge classified Starfleet information. Historical records confirm that Khan was the best of the genetic tyrants; although he ruled with an iron hand, there were no documented massacres under his reign. Even Scotty admits to having always had a sneaking admiration for Khan – at least until he actually meets him!

"Historical records confirm that Khan was the best of the genetic tyrants; although he ruled with an iron hand, there were no documented massacres under his reign."

Granted, one can already see hints of the darkness that will later consume Khan. Prodding from Captain Kirk and Mister Spock about his ouster back in the 1990s, provokes a bitter outburst: "We offered the world order!" He also attempts to destroy the *Enterprise,* and everyone on it, rather than surrender to Kirk. Such self-destructive fury would have tragic consequences many years down the road.

Still, the Khan of 2267 is ultimately gracious in defeat. Having lost his bid for control of the *Enterprise,* he gratefully accepts Kirk's offer to colonize the harsh, forbidding wilderness of Ceti Alpha V in lieu of incarceration in a Federation reorientation center. He also gladly accepts McGivers as his consort, judging her "a superior woman." Alas, he would live to regret his decision to "reign in hell" on Ceti Alpha V.

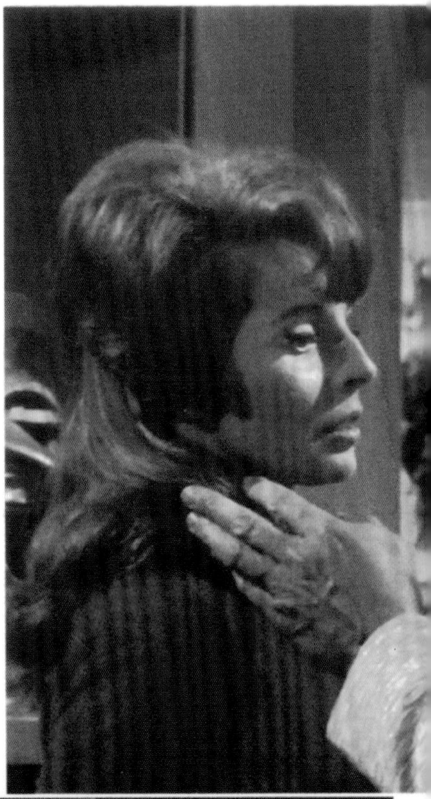

The Khan of *The Wrath of Khan* is a very different man. Seventeen years of hardship on Ceti Alpha V, after the freak explosion of a neighboring planet reduced the planet to a barren wasteland, along with the heart-breaking death of his beloved wife (Marla, we presume), transform Khan into a bitter, half-crazed Ahab obsessed with revenge on James T. Kirk, whom he comes to blame for his long exile on the dying planet. At least 20 of his 73 followers, including McGivers, are killed by the parasitic Ceti Eels alone, and it is only Khan's superior intellect (now identified as "genetically engineered") that keeps the rest of his people alive all those years. By the time the *U.S.S. Reliant* carelessly stumbles onto Khan in 2285, Khan is a weathered, ragged parody of his former glory, living only for vengeance.

That Khan is far more reckless and bloodthirsty than the man Kirk encountered years before. He infects the *Reliant*'s Captain Terrell and First Officer Pavel Chekov with the mind-controlling eels, condemning them to madness and an agonizing death. (Thankfully, however, Chekov survives.) Later, when the defenseless scientists at the Regula I space station refuse to turn over the secrets of the Genesis Device, Khan loses control entirely and slaughters them all (albeit offscreen). His obsessive hatred of Kirk dooms even his own devoted followers; despite the prudent advice of his trusted lieutenant Joachim, Khan cannot resist tossing the hijacked *Reliant* into a catastrophic final battle with the *Enterprise.* Losing that conflict, due to his inability to fully grasp the three-dimensional nature of starship combat, Khan sacrifices his ship, his crew, and his life by igniting the Genesis Device in one last attempt to achieve a pyrrhic victory over Kirk.

Spitting his last breath at Kirk, Khan fails to kill his foe, but his maddened lust for revenge claims the life of Mister Spock – and sets in motion events that ultimately lead to the destruction of the original *Starship Enterprise* in *The Search for Spock.* No wonder Khan is widely regarded as the greatest – and most deadly – villain in all of *Star Trek.*

Greg Cox

RICARDO MONTALBAN

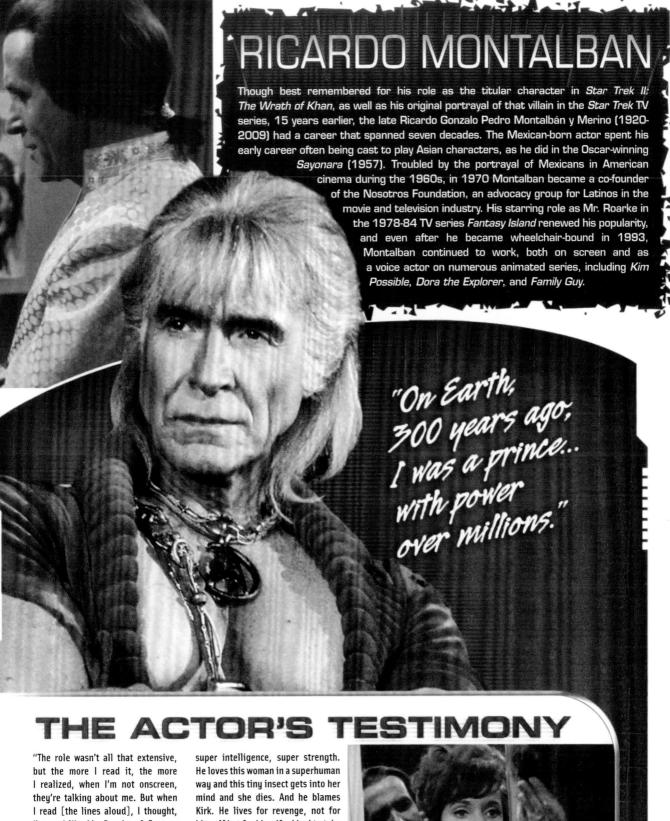

Though best remembered for his role as the titular character in *Star Trek II: The Wrath of Khan*, as well as his original portrayal of that villain in the *Star Trek* TV series, 15 years earlier, the late Ricardo Gonzalo Pedro Montalbán y Merino (1920-2009) had a career that spanned seven decades. The Mexican-born actor spent his early career often being cast to play Asian characters, as he did in the Oscar-winning *Sayonara* (1957). Troubled by the portrayal of Mexicans in American cinema during the 1960s, in 1970 Montalban became a co-founder of the Nosotros Foundation, an advocacy group for Latinos in the movie and television industry. His starring role as Mr. Roarke in the 1978-84 TV series *Fantasy Island* renewed his popularity, and even after he became wheelchair-bound in 1993, Montalban continued to work, both on screen and as a voice actor on numerous animated series, including *Kim Possible*, *Dora the Explorer*, and *Family Guy*.

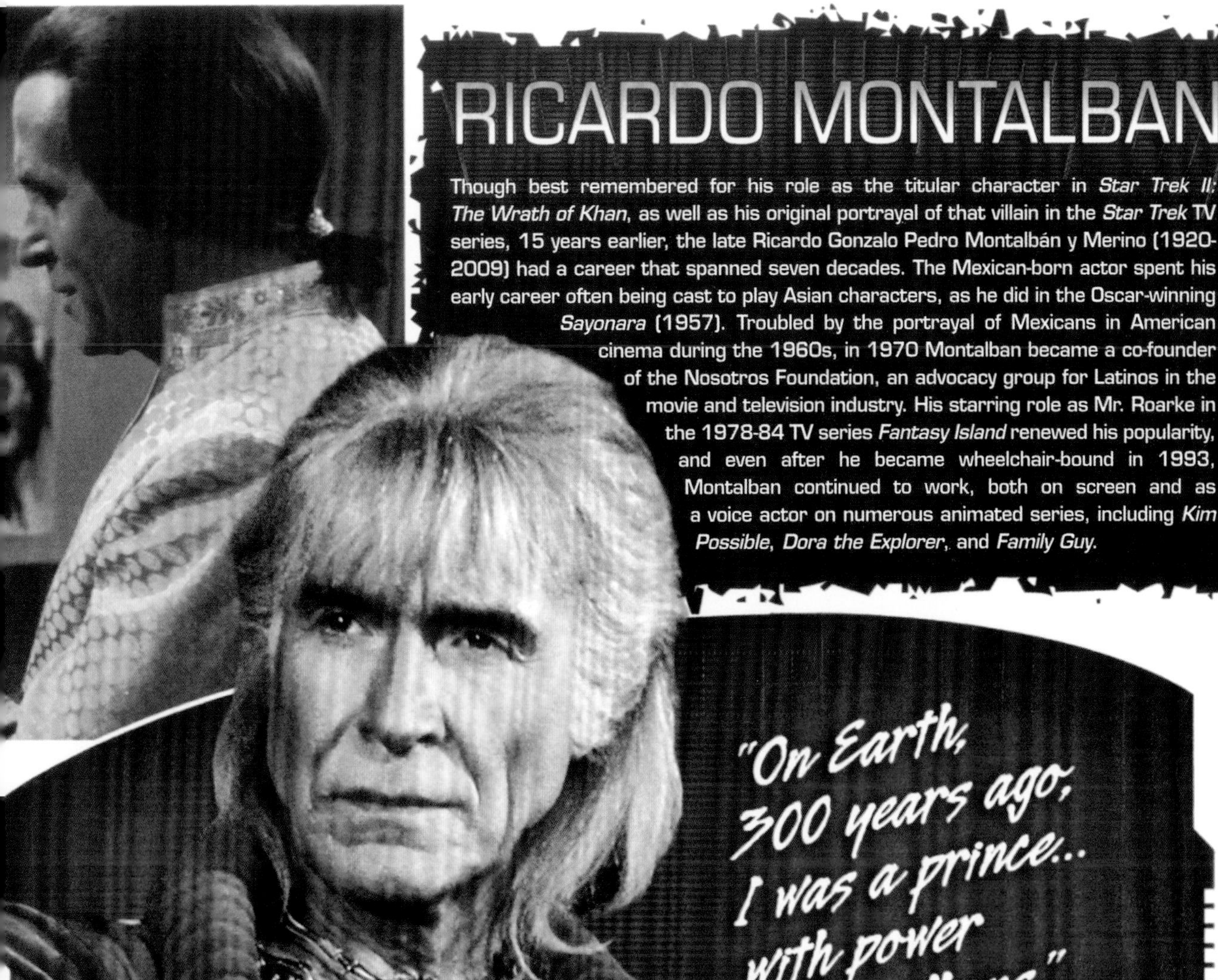
"On Earth, 300 years ago, I was a prince... with power over millions."

THE ACTOR'S TESTIMONY

"The role wasn't all that extensive, but the more I read it, the more I realized, when I'm not onscreen, they're talking about me. But when I read [the lines aloud], I thought, 'I sound like Mr. Roarke of *Fantasy Island*! People will laugh!'

I panicked. I called Harve Bennett, the producer, got a tape [of "Space Seed"], I watched it four or five times and I remember what I tried to do with this part. He has super intelligence, super strength. He loves this woman in a superhuman way and this tiny insect gets into her mind and she dies. And he blames Kirk. He lives for revenge, not for himself but for his wife. I had to take the performance to the top of the mountain, to the peak without going over the top. I had a wonderful director, Nicholas Meyer, who would say, 'You're going over the top, just a little. Take it down.'"

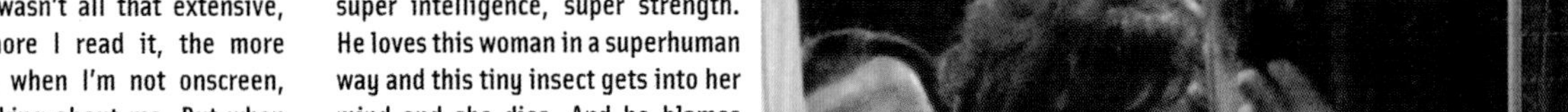

Lost & Found

Star Trek historian Larry Nemecek explains the origin of this issue's previously unseen shots of Khan Noonien Singh...

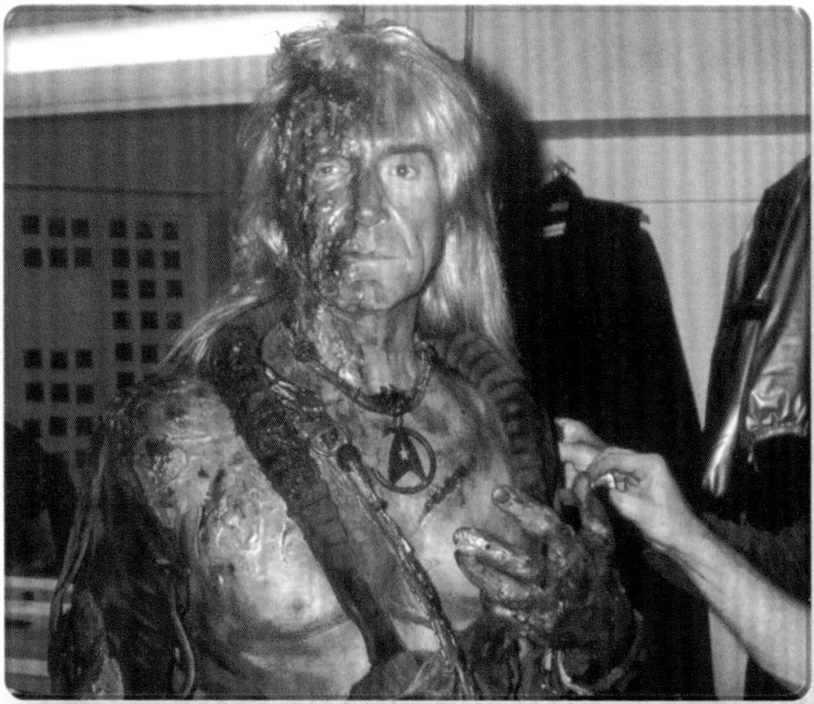

The climax of *Star Trek II: The Wrath of Khan* required an all-out makeup effort on star Ricardo Montalban, as his mortally wounded frame's final rise fills the screen, looming spooky and defiant in order to finish off his hated foe James T. – just when you thought the Big "E" had carried the day cleanly.

Veteran makeup artist Werner Keppler was assigned to share duties for the sequel with James L. McCoy.

Our opening shot on page 49, taken on set in early 1982, is Keppler's masterpiece of "body art" on Montalban, in a rare reference shot showing all the burns and scars of his handiwork unobstructed.

It also proves once and for all the answer to the question asked most frequently of both Montalban and director Nicholas Meyer: yes, that really was Montalban's chest!

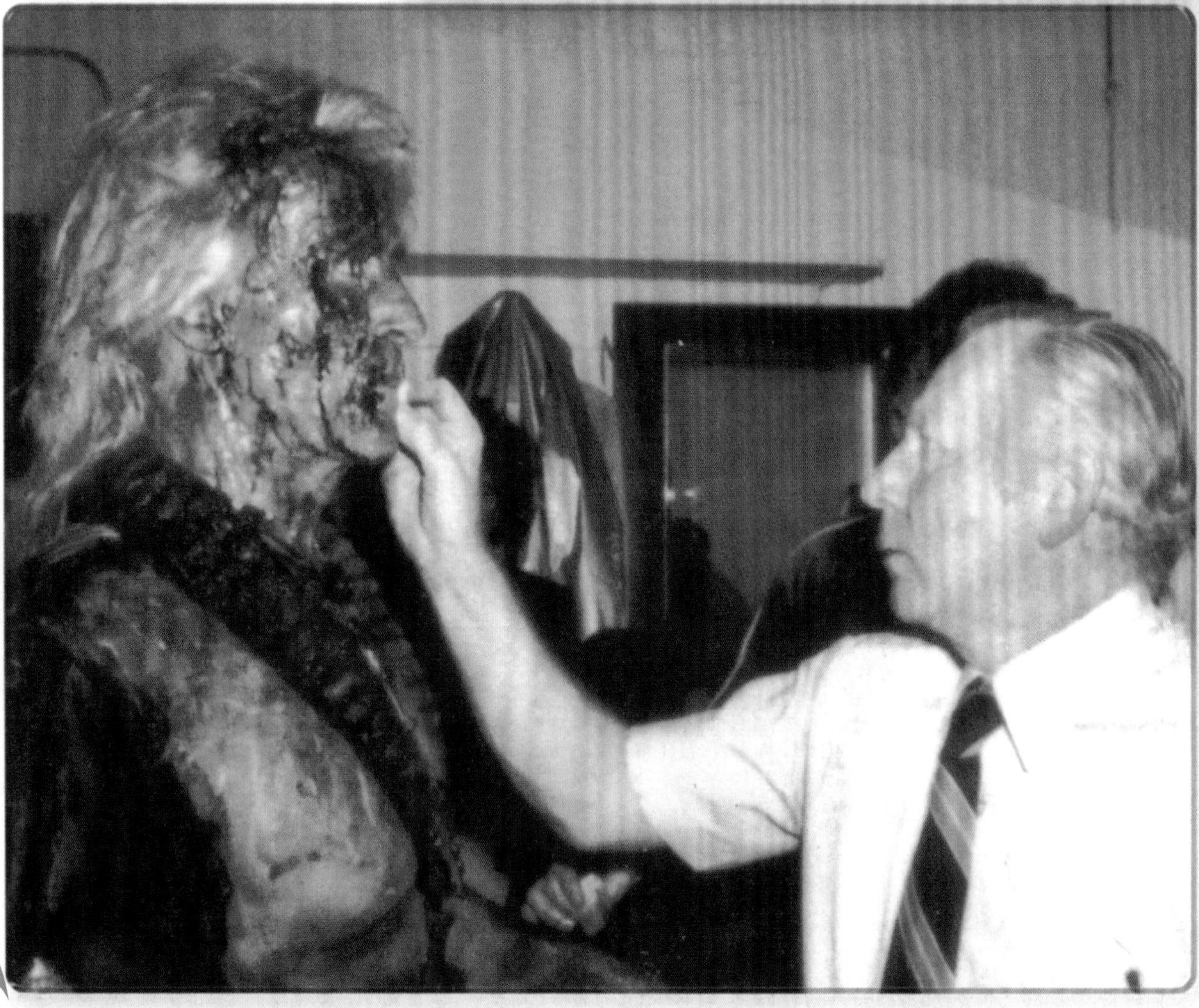

STAR TREK C.U.E.

KHAN

The first *Star Trek* villain promoted from TV series to movie – and, although we had hoped for *Star Trek II: The Wrath of Gorn*, things seem to have turned out okay. Khan was a prime mover in the Eugenics Wars of 1992-1996, remember them? Apparently there were 37 million deaths, Khan controlled a quarter of the world and, er, we just didn't notice. By the time of *Star Trek II*, Ricardo Montalban had become well known as the proprietor of TV's *Fantasy Island*. So, it would have been nice if he'd brought his sidekick Tattoo aboard the *U.S.S. Reliant* with him – instead of shouting 'da plane, da plane,' the little guy could have gone 'da *Enterprise*, da *Enterprise*,' thus lightening up those tense cat-and-mouse scenes in the nebula.

SIDESTEPS:

Other appearances in the *Star Trek* universe

from left to right: *The Eugenics Wars* Volumes 1 and 2; *To Reign In Hell*; *Seeds of Dissent* (set in an alternate reality where Khan and his supporters triumphed in the 20th Century); "Space Seed" – James Blish's adaptation in *Star Trek 2*, based on an earlier version of the script

TREK LIT VILLAINS
DR. ETHAN LOCKEN

Ethan Locken was the tragic villain of the *Star Trek: Deep Space Nine* novel, *Section 31: Abyss* by David Weddle & Jeffrey Lang. His roots are in the fifth-season *DS9* episode, "Doctor Bashir, I Presume?" in which it's revealed that as a child, Bashir underwent extensive and forbidden genetic enhancement. In the final act, Starfleet Rear Admiral Bennett explains the old fear that led to the illegalization of such practices: "For every Julian Bashir that can be created, there's a Khan Singh waiting in the wings – a 'superman' whose ambition and thirst for power have been enhanced along with his intellect."

That ominous warning inspired the creation of Locken, another genetically enhanced doctor who differed from Bashir primarily in the fact that Section 31 successfully manipulated him into embracing his own superiority before the shadowy organization lost control of him. In the midst of the Dominion War, Locken became convinced that his augmented nature offered him the best chance of imposing order upon an increasingly chaotic Alpha Quadrant. Turning the tables on Section 31, Locken used its agenda to advance his own, and became the very thing the Federation had so long tried to guard against: a fledgling new Khan.

In reluctantly undertaking the mission to neutralize Locken, the peril for Bashir was in identifying too closely with this man who was unsettlingly like himself. For Bashir, Locken was a reminder of his own terrible potential to abuse his gifts in the name of creating a better world. Could Locken, and by extension, Bashir, overcome the ruinous legacy of Khan? Or were they doomed by it?

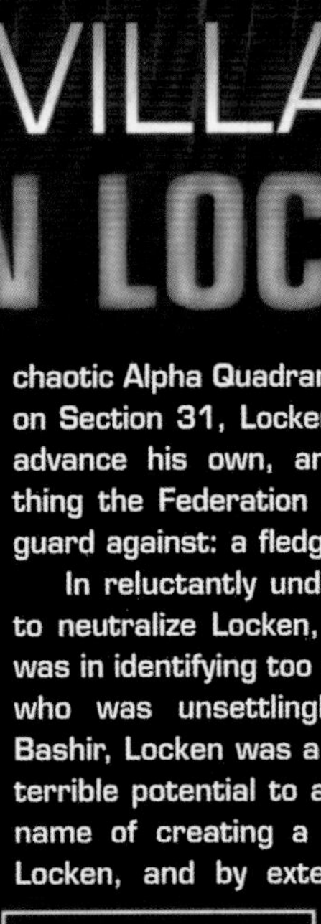

Nature verus nurture was one of the core conflicts of the story, one that would be revisited in later novels that continued the *Deep Space Nine* saga.

Marco Palmieri

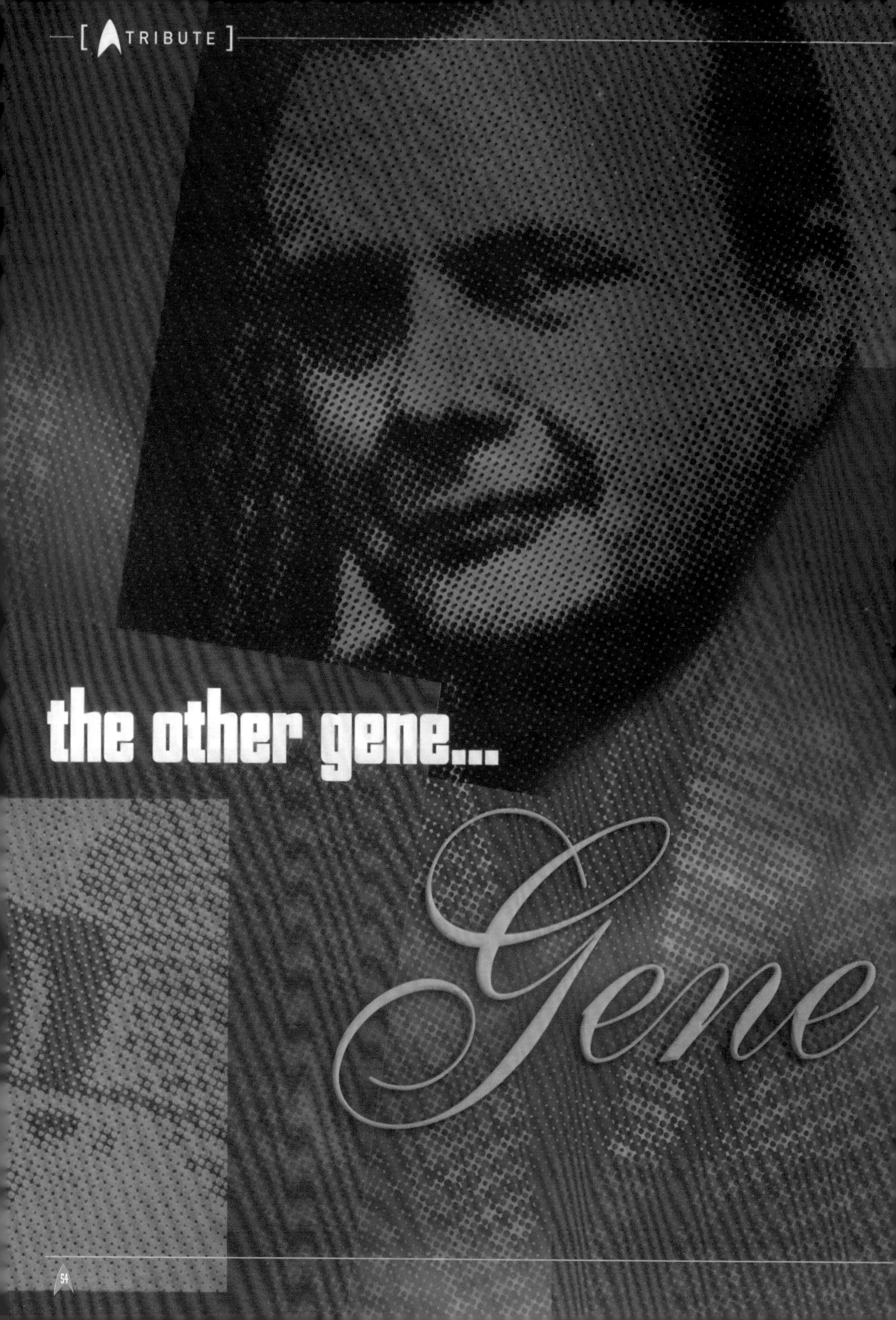

the other gene...

Gene

"He was an ever-fertile source of story ideas and 'the fastest typewriter in the West.'"
Robert Justman

While entire books have been devoted to the undisputed creator of *Star Trek*, Gene Roddenberry, there's sadly few mentions for the work of producer Gene Coon. Joe Nazzaro pays tribute to an unsung hero...

In David Gerrold's 1973 book, *The Trouble with Tribbles*, the then-fledgling television writer remembers his first meeting with *Star Trek* producer Gene Coon to discuss a possible assignment for the series. "Needless to say," he recounts, "I felt like Dorothy being ushered into the presence of the Wizard of Oz. That Gene Coon was on a 20-foot throne, surrounded by pillars of lighting and thunder didn't help much either." And looking back, the awestruck Gerrold doesn't recall his potential boss's first words to him either. "I was too awed by the effect of seeing them materialise in puffs of flame," he quips.

Exaggeration? Almost certainly, based on the fact that no records exist of any lighting/thunder-based thrones being used at the former Desilu Studios in the mid-1960s. But Gerrold's tongue-in-cheek anecdote only helps to demonstrate the high regard (and in the case of young writers, a healthy dose of fear) that people felt for the producer, who died in 1973 before *Star Trek* fandom had truly begun. "He was an ever-fertile source of story ideas and 'the fastest typewriter in the West'," recalls associate producer Robert Justman in his 1996 memoir *Inside Star Trek: The Real Story* written with former production executive Herb Solow. "Gene Coon was certainly one of the more inventive people on the show," adds veteran writer D.C. Fontana, who contributed a number of scripts to the original series. "He had a great sense of humour, and was always willing to try something or let somebody else try something."

Harve Bennettt, who used Coon's *Space Seed* as the basis for *Star Trek II: The Wrath of Khan*, has enormous admiration for the producer, a respect for which grew from marathon screenings of *Star Trek* as he tried to come up with the story for the second film.

"Roddenberry was the man behind *Star Trek*," Bennett told startrek.com's Kevin Dilmore in 1999. "He was the visionary and its great promoter. But it was Gene Coon who did the day-to-day aspects of production... I consider [him] an honourable, wonderful man."

"Poor Gene Coon... I think we killed him," feels Majel Barrett-Roddenberry talking to the BBC about the team that helped her husband Gene

L. Coon

REMEMBERING THE UNSUNG HERO OF STAR TREK

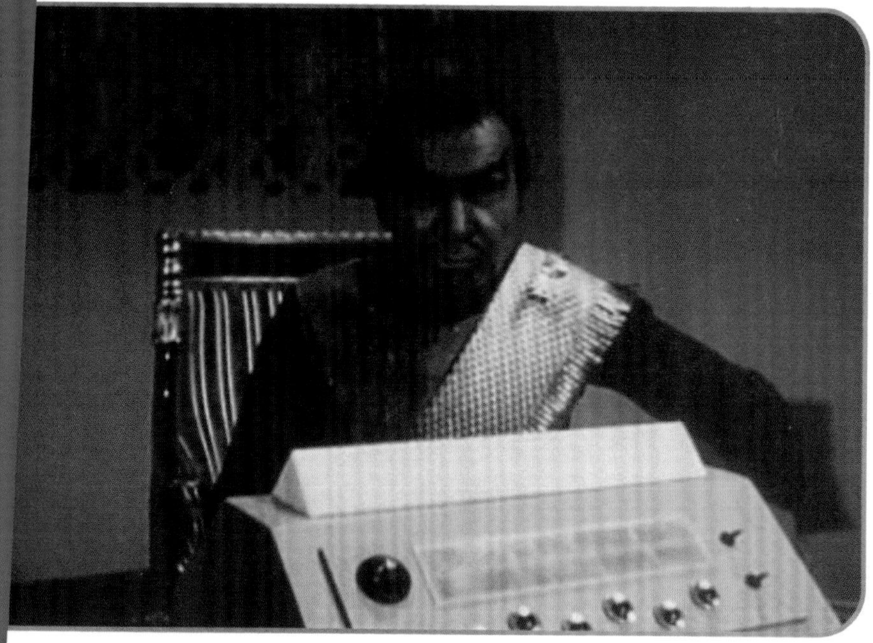

COON'S LEGACY

For many of the people who worked with Gene Coon on *Star Trek*, his influence was strongly felt while he was on the series, and long after he departed. "For both Gene Coon and Gene Roddenberry," notes Bob Justman, "their major function was not necessarily to write original scripts, although they both did. Their job was to ride herd on the writers that we had corralled and get something wondrous out of them, which seldom happened, because it was a difficult show to write. You had to have an interest and knowledge not only of the world of SF, but also the way Gene Roddenberry predicted the future. That's a tough call.

"Gene Coon was so skilled and enthusiastic that he would sit there typing with a cigarette between his lips, the smoke curling in front of just nose, just jamming out ideas, the richness of which never ceased to make me happy."

D.C. Fontana has no difficulty revealing some of the lessons she learned from working with Coon. "I think being a good, fast writer was a very strong asset to offer anybody who's hiring you," she elaborates, "so I worked on getting down my material faster, and I'm still able to do a script very quickly if I have to, and sometimes you do. In order to write faster, it's a matter of using your time best, so I took that to heart.

"I teach at the American Film Institute and what I tell them is, being a fast writer is a very valuable asset. If you become known as a good, fast writer, it's great for your reputation. Some people ponder over every word, while others can put down their thoughts very quickly and produce a solid first draft. After that, it's all rewrite; the toning of it, making it better and sharper, trimming the fat, that sort of thing; but one of the things I learned was that a good, solid, fast first draft is extremely valuable."

Gene Coon's powerful script for *Space Seed* was to prove the basis for one of the most successful *Star Trek* films years later.

Roddenberry create *Star Trek*. "You'd give him a script overnight and he would bring back a shooting script the next morning. One that we could actually go up on the stage, point the camera, light the lights and say, 'roll them.' It was remarkable. I'd say if anybody was really closest to helping Gene put those out I would say it was Gene Coon."

When the definitive history of *Star Trek* is finally told, there is no doubt that Gene Coon's contributions will play a vital role in that account. In addition to writing or rewriting numerous episodes over the show's three-season history, he was also responsible for a number of elements that became part of *Star Trek* mythology, from the Horta and Gorn, to the villainous Klingons. If there is one reason that Coon's influence is often overlooked, it may be that he died more than three decades ago, long before *Star Trek* was a bona-fide international SF phenomenon. "Unfortunately, he died quite young," agrees Fontana, "and didn't get to reap the rewards of people realising that he made an enormous contribution."

Born 7 January 1924, Gene L. Coon had already lived a fascinating life long before he became a successful television writer. A former World War II veteran and Korean War combat radio correspondent, his military experiences provided the backdrop for novels such as *Meanwhile, Back at the Front* and *The Wrong End of the Stick*. By the early 1950s, he found himself working in television, proving equally adept in everything from westerns to police dramas. For a decade and a half, he churned out scripts for an impressive number of programmes, including *Dragnet, Wagon Train, Man in the Shadow, Zorro, Maverick, Rawhide, Bonanza, Mr. Lucky, The Rebel, Acapulco, McHale's Navy, The Raiders, The Killers, The Chrysler Theatre, Laredo* and *The Wild Wild West* – to name just a partial list of credits. Within a relatively short period of time, Coon had established himself as fast and dependable, both of which were important qualities for any successful TV professional.

"He was a very fast writer," recalls Fontana. "Once he knew what the story was, he could write very quickly. He worked very intensely, and I think his scripts were always very good and very solid. On *Star Trek*, he'd arrive at 9am and leave at six, but in-between, he was always writing and it was very intense."

Coon had been working as a writer/producer on the CBS western *The Wild Wild West* when *Star Trek* began looking for a 'writing machine' to work with series creator Gene Roddenberry. It was the summer of 1966, not long before Season One began airing, and the new arrival made a big difference in terms of workload. "Although his title was 'producer,' Coon knew he was hired to write and write he did," recalls Justman. "Coon churned out page after page of shootable and exciting scripts, while chain-smoking his way through pack after pack of Sherman Cigarillos."

Coon only incorporated the Horta more fully into the script of *The Devil in the Dark* after seeing the creature the effects team had made in action

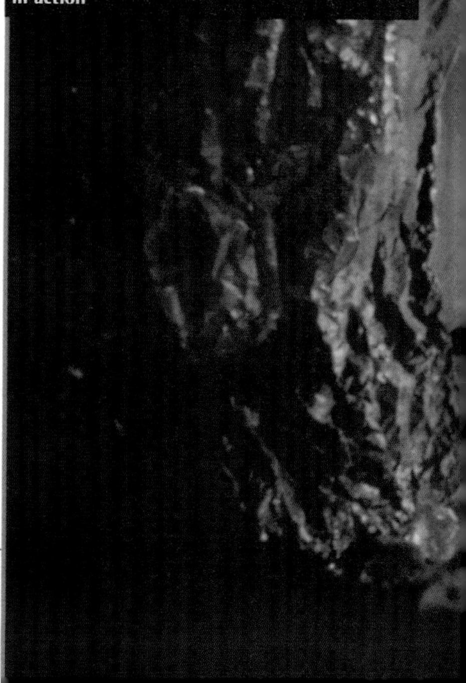

Coon inadvertently used a 1944 story by Frederic Brown as the basis for the script of *Arena*, but Brown was paid for the use. (In Brown's original story, on the eve of an epic battle for the solar system between an Earth armada and an alien Outsider fleet the human Carson is designated by a superior entity to represent Earth against an Outsider in a duel of champions to settle which race will survive).

Gene Coon's trademark humour litters *Spock's Brain*, although many fans villify the resulting episode.

Justman still remembers his first introduction to Coon, which took place in a Desilu corridor. "The executives at that time," he explains, "were Gene Roddenberry, yours truly and John D.F. Black, and John had either left or was going to leave shortly, so we very much needed somebody in story. I had never met Gene Coon before and was unaware of what he had done previously, but when I first saw him walking towards me down the hallway of E Building, I knew it must be him even though he didn't look at all how he turned out to be.

"To me, he looked like the banker who forecloses on a young person's mortgage: very cold and dry and not very fun-filled, all of which goes to show you that first impressions are often totally incorrect. It didn't take long for Gene's personality to emerge. He understood the concept of *Star Trek*, and the more I worked with him, the better I liked him, both personally as someone that was after the same things that Gene Roddenberry and I were after, and also because he was a very likeable fellow, not at all like I thought when I first saw him."

"You'd give him a script overnight and he would bring back a shooting script the next morning. One that we could actually go up on the stage, point the camera, light the lights and say, 'roll them.' It was remarkable."
Majel Barrett - Roddenberry

Fontana, who was working as Roddenberry's production secretary at the time, has a slightly different first impression of Coon. "I liked him," she recalls. "He was a very genial man (no pun intended), always pleasant, who liked to smile and laugh a lot. My feeling was that you got to know him right away, in the sense that he didn't shut any doors on you. He was always open and friendly, and as producer, he didn't look down at the staff at all. He was one of us."

With production on *Star Trek*'s first season well underway by the time Coon joined, one of his biggest responsibilities was to make sure that several workable scripts were making their way through the pipeline. Unfortunately, as Herb Solow relates in *Inside Star Trek*, when several writers didn't deliver as promised, the

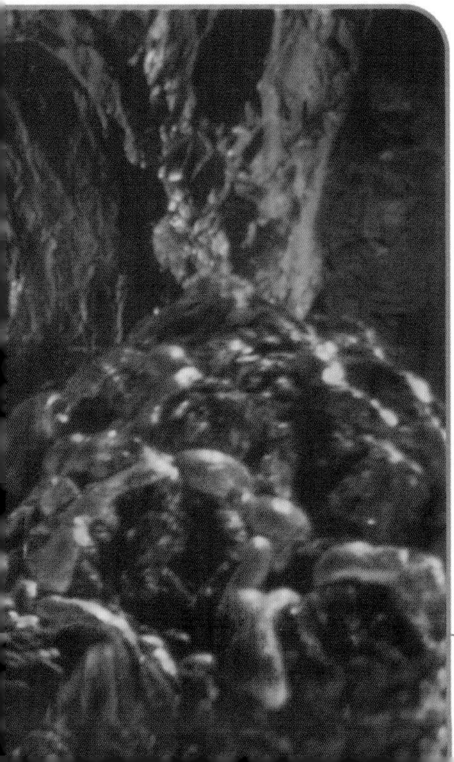

Captain Kirk's character benefited hugely from Coon's many scripts

producers suddenly found themselves running out of scripts. Coon offered to leave the office early on a Friday, lock himself in a room for the weekend and emerge on Monday morning with a new script. That became the episode *Arena*. On the following Monday, he arrived in the office with script in hand, which was quickly distributed for network and legal approval. "But suddenly the thrill was gone," Solow remembers. "Coon, an ardent reader of science fiction since he was a child, in his haste to create a story, had inadvertently based part of his script on a short story that had been written by Fredric Brown."

Coon was horrified that he had unknowingly used part of Brown's 1944 story *Arena*, but instead of scrapping the script, the producers decided to contact the author directly. "We went ahead and had the studio purchase the right to use his material," continues Justman, "and he was flattered and pleased, and we were happy to be able to use it. How it all occurred one never really knows, but it was certainly done without any attempt to piggyback somebody else's work onto his. If the author had said he didn't want it to happen, we would have junked it."

Justman remembers another incident, in which Coon was in the middle of writing *Devil in the Dark*, when stuntman/performer Janos Prohaska arrived at the studio with a new alien costume he wanted to 'demonstrate.' "Janos came in with this creature that was to become the Horta, so we went outside to see it. Gene had no idea what this creature was supposed to look like, except that it was supposed to look ominous and it was protecting its young, so I brought Gene Coon out to the studio street and Janos moved the creature around while inside it. At the end of the demonstration, he reared up a little bit, depositing a large plastic ball as an egg, and when Gene saw that, he laughed so hard that he almost choked to death, and ran back to his office where he incorporated the creature into his script."

Coon's own sense of humour was highly developed, if somewhat subtle on occasion. Fontana remembers the writer playing a joke on director Marc Daniels during production of *Who Mourns for Adonais* on which they had just done a rewrite during Season Two. "Marc went out of the office to go to the men's room or something like that, and Gene said, 'Let's do this...' and told me what it was. When Marc came back, we said, 'Marc, this last line, "Let's head for Starbase 21," we can't have that!' He asked what was wrong, and we said, 'Starbase 21 isn't anywhere near there!' You had to be a

"He was a very genial man (no pun intended), always pleasant, who liked to smile and laugh a lot." Dorothy Fontana

Kirk tries to stun the alien Deela, in *Wink of an Eye*

A Taste of Armageddon was a powerful polemic against the dehumanising impact of computers – a theme often visited in *Star Trek*

Trekker to understand that one, but we knew our universe so well that we could pull something like that, and of course Marc burst out laughing and we left the line alone."

The list of characters and concepts that Coon added to *Star Trek* is considerable, but that wasn't necessarily apparent at the time; take the Klingons for example. "We didn't plan for them to become part of the fabric of the series," claims Justman, "and it didn't happen at first, but they were good villains. A lot of these things didn't enter my consciousness at the time, but looking back on it now, I can see how unerring Gene's instincts were."

"We originally brought the Klingons in for one episode," adds Fontana. "It became very clear that the Romulans were hard to do, because we had all the problems with the ears. *In Balance of Terror*, we were able to cover the ears with helmets and stuff like that, but for leading characters, you had more sets of ears and eyebrows, and that was a little harder to do than the Klingons, who were easier. So they developed into being the heavies we could go to when we needed to, but at the time, it was purely a matter of make-up consideration: how long are we going to put these guys in the make-up trailer when we have to have them on stage? The Klingons were just easier to do." Justman is quick to point out by the way, that this is obviously before the make-up-intensive Klingons of the *Star Trek* films and *Star Trek: The Next Generation*.

Coon left *Star Trek* in September of 1967, but he continued to write scripts for the series under the pseudonym of Lee Cronin. Other credits included *It Takes a Thief, Journey to Shiloh, Nichols, The Sixth Sense, The Streets of San Francisco* and *Kung Fu*. In 1973, he was working on *The Questor Tapes*, which re-teamed him with Gene Roddenberry for the last time when the Sherman cigarillos that had been his constant companion, finally cut short his writing career. Coon died of lung cancer on 8 July of that year.

Having added so much to the mythology of *Star Trek*, it's a bit difficult to understand why Gene Coon's contributions to the series are sometimes overlooked. "I think part of it is that he's not around to talk to conventions and doing interviews and so on," reflects Fontana. "Because he's not here, his presence is no longer felt, but if you look at the number of scripts that he wrote, I think he wrote 10 or 12 *Star Treks*, and I did 10, so he beat me, and I was there a little longer than he was!

"I think Gene put his mark on the show just by his humour," Fontana adds. "The characters developed more of a sense of humour, because Gene Coon was there, and if you look at his episodes, you'll find that most of them are outstanding. A few, people don't like; he wrote *Spock's Brain* (under the name Lee Cronin), which is usually reviled, but it was one of those episodes where he was actually having fun. He was jerking everybody's chain, and people took it seriously. Gene was really a tough guy, but he had that saving sense of humour, and he was also a very giving kind of guy."

"I don't think Gene *has* been overlooked," counters Justman. "We're talking about him now, and he's certainly known to the world of *Star Trek* fans. I think his contributions were massive, and he certainly helped make the show what it was. He also understood almost instinctively what Gene Roddenberry's view of the future would be, and could write *Star Trek* better than anyone else other than Roddenberry, so that's pretty good to say the least." ■

TROUBLE WITH TRIBBLES

One of the true *Star Trek* success stories was David Gerrold, a 22 year-old screenwriter who had been invited by Gene Coon to come in and pitch potential story ideas for the series. As Gerrold recalls, he spent three months putting together five different premises, including a whimsical story about some ultra-prolific creatures called 'Fuzzies'. "I wasn't exactly sure how to tell it," he chronicles in his behind-the-scenes memoir, *The Trouble with Tribbles*. "The premise wasn't very well drawn. It may have been the worst written of the five – but it was the one that sold."

To Gerrold's surprise, Coon was not only intrigued by the premise of *The Fuzzies*, which eventually became *The Trouble with Tribbles*, but he also took the young writer under his wing, allowing him to take the story from outline to script. It was a privilege rarely accorded in the high pressure world of series television. "At the very beginning of the show," he happily relates, "where the credits come on, where it says 'Written by,' there is only one name on the screen."

"I think David was sort of unique in that way," recalls D.C. Fontana, "because the story came in as a treatment submitted through his agent. I thought it was a fun concept, and we should assign a writer with some credits to it. But Gene Coon said, "No, let's let him take a shot at it," so David ultimately delivered a very fine script, and he wrote it himself. Whatever notes and comments Gene Coon made to him, he then incorporated, so Gene did not do any writing on the script. Nor did I for that matter. I think the only changes that were done on staff were a few minor points needed for production purposes."

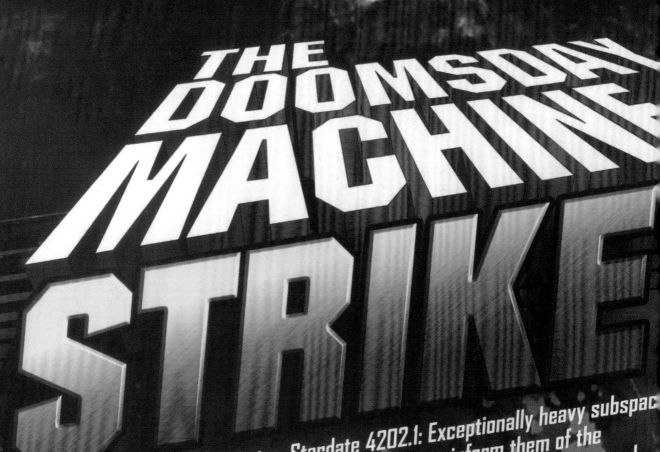

THE DOOMSDAY MACHINE STRIKES

Captain's Log: U.S.S Constellation: Stardate 4202.1: Exceptionally heavy subspace interference still prevents our contacting Starfleet to inform them of the destroyed solar systems we have encountered. We are now entering system L-374, Science Officer Masada reports the fourth planet seems to be breaking up. We are going to investigate...

CREATING THE DEVIL

Every episode of *Star Trek* starts from an initial idea, which can come from the writer or producers. Anthony Pascale talks to Norman Spinrad about the genesis of Commodore Decker's battle with *The Doomsday Machine*...

"THE DOOMSDAY MACHINE"

WRITTEN BY NORMAN SPINRAD

Sent to investigate the destruction of several planetary systems, the *U.S.S. Enterprise* discovers a crippled starship, the *U.S.S. Constellation*, floating in space. Commodore Matthew Decker is the only one left on the ship. Kirk and Scotty remain on board the *Constellation* to try and repair the starship, while McCoy beams Decker aboard the *Enterprise*.

Decker informs the crew that a giant robot ship, a planet-eating machine made by a long-dead alien race, is roaming the galaxies, consuming all in its path for fuel, including whole planets. When Decker challenged it, the "berserker," as he calls it, attacked. Decker beamed his entire crew to the planet's surface below, only to have the robot consume that planet, killing the *Constellation*'s entire crew.

When the "berserker" returns, Decker, consumed with guilt over the loss of his crew, pulls rank on Spock and takes control of the *U.S.S. Enterprise*. He seems determined to destroy the machine, even at the cost of another ship and crew. Kirk, still on board the *Constellation*, contacts Spock and supports his claim that Decker is exhibiting suicidal behavior and is therefore unfit to command. Thwarted, Decker steals a shuttlecraft and flies it down the 'throat' of the giant robot ship, killing himself.

Realizing that Decker's idea, on a larger scale, might work, Kirk sets the *Constellation* to self-destruct and sendS it after Decker's shuttlecraft. Due to a transporter glitch, Kirk barely makes it back to the *U.S.S. Enterprise* before the *Constellation* explodes, destroying the planet killer in its path.

Synopsis courtesy of StarTrek.com

It is said that one good turn deserves another, and so it was that one good turn by Norman Spinrad got him the opportunity to write a *Star Trek* classic. In 1967 Spinrad was a 26 year old burgeoning science fiction author who also did some magazine writing on the side. A favorable mention of *Star Trek* garnered the young writer a fateful phone call.

"I wrote a feature on the making of the film *2001* in which I compared it somewhat invidiously to Gene Roddenberry's *Star Trek* pilots," explains Spinrad. "He was showing them around to conventions at the time and I thought that it was better done. So I got a call from Gene Roddenberry thanking me for what I had written and as a courtesy asking me to pitch a *Star Trek* if I'd like. I was busy writing *Bug Jack Barron* at the time and so I asked him to call me back in six weeks, and six weeks later he did."

At the time Spinrad had published three novels, but was not yet the star that *Bug Jack Barron* would make him. He had also never written for television, but Roddenberry respected his work and wanted to give him a chance. The brief given to him by Roddenberry was more practical than creative. "Gene told me that they were running out of money and needed a show that could be shot on standing sets," Spinrad explains.

The Doomsday Machine was written after there had been only one season of *Star Trek*. At the time there wasn't the mountain of *Star Trek* history to deal with so writers were given a lot of flexibility, but with some guidance. "We could do pretty much anything we wanted as long as it didn't violate anything already done or violate science," explains Spinrad. "There was a big bible and that ship was designed down to every nut and bolt. But mostly there was Gene who had very firm ideas about what this universe was. It was pretty damn real to him.

"The genius of *Star Trek* was that by setting it on a space ship with the same basic cast you can do both an episodic series and an anthology in the same format. Each story was free standing. What you couldn't do is kill somebody off, and if they went crazy they had to be sane by the end."

The story for the script was actually not originally intended for *Star Trek*. "The idea for the story actually came from a novella I had wanted to write that never went anywhere," explains the writer. "I had this notion of doing Melville's *Moby Dick* in space. That is where *The Doomsday Machine* came from. It was where the idea of Decker came from. He was Ahab. There was a single ship he hunted which was his white whale. Gene liked the idea and asked me to write it up with the actor Robert Ryan in mind as

Commodore Decker. Ryan, like many other actors of time, was interesting in doing a *Star Trek*."

One of the signature items of the show is Decker's white whale – the planet killer. A decade before the Death Star and two decades before the Borg, Spinrad had envisioned a seemingly unstoppable machine that could destroy planets. Some have wondered if the Doomsday Machine was inspired by the 'berserker' machines described in the Fred Saberhagen book *Berserker* (also published in 1967). However, as with

"I ASKED GENE WHAT HAPPENED AND HE AGREED WITH ME THAT IT LOOKED LIKE A WINDSOCK DIPPED IN CEMENT"

Decker, the writer was using his own unused work for inspiration. "In 1965 Del Books wanted me to do what they called 'short 10 cent sci-fi novellas for the moron mentality.'" recalls Spinrad. "I was mad, but I came up with two ideas. One was called *Giant Green Bugs of Mars* and the other was called *The Planet Eater*. I didn't really want to write them, but that is where the planet killer came from. I envisioned it as a slick machine with some complexity. It had tractor beams and destructive beams on flexible stalks, vaguely like a squid. In the original script the idea was that they didn't know if it was alive or a robot, or if the lost alien civilization made an artificial organism."

After getting the script Roddenberry asked Spinrad to sketch out the Doomsday Machine itself. Even though he wasn't an artist he complied with the request and actually spent quite a bit of time drawing out his planet killer. "I presented it to Gene and he liked it," Spinrad enthuses.

When production began Spinrad was invited to the set. His first surprise was to find out that Robert Ryan would not be playing the part of Commodore Matt Decker. Apparently Ryan's schedule wouldn't allow it so William Windom stepped into the role. This was actually a bit disconcerting to the writer. "He played a different sort of part," laments the writer. "Windom was more subtle, more psychologically soft than Ryan who played more tough characters, like the Ahab I had imagined."

Windom's portrayal of Decker seems to have a bit of Captain Queeg of *Mutiny on the Bounty* in him. Spinrad sees this element, saying "they softened it and made him weaker." Spinrad notes that the biggest differences were in the scenes taking place between Kirk and Decker on the *Constellation*. When they meet Decker he is slumped and seems like a broken man, whereas it was initially written for him to be alert with an Ahab-like obsession. However the writer still has high praise for the guest star, saying "he was an excellent actor and once they got him over onto the *Enterprise* he played it much closer to the script – perhaps they underestimated him."

Adjustments to suit Windom weren't the only changes that Spinrad noted when on set. There was

"I HAD THIS NOTION OF DOING MELVILLE'S *MOBY DICK* IN SPACE. THAT IS WHERE *THE DOOMSDAY MACHINE* CAME FROM."

scene between Kirk and Spock that director Marc Daniels could not make work even after five takes. Spinrad attributes this to William Shatner's trimming of the script to ensure that Spock didn't have more dialogue than Kirk. Spinrad decided that even though he was just a young writer he would make a suggestion. "I pulled Marc aside and told him, 'I know you can't put the line back, but maybe Leonard Nimoy can just sort of grunt,'" says the writer laughing.

Even though *The Doomsday Machine* is a science fiction homage to a classic novel, it was still relevant to the day. Like many *Star Trek* episodes it was an allegory for the issues of the 1960s. Spinrad says that he meant it to be a cautionary tale, saying "I was drawing the obvious parallels." In fact the writer meant for the episode to end on the exchange with Kirk and Spock where Kirk talks of "way back in the 20th Century the H-Bomb was their ultimate weapon – *their* doomsday machine." However Roddenberry added the extra bit after that where Spock ponders if there are more doomsday machines out there and Kirk quips back, "I found one quite sufficient." Spinrad wasn't a fan of the *Trek* penchant for these light hearted moments, saying "they always added those cutesy pie codas after the real ending of the show."

Regardless of the minor edits, Spinrad says he was very happy with the resulting episode. However, after seeing the episode he did note that they didn't use his original sketch for the Doomsday Machine itself. "I asked Gene what happened and he agreed with me that it looked like a windsock dipped in cement, but said that they ran out of money and that was the best they could do," says Spinrad.

Now that he has had a chance to see the digitally remastered version of the show the writer is quite impressed. He notes how it much cleaner it looks than even the original in terms of both detail and the new effects. Spinrad was impressed with many of the effects that were just not possible with the technology available back in the 1960s. However, he did wish that they took another crack at his original design for the Doomsday device. "What they made was a slightly more sophisticated windsock," he jokes.

When looking back at the series, Spinrad gives Gene Roddenberry high marks for his support of fellow science fiction authors. "Gene wanted serious science fiction, and he got stuff from serious science fiction writers," explains Spinrad. He notes how the show reached out to writers such as Harlan Ellison, Theodore Sturgeon and George Clayton Johnson. Spinrad, who is the former president of the Science Fiction and Fantasy Writers Associates, pays Roddenberry the ultimate compliment when he says "as a writer he was a real science fiction writer."

As for his time with the franchise, Spinrad looks back fondly, saying "it was good writing experience. *Star Trek* had a very positive effect on sci-fi in culture, and I am very happy to be associated with it and still have fond feeling for it."

PSYCH-FILE:

COMMODORE MATTHEW B. DECKER,
COMMANDING OFFICER,
U.S.S. CONSTELLATION, NCC-1017

EXCERPTED FROM MEDICAL LOG OF *U.S.S. CONSTELLATION*, STARDATE 4194.6: DR. LEWIS ROSENHAUS, CHIEF MEDICAL OFFICER
CLEARED FOR GENERAL RELEASE BY DAYTON WARD AND KEVIN DILMORE

STARDATE 4194.6

This is to certify that I have conducted the annual psychological profile on Commodore Matthew Decker as part of routine testing to determine ongoing fitness for command.

I am obligated to note initial hesitation on the Commodore's part even to submit to the profile, but nothing that is uncommon to my dealings with him since my joining the *Constellation*. Upon reporting for the test, he remarked that not only did he distrust my psycho-tricorder's ability to function properly, he also wished to verify that my certification to operate the device was in proper order. I also must admit that my ability to discern when the commodore is joking is low, especially compared to those with whom he has served for a greater period of time.

I have rated Commodore Decker's psychological responses within the following parameters as prescribed by Starfleet Medical for command competency:

DUTY/LOYALTY:

The Commodore fulfills all obligations as commanding officer of the *Constellation* and as bound by the authority of Starfleet Command. As he has throughout his career, he consistently bears true faith and allegiance to the United Federation of Planets, Starfleet, their policies and general orders, as well as his vessel's command structure and crew. The Commodore is very much results-oriented, often giving the appearance that he cares little for the details involved in the tasks he requires so long as the mission is accomplished.

SELFLESS SERVICE:

Commodore Decker has an established record of placing the welfare of subordinates, Starfleet, and the Federation before his own. His responses to such situations stem from genuine motivation rather than any perceived sense of obligation.

HONOR/INTEGRITY:

While he may not provide a polished or exemplary role model for command, the Commodore conducts himself within the boundaries of what is good, proper and just, both legally and morally. On those occasions where he has felt the need to observe the "spirit of the law" rather than the letter, he always has reported said "interpretations" both in the *Constellation*'s official log as well as his reports to Starfleet Command.

PERSONAL COURAGE:

Decker has shown himself willing to face fear, danger and adversity on physical and moral grounds. This trait evokes similar behavior from his subordinates, and it is not uncommon for the Commodore and those on duty with him to remain at their posts until such time as I order mandatory rest and recuperation periods after crises have passed.

RESPECT:

As noted in my last report, Commodore Decker continually struggles with issues of respect toward persons in authority as well as for those under his command. His displays of superiority and self-importance can border on the offensive when directed at subordinates. To his credit, he usually recognizes when he has crossed a line with his behavior, and makes genuine attempts toward reconciliation – but only when he sees fit to do so.

Cross-reference these findings with the results of the Commodore's latest psycho-simulator test, conducted on Stardate 3925.8 at Starbase 2. Note those results are consistent with previous biennial tests, which indicate Commodore Decker's overall ability to command with objectivity and decisiveness.

There is one notable exception to Commodore Decker's command ability, according to these tests: Should he second-guess one of his own decisions and find himself unable to correct it, particularly in a scenario that puts his ship or crew in harm's way, it is possible that marked increases in anxiety and any consequent outward displays of emotional stress may well affect the commodore's critical thinking skills and impact his faculties for command. However, as he is currently being considered for promotion to a rank and billet which likely will remove him from active starship command and place him in an administrative position at a starbase or Starfleet Command Headquarters, the risk of the aforementioned scenario coming to pass is admittedly low.

All previously stated concerns under consideration, with this report I do certify that Commodore Decker remains psychologically fit for active duty and for command of this vessel.

END LOG ENTRY.

CAPTAINING THE CONSTELLATION

Charming character actor William Windom has a recognizable face and voice, in a career that has spanned 60 years and over 100 roles in movies like *To Kill A Mockingbird* ("That was a real privilege to be in!") and television shows like *The Twilight Zone*. He was also a memorable guest on classic *Star Trek* as Matthew Decker, Captain of the *U.S.S. Constellation* in the second season episode, *The Doomsday Machine*. Pat Jankiewicz caught up with him recently...

The "83 and a half year old" Windom, who was born "on a small island off the coast of New York called Manhattan," has a frank and funny honesty. The actor notes that Captain Decker "is an emotional wreck. I used to be known in those days as 'Willie the Weeper,'" Windom says proudly. "Whenever they needed someone to break down on a show confessing a murder or infidelity, anything where something happened to this guy and we watch him disintegrate on camera, they would say, 'Get Windom – bring in Willie the weeper!'

"They would give me these terrible parts that never went anywhere, including, God help me, that one on *Star Trek*," he chuckles. "It would always lead up to me falling apart on camera. Of course, Decker falls apart telling Captain Kirk and company what happened to his ship and crew, how he lost everything because of the Planet Eater!"

As you may have guessed, Windom has an irreverent take on doing *Star Trek*. "I was not a fan of *Star Trek* when I did it and I never got that way," he confesses. "I am a fan of [William] Shatner now, only after he turned funny about five years ago, but I wasn't a fan of anybody involved with that thing! Not the storyline or any part of it. Because I'm a Starship Captain, I'm wearing the same silly shirt as Captain Kirk, and I couldn't think of anything else besides stubble to show that Captain Decker had been holed up in this wrecked starship for a couple of weeks. To me, it was like doing a fairy tale!"

Windom is thrilled to remember how he landed the role of Decker. "My agent called me," he says dryly. "The episode was okay, but the premise was just beyond me – I thought the whole thing was ludicrous! The distances involved, the time and effort to move a machine between here and there through space, except in your imagination, was just unbelievable.

"It seemed kind of silly, with the Planet Eater and spaceships. It's like doing a cartoon, so I acted accordingly! It was mildly amusing, but certainly nothing to drive my imagination! The whole thing was a take-off on *Moby Dick*. I was playing 'Captain Ahab in Outer Space' but I didn't think about it that way until years after I did it, when I read it in an article!"

While Captain Kirk and Mr. Spock were best friends onscreen, Windom saw a different side to them. "When I did the show, Shatner was at war with Nimoy! Shatner was not funny then. Not when I saw him – Shatner was quiet, business-like. I felt it was an unhappy set. I like to clown around, so when I get on a set where the actors don't clown around, I get a little suspicious. That put me off right away.

"Shatner was the one who teased the fans by saying 'Will you people get a life?' I never did that. But I'm more than happy to point out I was not a *Star Trek* fan," he laughs.

"I'm happy to do the work, I am happy people liked it, but I did not memorize every line from the part! In fact, I never saw another episode besides my own. I love actors and I admire any audience that goes to see them, I don't knock that, even if I don't really like the show.

"The episode has followed me around for 40 years, probably because it's the only thing of mine *Star Trek* fans have ever seen. Loving that episode as a *Star Trek* fan is like saying to someone who lives on a farm, 'Would you like some more of this cow feed?' Most people would say 'No, I'm a human being', but they say 'Yeah, but the cows all love it!' Fans shouldn't be bothered I don't like my *Star Trek* – I also don't like Cruise Ships or Disneyland!"

At the climax of *The Doomsday Machine*, Windom bravely pilots his shuttle into the heart of the Planet Eater in a suicidal bid to kill it. "There's that great close-up at the end of the show when I do that," he recalls. "The director, Marc Daniels, and I got along famously. Marc was a great guy – he was the only guy on the show who would talk to me, because the rest of the cast was too busy. I couldn't get a smile out of anybody on that set. They were taking the show so seriously, like it was the latest from The Western Front.

"The whole thing gave me the giggles. The director, Marc, and I got to that scene where I had to do my close-up, where I'm being swallowed by the thing. Marc said to me, 'I don't know what to tell you to do, Bill... This is your close-up, going down into the center of the Planet Destroyer. Sit in this chair, turn it around, face the camera, do what you want, I'm going out for a smoke!' For my close-up, I'm just leaning back in this chair, thinking about lunch! Marc liked it and they used it. I just wanted to make this for the multitude of eager beavers sitting out there watching it!"

He reprised his role as the late Captain Decker for the fan film, *Star Trek: In Harm's Way*. "That was fun. I was surprised to be Decker in that, because I died in the episode! I think there was a character playing my son in that, too. They did tell me that the Decker in *Star Trek: The Motion Picture* was supposed to be the son of my character from *Doomsday Machine*."

In what he considers the most symbolic part of *The Doomsday Machine*, William Windom notes that "The Planet Eater turned out to be the center roll of toilet paper: that's what they made the model out of. I tell people, 'Every time you change a roll of toilet paper, and you will at least once in your lifetime, think of me diving into that and saving your whole civilization!'"

PREVIOUSLY ON *STAR TREK*...

In *The Doomsday Machine*, only one crewmember of the *U.S.S. Constellation* was named besides Commodore Decker (Science Officer Masada, named in the Commodore's log entry). However two novels gave us a more detailed look at the *Constellation* and its crew in happier times: *The Brave and the Bold* Book 1 by Keith R.A. DeCandido and *Vanguard: Harbinger* by David Mack. Keith DeCandido presents details on the people whose lives were lost in that episode.

Commodore Matt Decker
Commanding officer
Decker came up through security, and was never expected to get a command. Has a tendency to make a decision and stick to it, sometimes flying in the face of reality. Hates shaving, but never actually grows the beard. He also has difficulty remembering the names of his crew. He's a tough-but-fair leader, with a relaxed charisma that the crew responds to. Has succeeded due to a combination of instinct and dumb luck. His son is Willard Decker, who would later become captain of the *U.S.S. Enterprise*.

Commander Hiromi Takeshewada
First officer
A petite woman whom no one makes the mistake of underestimating twice. Her job is to kick Decker back in bounds. Sometimes this results in very loud arguments between the two (though never in front of the crew), and often the yelling pays off, as Decker will sometimes listen to the advice of his Number One.

Lieutenant Guillermo Masada
Science officer
Far more of a scientist than he is an officer, Masada is very much dedicated to his job of learning about the unknown, making him well suited to the *Constellation*'s mission to seek out new life and new civilizations. Can be cheerfully oblivious at times, and also has a good sense of humor – he also is amused by Spock's subtle sense of humor when they work together, though Spock himself refuses to admit to it.

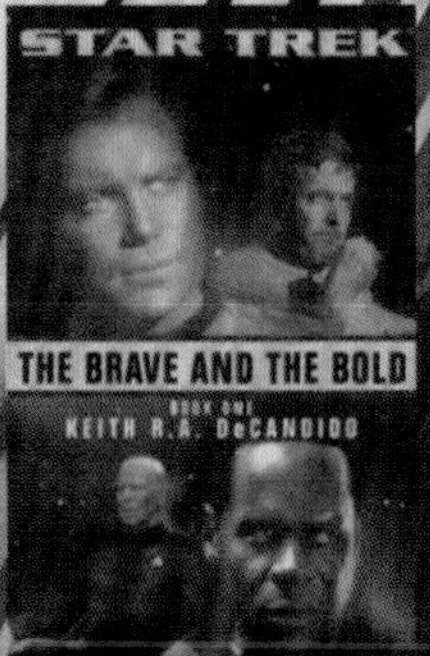

Dr. Lewis Rosenhaus
Chief medical officer
Rosenhaus is an eager young doctor, who graduated from Starfleet Medical Academy with honors. He butts heads with Dr. McCoy when they work together, as the veteran surgeon has little patience for eager youth – though, oddly, when Rosenhaus lets his enthusiasm get away from him, accidentally endangering the life of a patient, McCoy goes easier on him. He wasn't Decker's first choice for a new CMO, but Admiral Fitzgerald all but forced Decker to take him on after his predecessor retired.

Lieutenant Etienne Vascogne
Chief of security
A native of the human colony of Gammac, Vascogne joined Starfleet rather than the local police force, which was what his uncle Claude wanted him to do. He's an easy-going sort who prefers quick and simple solutions to problems.

Other characters:
Lieutenant George Howard, communications officer
Lieutenant (j.g.) Chaoyang Soo, sensor officer
Ensign Sontor, sensor officer (Vulcan)
Nurse Emil Jazayerli, head nurse
Yeoman Guthrie, captain's yeoman
Norma Shickele, sickbay lab technician

FILLING THE BOTTLE

Andy Lane examines how author Norman Spinrad turned a "bottle show" into one of *Star Trek*'s classic episodes...

Gene Roddenberry did a great many things to help make *Star Trek* into a phenomenon which has lasted to this day, including basing the series on a mythic archetype, choosing the right actors, and recognizing that science fiction should still follow the normal rules of character-based drama. One of the most important and least recognized was to use, as his scriptwriters, a mixture of seasoned TV professionals who weren't as concerned about the themes and tropes of SF as they were the budgetary constraints of TV drama, and SF writers whose attitude was that the story was paramount. Roddenberry realized, consciously or unconsciously, that the fledgling series needed a balance, that a weak episode could be bolstered by a strong episode on either side of it, and that his best chance of ensuring that his series lasted the course was to make sure that it had variety. Lots of variety. And so, alongside the likes of Gene L. Coon and Stephen Kandel he employed Norman Spinrad, Harlan Ellison and Jerome Bixby.

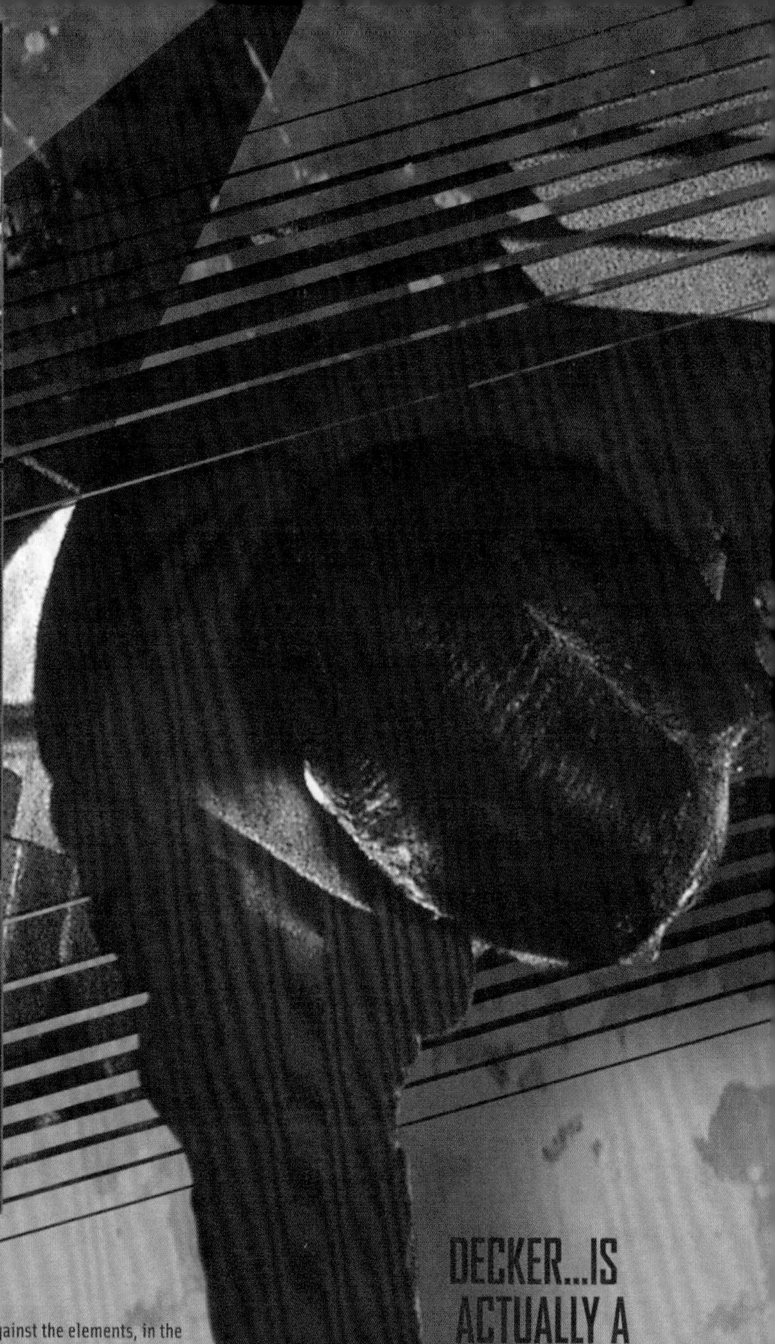

DECKER...IS ACTUALLY A SURROGATE KIRK. HE SACRIFICES HIMSELF SO THAT KIRK DOESN'T HAVE TO...

Norman Spinrad's episode *The Doomsday Machine* has rightly come to be regarded as one of the show's classics, but it's worth taking a moment to examine why. It has no alien worlds, no alien creatures, and it doesn't feature Captain Kirk with a ripped shirt inflicting his famous drop-kick on an adversary. Stripped to its essentials, *The Doomsday Machine* has the crew of the *Enterprise* fighting against a large special effect for 50 minutes – a large special effect that cannot even talk back or justify its own actions – and yet it is compelling drama. Why?

The obvious answer is that Spinrad – briefed by Roddenberry that he wanted a "bottle" show set just on the *Enterprise* in order to save money that might otherwise have been spent on building sets – sensibly returned to classic dramatic elements that have served writers well, from Shakespeare to Henry Melville and beyond. His script has a small band of men pitted against the elements, in the same way as did Melville's *Moby Dick*. The comparison with Melville is deliberate: *The Doomsday Machine* can be seen as an updating of *Moby Dick*, with a massive robotic vessel of immense destructive power in the place of a white whale, but Spinrad creates, in the character of the obsessed Commodore Decker, more than just a carbon copy of Captain Ahab. No, Decker is a man who has been driven almost to the point of insanity by his own powerlessness in the face of disaster. A Starfleet captain whose remit is to protect the planets of the Federation, Decker can do nothing but watch as the robotic behemoth – left over, one is led to believe, from some long-ago war between alien races – just keeps blindly following its programming.

Interestingly, other episodes of *Star Trek* and its various offspring, including the movies, have shown us planets being laid waste, but nowhere else have we felt the sheer gut-wrenching horror of what it actually means. Compare, for instance, *The Doomsday Machine* with the episode *The Immunity Syndrome*, in which Kirk and his compatriots fight against a large special effect that also eats planets and also cannot talk back or justify its own actions. In *The Immunity Syndrome* (another "bottle show") the special effect is a massive space-going amoeba rather than a giant robot, but the principle is exactly the same. The former episode is a classic, the latter is just quite fun to watch. What's the difference? Well, it's in the way Spinrad personalizes the drama in the character of Decker. Decker can argue with Kirk, he can put obstacles in Kirk's way and, at the end of the day, he can even provide the solution to the insoluble problem by sacrificing his own life. Decker provides us with a viewpoint character. Through his mental breakdown we can emotionally understand the threat that the massive robot poses, and in his ultimately redemptive act we feel a catharsis. By comparison, *The Immunity Syndrome* has nobody who is deeply affected by events, and nobody who sacrifices themselves in order to save the day. It's a plot in which the events are never made important to us, the audience. We just watch them; we don't feel them.

The Doomsday Machine has one other trick to play on us, and it's quite a subtle one. Decker – the committed Starfleet officer – is actually a surrogate Kirk. He sacrifices himself so that Kirk doesn't have to, but when we stare into his haunted eyes, when we hear his cracked voice talking about how he could do nothing while millions of people died, part of us knows that Captain Kirk, under the same circumstances, would probably go the same way. Without ever having to show Kirk having a mental breakdown, Spinrad plants a picture in our mind of what might happen if he did. And that's great drama.

CONTROLLING THE DOOMSDAY DAMAGE

Like so many others, Richard Compton was a young man trying to make it in Hollywood when he snagged two days' work in yet another bit role for TV. Unlike most, though, those two days were in the 1960s on a show called *Star Trek* – and his bit part became enshrined to millions as dutiful damage control officer Lt. Washburn of *The Doomsday Machine*. Larry Nemecek takes him back...

His memories are hazy now, but Richard Compton – who went on to a long career in directing TV and films alike – will never forget how his "audition" was hardly the anxious trauma most actors face.

"I was not looking for acting work – I was at that point only directing in little theatres, and going back and forth between New York and here," he said during a recent Los Angeles chat. "When my dad passed away, I flew to Washington, D.C. On my way back, I get on the plane in Washington and I have a script I'm reading; the guy sitting next to me – *he* opens a script. So we start chatting; he reaches over and says, 'Hello, I'm the creator of *Star Trek* – do you know the show?' So I had him as a captive audience from Washington to L.A. – a four and a half hour flight!"

The two struck up a long talk, exchanged numbers, and the producer asked how work was going. Compton confided that he was doing bit parts but really aimed for writing and directing, and Roddenberry invited him to "send his stuff along." But then, he recalls, the producer turned paternal and asked, "Are you earning enough to survive?" "And I said, 'Well, my sister was kind enough to send me this first-class ticket to go to my dad's funeral,' so he said, 'Look me up and I'll find you some stuff to do.' "

"Some stuff" turned into the extended face time of Washburn, plus a Romulan crewman on *The Enterprise Incident* – "I got to keep the ears," he laughs – and even more work as voiceovers for intercom crew. "They weren't big parts or anything," he notes. "It was a little bit of a pay check, but back in that time I definitely could use every single bit I had."

On set, he recalls Marc Daniels as a no-nonsense but actor-friendly director. "It was not a cut-and-dried shoot; it moved quickly, but there was definitely discussion on the set – mostly by [William] Shatner," Compton says. He smiles when reminded of his biggest scene with Shatner, with Compton placed behind a see-through but background red-orange grille: "When Daniels put me there, I thought he was mad at me!

"He actually liked me, Shatner did," he adds. "I made him laugh a little. That was good.

"It was a very diverse set, y'know, which wasn't that common back then," Compton recalls. "I mean, it had every ethnic representation – I think Charlie [Washburn, his role's namesake] was the first black assistant director in Hollywood. I just remember that it was a very cool set, and the actors were wonderful in the sense that they all were feeling their oats, y'know? They had a series – a series that was a little different than what was on the air at that time."

Well into his career, Compton was later invited by Roddenberry and friend Maurice Hurley to be one of the first directors on *Star Trek: The Next Generation* with *Haven* – coincidentally, exactly 20 years and one month after his two days as Washburn! And while he's never guested at a convention, Compton marvels at the fact he's autographed Washburn trading cards for the manufacturer.

"It was never a big part of my life – it was just one of those things that happened, just an accident that happened with Gene," he muses. "I really liked him – what a *really* nice man."

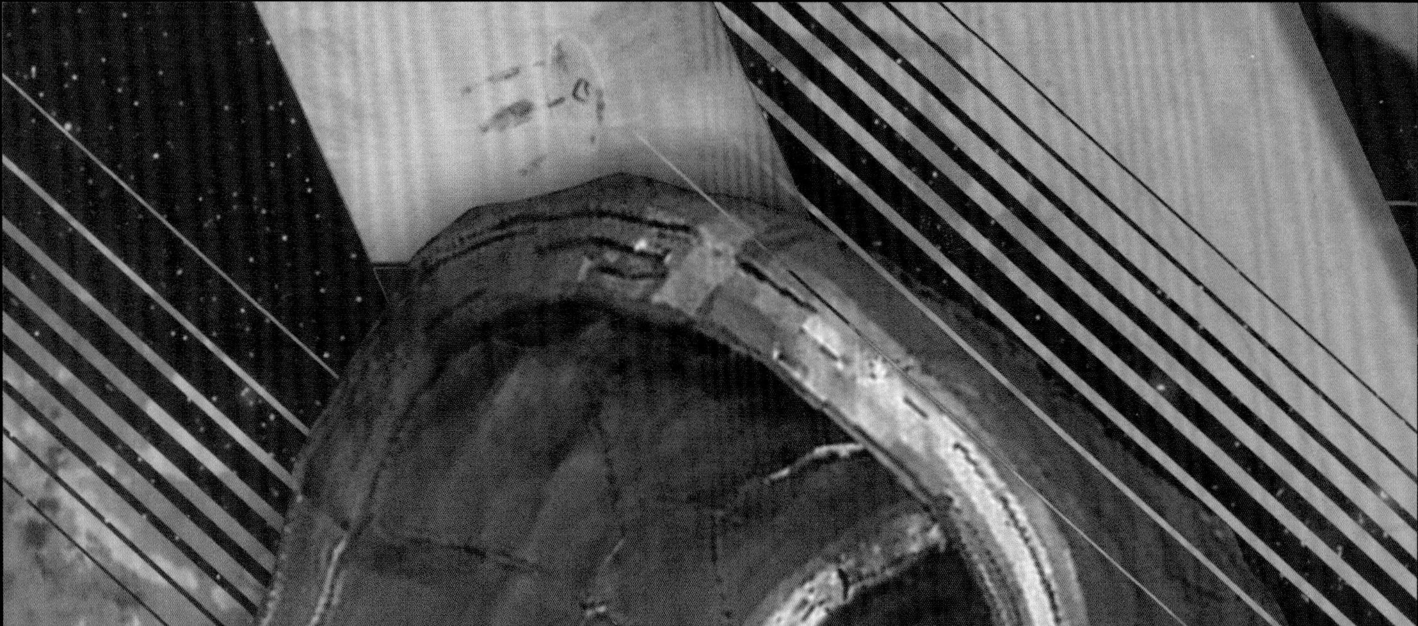

REMASTERING DOOMSDAY

Dave Rossi describes the process by which the Doomsday Machine fulfilled its potential...

You may have heard about a project that's been ongoing for the last few months known as *Star Trek Remastered*. My job, along with Co-Creative/Line Producer Mike Okuda and Associate Producer Denise Okuda, is to watch every episode of *Star Trek: The Original Series*, identify every exterior space shot, viewscreen shot, and scenic background shot and then suggest new shots using today's CGI techniques. Yeah, I know, tough gig. While the scope of work is what I mentioned above, on occasion, time permitting, we've also done some work on other types of shots, such as Norman's internal circuitry in *I, Mudd* and adding a beam to Scotty's phaser in *The Naked Time*.

The project started up in June of 2006. Working with Niel Wray, Visual Effects Producer at CBS-Digital, we've been delivering an episode a week. These new episodes, also wonderfully remastered, are airing in syndication around the United States with plans to release them on DVD underway.

While we've been giving every episode all the tender loving care we can, one episode in particular seemed to jump out as a watermark: *The Doomsday Machine*.

From the time we started *Star Trek Remastered*, there seemed to be this undercurrent of whisperings that *this* was the show everyone wanted to see done. While it was full of battle sequences that we could sink our teeth into, the most important thing for Mike, Denise, and me was to do what we've been attempting to do in every show: use the effects to broaden the story. For us, this project is about taking people out of their living rooms and slamming them into the 23rd Century so firmly that things like the AMT *Constellation* model, with its matchstick-burned nacelle, no longer takes viewers out of the story with a titter and an eye-roll.

We've found that things like matte paintings used as establishing shots, such as the castle in *Catspaw* or what we did for the Rigel mining encampment in *Mudd's Women*, can evoke a feeling that helps advance the story and makes this universe more of a real place for the viewer. Likewise, exterior ship shots, like the Big E releasing the Botany Bay from her tractor beam, do the same thing. *The Doomsday Machine* was no different. In fact, this brilliant story of a half-crazed, defeated Commodore, a wrecked ship, and a relentless killing machine deserved our best efforts. There were things I absolutely needed to see to make it real for me.

"It's miles long, with a maw that could swallow a dozen starships!" That was number one on my list. It always bothered me that the ill-fated *Constellation*, entering the maw of the Doomsday Machine, made Commodore Decker look like a terrible liar. I wanted to capture the scope of the monster in a new way that led us to believe it *could* in fact swallow a dozen starships.

The problem presented to us was twofold: The shuttlecraft would all but disappear in any wide shots, which would completely drown any of the drama we get from Decker's sacrifice, and secondly, the geography of

the battle overall would suffer (which was the other hot button for me. I was hell-bent on making sure the battle made sense!). So we had to compromise by increasing the Doomsday Machine to a size we felt supported Decker's statement, but let us show a compelling visual element that allowed viewers to see the Doomsday Machine, while not obscuring other ships in the same shots.

Being something of a naval combat history buff, the geography of the battle was very important to me. The original episode is a series of reused shots that make very little sense in relation to what people are saying and what's actually happening during the battle. That same shot of the phasers hitting the Doomsday Machine they used over and over reminded me of that reuse of the Cylon ship blowing up in the original *Battlestar Galactica* TV series or the pirate ship exploding in *Buck Rogers*. While I understand (and now *fully* appreciate) the kind of schedule and budget restraints the *ST:TOS* folks were under, *Star Trek* deserved better and I was intent on doing whatever we could to make that battle real. I just about held a phaser to everyone's head regarding it. It was also again a chance for us to help tell more of the story and that was an opportunity we couldn't lose.

We screened the episode among ourselves about six or seven times before we showed it to CBS-Digital. We needed to have a real grasp of what was supposed to be happening according to dialogue before we started on animatics for the visual effects. Once we talked it out for the 600th time, Mike set to task developing highly elaborate planning sheets that spelled out what was happening in each scene (see overleaf). Those little pieces of paper became our bible for the length of the work. I think at one point everyone in my dreams was preceded by giant, sweeping red arrows that showed their relationship to each other and the direction they were moving in.

In conjunction with all this, Niel Wray set his CGI modelers to developing the look of the Doomsday Machine as well as the *Constellation*. Mike had a vision for the *Constellation* that took the poor ship way past crooked nacelles. Again, with story in mind, Mike wanted to illustrate how deadly the Doomsday Machine was, using the *Constellation* as a sign-post and I agreed. Without being able to see the true destructive power of the Doomsday Machine carving up a planet, we wanted the audience to see what the stakes were, and I think we did that with the mangled, horrific hulk of the *Constellation*.

As for the Doomsday Machine itself, we spent a lot of time discussing it. While the original Norman Spinrad concept was a machine that had been bristling with weapons, we decided to keep the basic shape because of its recognizability and start from there. If you look closely though, you can catch areas that have little bits and doo-dads along the large couplings to give the impression that while one day this thing may have been glistening with weapons, over the uncounted wars and attacks it sustained, they've been ground to almost nothing, leaving just its primary weapon: the pure anti-proton .

Next, we sat down and started getting into the specifics of each shot as CBS-Digital started creating animatics. Although there isn't time here to go into the thought behind every shot, I will talk about a couple that I pushed for that were very important to me and that turned out really well.

Pictures above: original and Remastered shots of the Doomsday Machine firing, and the Constellation entering the maw of the machine

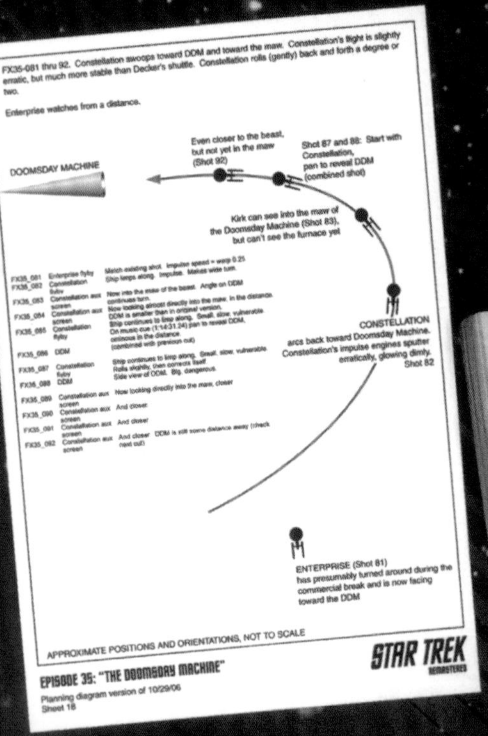
FX35-081 thru 92. Constellation swoops toward DDM and toward the maw. Constellation's flight is slightly erratic, but much more stable than Decker's shuttle. Constellation rolls (gently) back and forth a degree or two.
Enterprise watches from a distance.
DOOMSDAY MACHINE
Even closer to the beast, but not yet in the maw (Shot 92)
Shot 87 and 88: Start with Constellation, pan to reveal DDM (combined shot)
Kirk can see into the maw of the Doomsday Machine (Shot 83), but can't see the furnace yet
CONSTELLATION
arcs back toward Doomsday Machine. Constellation's impulse engines sputter erratically, glowing dimly. Shot 82
ENTERPRISE (Shot 81)
has presumably turned around during the commercial break and is now facing toward the DDM
APPROXIMATE POSITIONS AND ORIENTATIONS, NOT TO SCALE
STAR TREK REMASTERED
EPISODE 35: "THE DOOMSDAY MACHINE"
Planning diagram version of 10/29/06
Sheet 18

MEMORY CHEATS

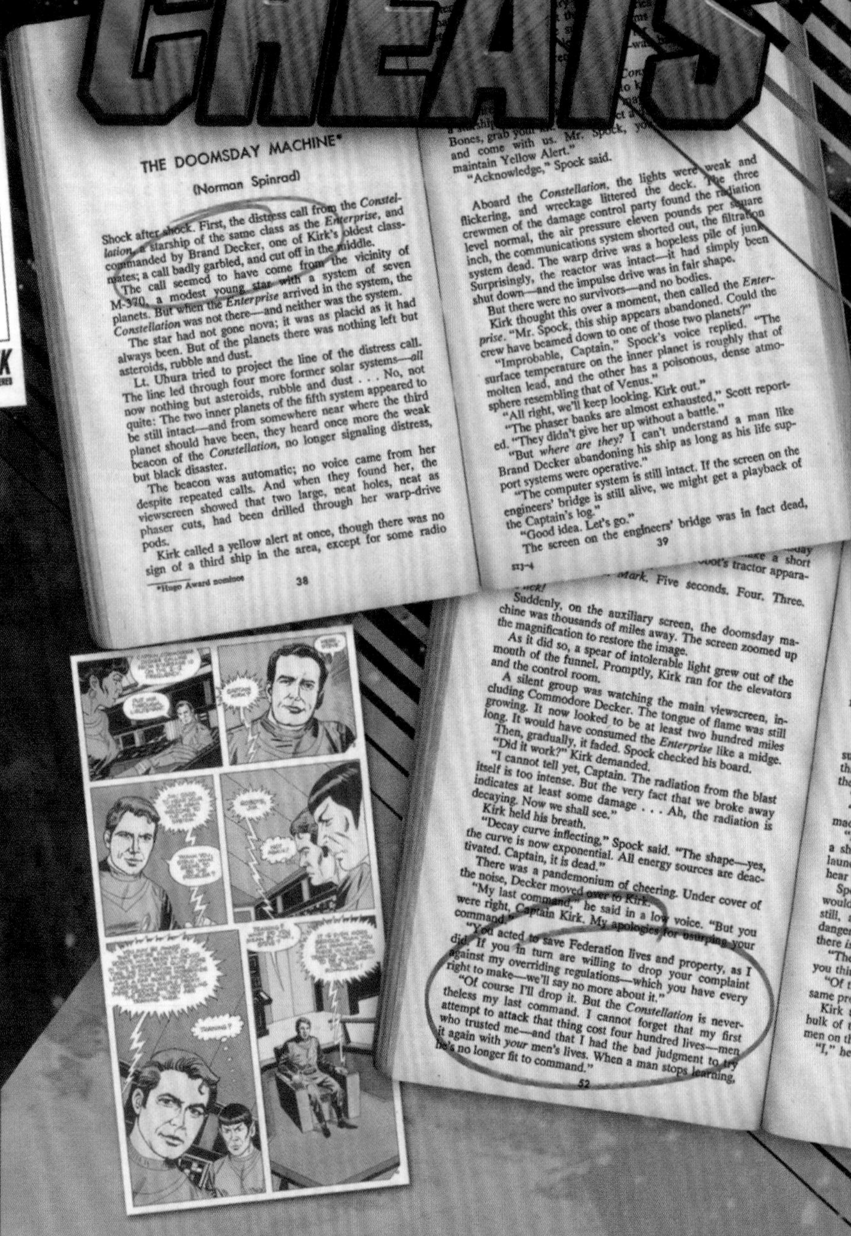

THE DOOMSDAY MACHINE*

(Norman Spinrad)

Shock after shock. First, the distress call from the *Constellation*, a starship of the same class as the *Enterprise*, and commanded by Brand Decker, one of Kirk's oldest classmates; a call badly garbled, and cut off in the middle.

The call seemed to have come from the vicinity of M-370, a modest young star with a system of seven planets. But when the *Enterprise* arrived in the system, the *Constellation* was not there—and neither was the system.

The star had not gone nova; it was as placid as it had always been. But of the planets there was nothing left but asteroids, rubble and dust.

Lt. Uhura tried to project the line of the distress call. The line led through four more former solar systems—*all* now nothing but asteroids, rubble and dust . . . No, not quite: The two inner planets of the fifth system appeared to be still intact—and from somewhere near where the third planet should have been, they heard once more the weak beacon of the *Constellation*, no longer signaling distress, but black disaster.

The beacon was automatic; no voice came from her despite repeated calls. And when they found her, the viewscreen showed that two large, neat holes, neat as phaser cuts, had been drilled through her warp-drive pods.

Kirk called a yellow alert at once, though there was no sign of a third ship in the area, except for some radio

*Hugo Award nominee

38

Bones, grab your ... and come with us. Mr. Spock, you ... maintain Yellow Alert."

"Acknowledge," Spock said.

Aboard the *Constellation*, the lights were weak and flickering, and wreckage littered the deck. The three crewmen of the damage control party found the radiation level normal, the air pressure eleven pounds per square inch, the communications system shorted out, the filtration system dead. The warp drive was a hopeless pile of junk. Surprisingly, the reactor was intact—it had simply been shut down—and the impulse drive was in fair shape.

But there were no survivors—and no bodies.

Kirk thought this over a moment, then called the *Enterprise*. "Mr. Spock, this ship appears abandoned. Could the crew have beamed down to one of those two planets?"

"Improbable, Captain," Spock's voice replied. "The surface temperature on the inner planet is roughly that of molten lead, and the other has a poisonous, dense atmosphere resembling that of Venus."

"All right, we'll keep looking. Kirk out."

"The phaser banks are almost exhausted," Scott reported. "They didn't give her up without a battle."

"But *where are they*? I can't understand a man like Brand Decker abandoning his ship as long as his life support systems were operative."

"The computer system is still intact. If the screen on the engineers' bridge is still alive, we might get a playback of the Captain's log."

"Good idea. Let's go."

The screen on the engineers' bridge was in fact dead,

39

ST3-4

... *Mark*. Five seconds. Four. Three.

Suddenly, on the auxiliary screen, the doomsday machine was thousands of miles away. The screen zoomed up the magnification to restore the image.

As it did so, a spear of intolerable light grew out of the mouth of the funnel. Promptly, Kirk ran for the elevators and the control room.

A silent group was watching the main viewscreen, including Commodore Decker. The tongue of flame was still growing. It now looked to be at least two hundred miles long. It would have consumed the *Enterprise* like a midge.

Then, gradually, it faded. Spock checked his board.

"Did it work?" Kirk demanded.

"I cannot tell yet, Captain. The radiation from the blast itself is too intense. But the very fact that we broke away indicates at least some damage . . . Ah, the radiation is decaying. Now we shall see."

Kirk held his breath.

"Decay curve inflecting," Spock said. "The shape—yes, the curve is now exponential. All energy sources are deactivated. Captain, it is dead."

There was a pandemonium of cheering. Under cover of the noise, Decker moved over to Kirk.

"My last command," he said in a low voice. "But you were right, Captain Kirk. My apologies for usurping your command."

"You acted to save Federation lives and property, as I did. If you in turn are willing to drop your complaint against my overriding regulations—which you have every right to make—we'll say no more about it."

"Of course I'll drop it. But the *Constellation* is nevertheless my last command. I cannot forget that my first attempt to attack that thing cost four hundred lives—men who trusted me—and that I had the bad judgment to try it again with *your* men's lives. When a man stops learning, he's no longer fit to command."

52

1. The small asteroid hitting the *Constellation*'s hull. I felt it was important to not only show the ship damaged, but also watch as the universe picked on it even more. I think that seeing this poor, defeated, defenseless ship getting kicked when it's down was a nice touch to illustrate its vulnerability. Niel's suggestion having the asteroid splinter into five pieces after it hit the hull, a sweet addition. Thanks Niel!
2. Decker stealing the shuttle. The original animatic was very like the original shot, but the more I looked at it, the more I felt it lacked a certain urgency. Again, this was a way for us to add to the story by demonstrating a couple of things. First, by not waiting for the shuttle's flight sequence to finish (which is a long, laborious process) we see Decker's impulsiveness and the fact that he's over the edge. Secondly it illustrates that Starship Captains are kick-ass pilots. It was an easy sell to Niel who set his animators to it straight away and it paid off in an amazing shot.
3. The *Enterprise* being drawn into the Doomsday Machine. To get a sense of the *Enterprise*'s helplessness in the clutches of the Doomsday Machine tractor beam, I loved the idea of the *Enterprise* falling towards the maw in a slow tumble. Not being able to maintain their own attitude made the crew's plight seem much more hopeless and dramatic.

Make no mistake, this was a tough episode: 105 shots of maybe the toughest single *ST:TOS* episode for visual effects. Everyone at CBS-Digital was sleep deprived by the time they delivered this one. We had to pry it out of Niel Wray's cold, clammy grasp. But all that effort was worth it. The day after the remastered *The Doomsday Machine* first aired, our mailboxes were flooded with e-mails from friends, fans, and colleagues who loved it. With people thanking us for being so respectful of the original work, and thanking us for "helping me rediscover what I loved about *Star Trek* in the first place." as one fan put it, how can we not be excited about the rest of the project and what's to come?

With Doomsday behind us, we're currently tackling giant amoebas, Leo Walsh's stolen ship, a planet called Gothos, and an angry God's hand among other things. Here's an insider tip: Keep an eye out for *All Our Yesterdays*. The Sarpeidon sun's supernova is simply breathtaking! It's a great time to be a *Star Trek* fan.

In the days before video tapes of every episode, let alone DVDs, were commonly available, the only resource that many fans could tap, if they wanted to relive a story that wasn't currently rerunning, was James Blish's novelisations of the scripts. Published between 1967 and 1975, the 13 books (completed by his wife Judith Lawrence after Blish's death) gave prose versions of each episode.

However, particularly in the first four books, Blish departed from the televised material where he felt that stories either didn't work on the printed page, or where alternative versions were provided to him. *The Doomsday Machine* is a case in point: the *Enterprise* meets up with Kirk's classmate *Brand* Decker, who doesn't sacrifice himself in a shuttle, but instead watches as Kirk destroys the *Constellation*, then decides to retire.

When asked about this, author Norman Spinrad was amazed, "I can't imagine why they would bother changing Decker's name. On Wikipedia someone said that in an earlier version he didn't die. I never wrote anything like that and I don't remember anyone bringing up such a thing because it wouldn't make any sense. There is no story. He doesn't die, and then what happens? How do they kill the thing?" he said, adding emphatically that "I never wrote a thing where Decker didn't die... That is the whole end of the thing, that is *Moby Dick*! Dialogue got changed here and there but the fundamentals of the story were never changed."

However Blish's rewriting of the story might explain why the unknown author of the Power Records *Star Trek* story *The Robot Masters* thought he was still alive in the era of *Star Trek: The Motion Picture*...

RE-MASTE

IN THE FIRST OF A TWO PART FEATURE, LARRY NEMECEK TALKS TO THE TEAM BEHIND *STAR TREK REMASTERED*...

It was a dream project bandied about for years: "redo" the aging visual effects of classic 1960s *Star Trek*, but without jarring either the stories or the fan love that built a modern pop culture empire out of them. But would the awesome power to "update" Gene Roddenberry's classic really be a dream – or a nightmare that brings out angry fans and a million different reactions?

Longtime *Star Trek* staffers Dave Rossi and Mike and Denise Okuda brought the savvy of their fan and professional backgrounds alike to turn in an overwhelming effort as producers, and CBS's decision to use its CBS Digital group and visual effects supervisor Niel Wray's team made the project think tank complete.

With the two-year monster project now wrapped, we asked the quartet to share with us their favorites among the all-new visuals presented – especially the moments that did not originally get a big PR treatment – and the "how and why" behind these creative and potentially controversial choices.

In all things, says Mike Okuda, the team's philosophy was to enhance and honor the original. "Where we added things, we tried very hard to maintain the original flow of the storytelling. We wanted the ship shots to feel familiar, not jarring. We wanted the style of the new matte paintings to be evocative of the originals. In the places where we added new elements to the original show, we tried to do so in a way that supported the story rather than calling excessive attention to our work." Dave Rossi, for his part, was always pushing for more angles that would show off the original "Big E" starship in ways the overtaxed 1960s opticals houses could never hope for, and thus "show that Matt Jefferies was a genius and that his starship is a thing of beauty."

THE ALL-NEW SHIPS: "CHARLIE X"/"MUDD'S WOMEN"

Mike Okuda: The *Antares*, the Thasian ship, Mudd's ship: in all of these cases, the original episodes had been ingeniously designed to avoid having to show the ships, because *Star Trek* could rarely show "guest" ships. (We did see Mudd's ship in the original, but all we saw was a blob of light.) We were able to do digital models to give you a glimpse of those ships, and I think we were able to do it in a way that didn't feel jarring.

RPIECES

THE 'EASTER EGG': "THE CLOUD MINDERS"

MO: I love both of Max's Stratos matte paintings. After Niel created a digital model of the city, he rendered the model and turned that image over to Max Gabl, who used his artistic brilliance to give it a level of realism that would have been much harder to get with just a digital rendering. Anyway, the second angle really gives you a sense of "place," like you're really there. It's a delightful surprise, since you're so used to having only the one basic angle in the original. And there's one shot, if you look really, really closely, where you can see Droxine standing on her balcony! (She's really tiny, just seven pixels high.)

RETROFITTING THE COOL STUFF: "TOMORROW IS YESTERDAY"

Denise Okuda: The *Enterprise* whipping around the sun, skimming the surface... So dynamic, it adds so much to the excitement of that moment in Dorothy Fontana's story.

THE FORCEFIELD-HIT FIX: "WINK OF AN EYE"

MO: For some reason, the original shot – Kirk, Spock, and the two security guards firing toward the camera – really bugged me, even though it was an incredibly ingenious effect (the phasers essentially white out the screen). I wanted to show the beams hitting the force field, and I wanted a little bit of animated articulation on the arms.

"*STAR TREK* BELONGS TO GENE RODDENBERRY AND HIS TEAM, AND WE TRIED NEVER TO FORGET THAT."

MIKE OKUDA

RETHINKING VULCAN'S LANDSCAPE: "AMOK TIME"

MO: We originally wanted to improve the realism by replacing the sky in all of the planet shots, and maybe add a distant mountain range; the problem was that there were over 100 shots that would have to have been changed! Dave Rossi came up with a brilliant solution: we found a place, early in the episode, where we could insert two matte paintings. It was one of the very few times when we actually recut an episode. Max Gabl's paintings were so dramatic that they left a powerful impression that (hopefully) lasted for the rest of the episode.

SWEATING THE DETAILS: "REQUIEM FOR METHUSELAH"

DAVE ROSSI: What does "immortal" connote? What *would* we do if we were immortal? In designing Flint's home, we wanted to take what we felt would be his refined design and artistic sense and meld that with the scientific. Who the heck knows what he's been working on besides artificial people and the ability to shrink starships? But down to every detail, we discussed who he was. Take a look around and see what you can find. There's even a mini-spaceship in the background, at a steep angle ready to blast off, as if from some 1950s sci-fi movie! Props to Niel, who designed Flint's home and did an amazing job; Max Gabl did the full painting.

NIEL WRAY: Mike and Dave always had their own ideas, because although I was a fan, they'd been thinking about the series for years and years. So anytime they said, "Hey Niel, why don't you take a crack at this?" it was a major treat – and Flint's castle was one of those. I actually designed that and built a CG model – it was a labor of love. It's unfortunate we didn't get to do a couple of different angles of that model; having a 3-D model meant I could move the camera around and get some great angles.

FLASH

OPERATION: ANNIHILATE!

THE TEASER

Aboard the *U.S.S. Enterprise NCC-1701*, Lt. Uhura has been trying to make contact with the planet Deneva, home to Captain Kirk's brother and family, with no success. Kirk tells her to try his brother's private comm. channel, while Mr Spock reveals that Deneva is the next system along in a line of planets whose inhabitants were driven mad and then mysteriously died. Just as Dr McCoy is explaining that he is at a loss to explain the mass insanity, the *Enterprise* scanners spot a one-man shuttle heading directly into the Denevan sun. Kirk orders Sulu to intercept, but the *Enterprise* is out of tractor beam range and the shuttle is disintegrated in the intense heat of the sun. However, just before the ship blows up, its occupant screams out, "At last, I'm free!"

"I cannot let it spread, even if it means destroying a million people down there!"

THE STORY

The ship goes into orbit around Deneva, and Spock informs the Captain that the million or so inhabitants are still alive, but strangely inactive. Kirk, McCoy, Spock, Scotty and two 'red shirts' beam down to the planet to find it empty of life. As they start to explore, four screaming men waving clubs suddenly attack them and the landing party are forced to stun them. Bones scans their bodies and reports that even though they are unconscious, their nervous systems are being highly stimulated.

They continue to make their way to the home of Kirk's brother, Sam, when they suddenly hear a woman screaming. It's Aurelan, Kirk's sister-in-law, and when they burst into her home, she becomes psychotic, screaming, "They're here! They're here!" before Bones sedates her. Also in the futuristic house are two inert bodies – Bones reports that Sam, Kirk's brother, is dead but Kirk's young nephew, Peter, is alive but unconscious. Kirk beams up to the *Enterprise* with his family and Bones, leaving Spock in charge of the Away team.

In sickbay, Kirk tries to get Aurelan to tell him what happened on the planet, but she's in considerable pain and her babbling doesn't make much sense. She does manage to say, "They came eight months ago. Things, horrible things. Visitors brought them in their vessel from their planet, Ingraham B. Not the ship's crew's fault, the things made them bring their ship here." It all becomes too much for her, and she dies in agonising pain.

Seeking answers, Kirk beams back down to the planet where he is met by the Away team. Kirk warns them to set their phasers to kill, telling them, "We're

Spock and McCoy bake their soufflé

Kirk shoots to kill

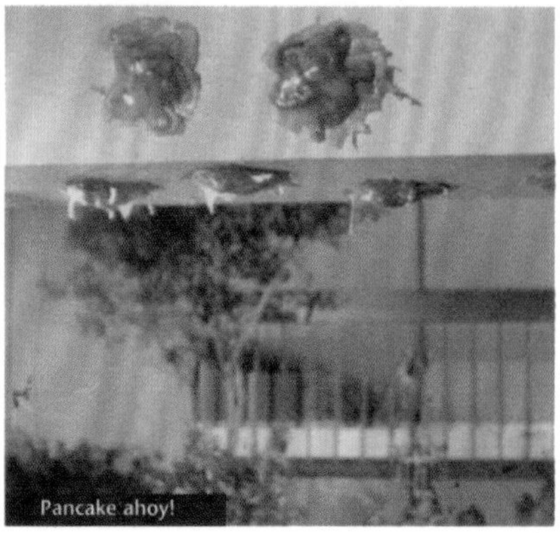
Pancake ahoy!

looking for some kind of creature, and we already know *it* will kill." While investigating a strange buzzing sound, they are suddenly attacked by these flying pancake-shaped creatures and their phasers prove to be virtually ineffective. Spock inspects a stunned creature, noting, "Incredible. Not only should it have been destroyed by our phasers, it does not even register on my tricorder... It is not life as we know or understand it."

As the Away team make a tactical retreat, the stunned creature suddenly flies at them and glues itself to Spock's back. Kirk rips it off, but Spock seems out for the count.

Retreating to the ship, McCoy operates on Spock and finds his nervous system has been intertwined with minute alien tentacles, which the creatures use to exact excruciating pain on its host as a means of controlling their victims. McCoy reports, "When the creature attacks, it leaves this stinger, much like a bee or a wasp, leaving one of these [tentacles] in the victim's body. It takes over the victim very rapidly. The intertwining is far too involved for conventional surgery to remove." The medical team are stumped and don't know how to free the victims from this control.

Spock awakes, and after initially running wild, informs the captain that he is now in control and is using his Vulcan mind control techniques to suppress the pain. He suggests he go to the planet to gather a creature so that they can find a way to kill it without harming the hosts. Bones notes that Spock, "may be controlling the pain, but you're far from all right." Kirk overrules him and Spock carries out the task, returning to the *Enterprise* with a captured creature.

After many tests, Spock discovers the secret to the parasites' power, it's a single cell creature, resembling a solitary brain cell. "Although it is not physically connected to the other cells, it is nevertheless part of the whole creature. Guided by the whole, drawing its strength from the whole, which probably accounts for its unusual resistance to our phaser weapons." Sadly, neither he nor Bones can find a way to kill it.

"They're here! They're here!"

Captain Kirk tells the pair of them that they must find a way to stop these parasites, or he will be forced to commit genocide. "I cannot let it spread, even if it means destroying a million people down there!"

THE CONCLUSION

Just then, Kirk remembers the Denevan who flew into the sun and suggests that these parasites may be sensitive to intense light. Spock volunteers to be a test patient and Bones bombards him with intense light. It works, destroying the parasite's hold on Spock, but unfortunately the beam was so strong that the Vulcan is left blinded for life.

Too late, a devastated Bones realises that only ultraviolet light is needed to kill the creatures, which would not have blinded Spock. At least Kirk can use the method to save the Denevans. The Captain sets off ultraviolet flares from satellites surrounding the planet, killing all the parasites and freeing its inhabitants.

However, in a fortunate twist (press that rewind button!), Spock regains his eyesight and takes up his post at the science station on the bridge. Kirk, Bones and the rest of the bridge crew are dumbfounded until Spock reveals that due to the intensity of Vulcan's sun, his species have developed a hereditary inner eyelid, and he was only temporarily blinded. "We tend to ignore it," Spock concludes, "as you ignore your own appendix."

And the ship sails off into the cosmos. ■

EPISODE TITBITS

- A phaser setting of force three is enough to kill.
- Captain Kirk's brother, George Samuel Kirk, his family and three sons were name-checked in the episode *What are Little Girls Made Of?*, where Kirk reveals they waved him off on his first five-year mission. Only Jim calls him Sam.
- The dead Sam Kirk was played by none other than William Shatner in make-up.
- The private transmitter channel of Sam Kirk is GSK783, subspace frequency three.
- The *Enterprise* has 14 science labs.
- Bones bombards Spock with the light of a million candles.

THE FACTS

EPISODE TITLE: *Operation: Annihilate!*
SERIES: *Star Trek: The Original Series*
SEASON: One
PRODUCTION NO.: 29
FIRST US TRANSMISSION: 13/4/67
STARDATE: 3287.2
WRITTEN BY: Stephen W. Carabatsos
DIRECTED BY: Herschel Daugherty
GUEST STARS: Majel Barrett (Nurse Chapel), Joan Swift (Aurelan Kirk), Craig Hundley (Peter Kirk), Dave Armstrong (voice of Kartan)

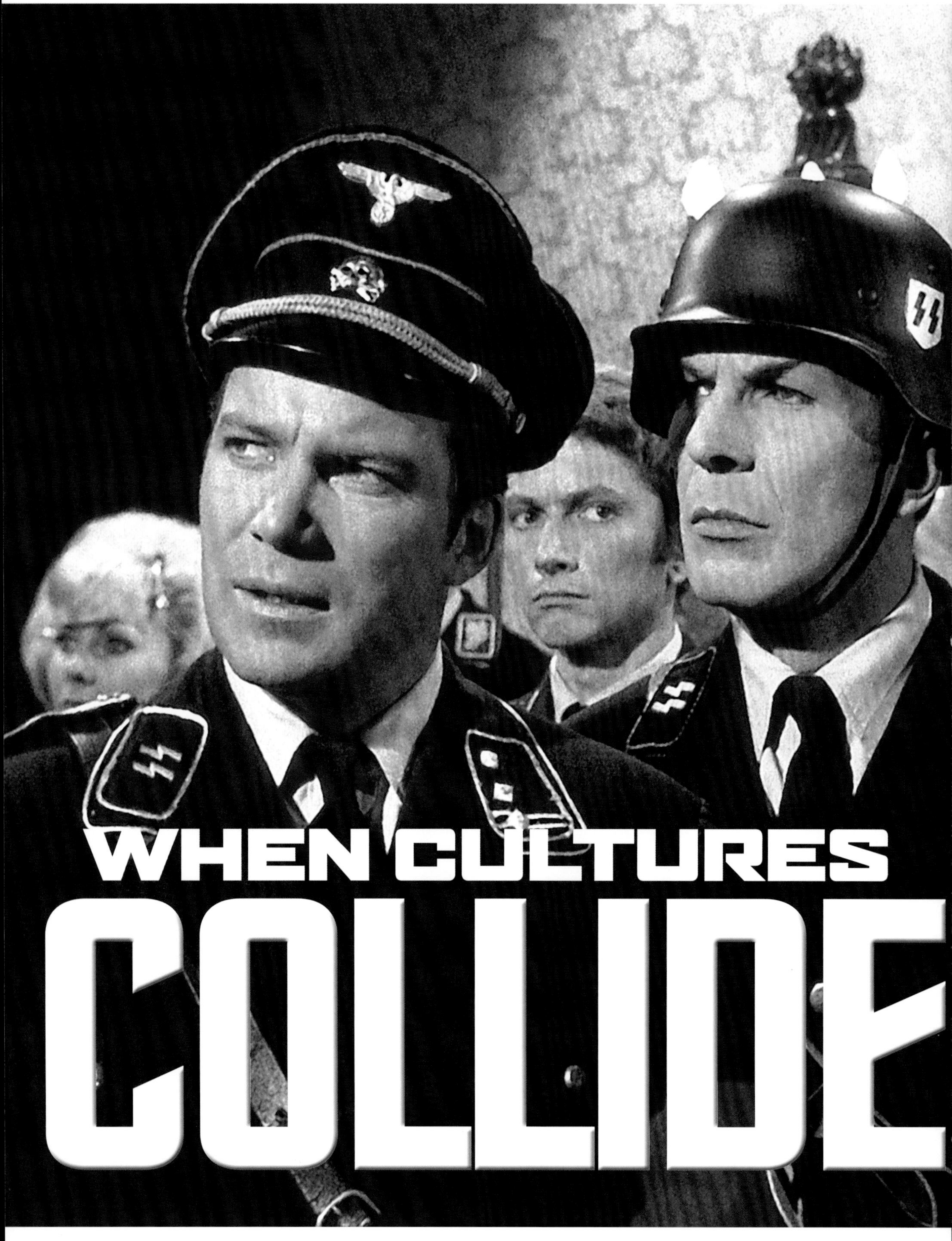

WHEN CULTURES COLLIDE

Space, the Final Frontier... or is it? The *U.S.S. Enterprise* traveled to many planets during Captain Kirk's first five-year mission. Some of those planets were fantastic realms of wonder, while others displayed more than a passing resemblance to Earth – much more!

***Timothy J. Tuohy* investigates those worlds far away yet so close...**

There are billions of planets in the Milky Way galaxy. Even if an explorer spent a lifetime traversing the Alpha Quadrant, they would only have time to visit a tiny fraction of them. Of that fraction, an even smaller number would be planets that could support life, and, of those, fewer still would be designated as Class-M – worlds suitable for human habitation.

The diversity of life on our own planet would seem to make the basic premise of Hodgkin's Law (first mentioned in the original *Star Trek* episode "Bread and Circuses" – see boxout overleaf) highly improbable. The Vulcan philosophy of IDIC – Infinite Diversity in Infinite Combinations – could even be considered a direct and compelling contradiction to Hodgkin. So can a concept of "Infinite Diversity" exist side by side with Hodgkin's Law of probable similarity? If you're talking truly infinite diversity, then yes – in a universe of infinite possibilities everything is possible, even parallel evolution.

"SIMILAR PLANETS WITH SIMILAR POPULATIONS AND SIMILAR ENVIRONMENTS WILL EVOLVE IN SIMILAR WAYS."

– A.E. HODGKIN'S LAW OF PARALLEL PLANET DEVELOPMENT

During its original five-year mission (or at least the 79 episodes that made it to television), the *U.S.S. Enterprise* trekked to 54 habitable planets. Conditions on those planets ranged from almost completely inhospitable, such as Rigel XII and Psi 2000, to idyllic paradises like Tyree's or Miramanee's planets. It was on the planets which could literally be mistaken for Earth where Kirk and crew would see Hodgkin's theory put to the test, in some thought-provoking episodes. What we would also learn is the importance of the Prime Directive, as it seems that comparative evolution often benefits from a little outside help.

NOT SO STRANGE NEW WORLDS

EXPLAINING HODGKIN'S LAW

During a scientific expedition to Loracus Prime, an inhospitable world in the heart of the Gagarin Radiation Belt, the biologist A.E. Hodgkin observed a species of termite similar to those found on Earth. This discovery inspired the scientist to investigate further, and once he had ruled out biological contamination of Loracus Prime from colonization or meteor impact, he began to develop his theory that in an infinite universe it was probable that evolution could follow similar paths on similar worlds entirely independently. Hodgkin continued his research and further expanded his hypothesis beyond simple biological coincidences to include comparative cultural development.

Hodgkin's theory explained in the Handbook of Exobiology (*Enterprise* "Strange New World")

Hodgkin's Law was first referenced in the captain's log, stardate 4040.07, during the original series episode "Bread and Circuses" (see When In Rome on page 86), and again in the *Enterprise* Season One episode "Strange New World".

THE FOURTH REICH?

On stardate 2534.0 ("Patterns of Force"), the *Enterprise* travels to the planet Ekos to learn what has become of John Gill, a Federation cultural observer stationed there. Following an unprovoked attack from Ekos, Kirk and Mr. Spock beam down to the planet's surface. They learn that Gill, in direct violation of the Federation's Prime Directive, attempted to guide the fractured Ekosian government into one that was more cohesive. Relying on Earth's own history, Gill unfortunately chose Nazi Germany as his template of efficiency.

The Wall Street Crash on Earth in 1929 devastated Germany's growing, post-WWI economy. The Germans, like many others in these situations, looked to a compelling figure to lead them from their despair. However, the person they found would only make matters worse. Adolf Hitler was a decorated officer who had been jailed in 1924 for high treason following a failed coup against the Weimar Republic. Imprisoned for less than a year, Hitler was swept into power with the Enabling Act of 1933, which gave him control of the legislative and executive braches of Germany's government. Along with his select group of military advisers and adroit propagandists, Hitler brought Germany, as Mr. Spock noted, "only one step away from global domination." It was Gill's belief, tempered with his knowledge, that successful strategies could be implemented while at the same time avoiding the infamous Nazi atrocities.

By his own account, Gill's plan had initially worked. Ekos had united and was moving away from generations of war. However, like Earth's Germany, the Ekosian propaganda machine looked for a scapegoat to blame for their world's previous troubles. For the Ekosians, it was people from the neighboring planet Zeon.

Melakon, the deputy Führer, eventually drugged Gill and perverted the cause of Ekos' military operations. He was mad with power and had initiated a campaign to inflame xenophobic racism to further his vile agenda of racial purity. Melakon was determined to exterminate all those he considered genetically impure by implementing his own version of Hitler's "Final Solution." Thankfully, Melakon was not able to fully set his plans into motion; he was killed after he gunned down a coherent and remorseful John Gill. Sadly, the horrors that man inflicts upon his fellow man are not limited only to our planet.

Due to Gill's interference, developments on Ekos do not make for a model example of Hodgkin's Law. Gill was also not the only member of Starfleet to cross the line.

Fascist ideology rears its ugly head in "Patterns of Force"

Kirk and Tracy battle for "The Omega Glory"

The Holiest of Holies

Stars and Stripes?

PATTERN BUFFER

In "Return of the Archons", the *Enterprise* journeys to the planet Beta III on stardate 3156.2. Her mission is to learn what had become of the *U.S.S. Archon*, missing for 100 years. But what begins simply as a look into the past quickly turns into a desperate rescue mission.

The planet's history was a tale heard all-too often; war followed by unification under a charismatic leader. Beta III's unifier, Landru, foresaw his own mortality and planned to have his influence continue after his own death. Landru programmed a powerful computer to continue his philosophy of unity, but the computer had no comprehension of human needs and emotions, and it quashed the population's individuality in favor of the conformity of "The Body".

Beta III presents an interesting extrapolation to Hodgkin's Law. Obviously, there are grounds for comparisons to Earth – the rescue party transports to the planet's surface wearing clothes passing for what was worn in the late 19th Century, and a clock in the town center reflects a very Earth-like 24-hour day – incredible coincidences for a world so very far away.

Landru's legacy, in "Return of the Archons"

Kirk cloaked

YIN AND YANG

During what seemed to be a routine patrol (in "The Omega Glory"), the *Enterprise* discovers the *U.S.S. Exeter* in orbit above the planet Omega IV. Receiving no response to hails, Kirk transports over to the ship with Spock, McCoy, and a security guard only to find the ship deserted. The final log entry – made by the ship's surgeon – explains that a terrible disease ravaged the *Exeter's* crew and the only chance for survival was to beam down to the planet as soon as possible.

On the planet, the *Exeter's* captain, Ron Tracy, has flagrantly broken the Prime Directive by getting involved in Omega IV's own world war. Tracy supplied phasers to the side he believed was superior, in an attempt to swing the balance of power. Kirk is obligated to stop his fellow captain's mad quest to sell the immortality he believes Omega IV offers.

The indigenous "Yangs" and "Kohms," metaphors for Earth's Yankees and Communists, were engaged in a prolonged war that, unlike Earth' s Cold War, involved actual conflicts. However, cultural similarities do not always imply identical outcomes, and the Kohms' initial triumph on Omega IV is irrelevant as an example of Hodgkin's Law. The truth is far more breathtaking – when the seemingly barbaric Yangs win the final battle, they parade a tattered American flag, and Kirk even recites from their "Holiest of Holies", Omega IV's own Constitution of The United States. This revelation is an astounding moment in galactic comparative evolution, as we witness a planet, light years away from Earth, forming duplicate government documents and symbols. This goes far beyond anything Hodgkin could have imagined, but seems a perfectly logical outcome of Infinite Diversity in Infinite Combinations.

WHEN IN ROME...

On a routine patrol near the planet 895IV, the *Enterprise* discovers debris of the Federation survey ship *S.S. Beagle* ("Bread and Circuses"). The *Beagle* had been lost for six years without any contact. When the *Enterprise* enters orbit, Lt. Uhura picks up video images from the surface showing what looks like a Roman gladiatorial contest, complete with a barbarian who computer records identify as a member of the *Beagle*'s crew.

After beaming down to the surface (and a quick reminder of the tenets of the Prime Directive), Kirk, Spock, and McCoy are captured by a rag-tag group of former slaves. The slaves have escaped the games and have dedicated themselves to following the "Sun." Kirk learns that the captain of the *Beagle*, R.M. Merick, is now "first-citizen" of a culture that rivals Earth's own ancient Roman Empire.

Kirk and his group are captured again, this time attempting to enter the city with the help of a former gladiator, Flavius Maximus. They are brought before Merick and Claudius Marcus, the leader of this new Rome. Spock and McCoy are forced to compete in the gladiatorial games as pawns to pressure Kirk into sacrificing the *Enterprise*'s crew. Thanks to the quick thinking of Chief Engineer Scott and redeeming heroics from Merick, the three *Enterprise* crewmembers escape back to their ship.

The existence of 895IV again proves the feasibility of Hodgkin's Law. The planet had developed on a path similar to Earth's even before the *Beagle*'s arrival. Their "Rome" supposedly encompassed the whole planet. While not achieving that geographical dominance, Earth's Western Roman Empire did last for almost 500 years. Merick comments that there has been no war on 895IV for over 400 years. That amount of time indicates an empire that is still strong and effective. In comparison, the peaceful period know as the Pax Romana on Earth lasted about 207 years.

A fascinating aspect about 895IV's development was that while the culture advanced into an Earth-like 20th Century, complete with television and automobiles, their martial traditions stayed decidedly 1st Century BCE to 3rd Century CE. Lt. Uhura had continued to monitor transmissions from the planet, and revealed to Kirk upon his return that the worshippers of the "Sun" were really the new followers of the "Son" of God. Christianity was beginning to spread across 895IV, much as it did on Earth. Could the fall of this world's "Rome" be far behind?

An imperial entanglement for Bones and Spock, in "Bread and Circuses"

GREECE IS THE WORD

The *Enterprise* wasn't just limited to encounters with Roman wannabes. On two different occasions, ancient Greece had its turn in the futuristic spotlight, in the form of aliens who – without their own version of the Prime Directive – may have influenced Earth's cultural history...

Apollo, the Greek God, literally stops the *Enterprise* in its tracks near Pollux IV, in "Who Mourns for Adonais?" Apollo and his brethren were members of a space-faring race who resided on Earth for a period of time. Eventually, the "gods" left Earth and returned to space, leaving behind them a profound change in human culture. Apollo still yearned for the worship of humans, however, and recreated a Greek temple on Pollux IV's surface.

The planet Platonius was another refuge of the Greek legacy in "Plato's Stepchildren". The Platonians, like Apollo's cohorts, had visited Earth's past and lived amongst the Greeks. When the Greek society they revered began to wither away, they left Earth and founded their own Grecian utopia light years away.

GOING GANGSTA

The *U.S.S. Horizon* visited the planet Sigma Iotia II 100 years before the *Enterprise* arrived in "A Piece of the Action". Much like the situation on Ekos, Hodgkin's Law and the Prime Directive once again proved each other's validity and worth, but unlike on Ekos, in which a Federation member became personally involved in the course of the planet's development, all the *Horizon* did was leave a book behind.

The Iotians took that book, *Chicago Mobs of the Twenties,* and used it as a foundation for their entire planet's culture. Mob bosses, flappers, flivvers and Tommy guns were ubiquitous. The Prime Directive's non-interference policy had not been in place when the *Horizon* arrived at Iotia, and the Iotians knew that they were not alone in the universe. It is possible that the Iotians would have developed on an entirely different path had the Prime Directive been in place.

There is no evidence that suggests Iotia was not already on a comparative evolutionary path to the Earth, although the Iotians were described as being highly imitative. Although the *Horizon*'s influence could be considered a focal point, the Iotians still achieved their technological and industrial capabilities without outside assistance. Therefore it is entirely conceivable that Iotia could have developed on its own evolutionary path and still borne remarkable similarities to ours.

Mob rule in "A Piece of the Action"

"The Paradise Syndrome"

Kirk finds true love in paradise

PARADISE LOST

"The Paradise Syndrome" is one of the most heartbreaking voyages of the original *Enterprise,* and provides an interesting twist on Hodgkin's theory, as an outside influence actively moves an entire culture to another world without its knowledge.

The mission seems simple enough: use the *Enterprise's* deflector beam to save a Class-M planet from an approaching asteroid. But when Kirk, Spock, and McCoy survey the planet, they make an astounding discovery – a village impossibly populated by a tribe of Native Americans from Earth.

Kirk falls into a hidden entrance in an ancient obelisk, and is temporarily robbed of his memory. During the months that he lives as one of the tribe, Kirk becomes their Chief Medicine Man and marries tribeswoman Miramanee.

Mr. Spock studies the writings he scanned on the obelisk as the *Enterprise* struggles to stop the deadly asteroid without her captain, and discovers that the planet's inhabitants had been transported there by a race of beings called The Preservers. The *Enterprise* returns to the planet with precious little time left, where Spock and Kirk (no longer suffering from amnesia) utilize the obelisk's true purpose and divert the asteroid, although tragically Kirk's wife and unborn child are killed before the planet is saved.

The Preservers and their actions are far from a validation of Hodgkin's Law, and their interference is precisely the kind of thing that the Prime Directive seeks to deter, as it only ever seems to end in disaster. However, while Miramanee's people did not naturally evolve on the world they were taken to, they did flourish and prosper. Who knows how closely their future society may have mirrored our own?

Certainly, many of these examples of comparative evolution rely on outside interference, whether deliberate or accidental, but adapting to change is surely a basic tenet of evolutionary theory. The existence of these worlds, their cultures, and peoples so far from Earth, proves that not just evolution, but comparative evolution is perhaps a possibility. From Darwin's finches to Hodgkin's termites, the vast expanse of the galaxy may not be as strange and unfamiliar as once thought.

Spock finds his own reflection "fascinating"

Kirk and co. step into the "Mirror Mirror"

THE MAN IN THE MIRROR MIRROR

Writer of four episodes of the original *Star Trek*, Jerome Bixby's biggest contribution to the show's mythos was his creation of the savage parallel reality known as the Mirror Universe. In this previously unpublished interview, he reveals the mundane reality behind its inspiration.

Interview by Pat Jankiewicz

Prolific screenwriter, novelist and author of 1,500 short stories, Jerome Lewis Bixby (1923–1998) remembered his reaction to first seeing the William Shatner/Leonard Nimoy television series *Star Trek* when he caught its debut run.

"I had seen three or four episodes and thought it was really good. I said, 'Wow, this is all right – they're really doing science fiction!' They were doing stories by guys like Dick Matheson and George Clayton Johnson. I said, 'This I would like to do."

Bixby, whose classic short story "It's a Good Life" (where a small child with omnipotent powers terrorizes a small town) is carried to this day in high school textbooks and was adapted by *The Twilight Zone*, wanted to write for *Star Trek*.

Inspired by the show, Bixby said, "I can do a complete script as fast as I can do an outline. I sat down and in about four days, I did a script. They flipped over it, but said, 'We don't usually put $7 million into a *Star Trek* episode' – the average budget was about $237,000," he laughed.

While he did four classic episodes, "By Any Other Name" (where aliens hijack the *Enterprise*), "Day Of The Dove" (where Captain Kirk and the Klingons unite aboard ship against a deadlier threat) and "Requiem For Methuselah," in which the crew meet a man who has lived through centuries, it's the first,

"I LIKED THAT EVEN IN THE MIRROR UNIVERSE, MR. SPOCK IS GUIDED BY LOGIC."

Photo © Lisa Orris

Jerome Bixby

"Mirror Mirror," that really made its mark in the *Trek* universe and on pop culture in general. Indeed, when seeking a single episode that best captured what *Star Trek* is all about, The Smithsonian Institute selected "Mirror Mirror."

"I'm pleased and very honored that it's so popular," Bixby mused. While it routinely tops '*Trek* top 10' lists, nods to "Mirror Mirror" have shown up in everything from *The Simpsons* and *Family Guy* to *Saturday Night Live.*

ONE WAY STREET

The writer came up with "Mirror Mirror" because, "a long time ago, I did a story called 'One Way Street', about a guy who gets into an automobile accident by a laboratory and is sent into a parallel universe. It's not totally alien, just jogged. Everything, including his family, wife and dog, are just a little different. That was my inspiration."

After his too-expensive-for-the-show sample script, Bixby was happy to be asked to take a second shot. "They wanted me to write another *Star Trek*, so, having written 'One Way Street,' I thought 'Okay, parallel universe!'" He envisioned an episode set aboard "another *Enterprise*, albeit slightly different, an *Enterprise* [that] is a savage – almost pirate – ship, governed by imperialists."

"Originally, I was only going to have Captain Kirk go into this parallel universe alone, and he would be affected by it the longer he was there," Bixby explains, "As I was searching for ideas, I knew that they loved to use their cast in unusual ways on *Star Trek*. Instead of just throwing the cast up against a group of bad guys or space monsters eating planets, they got a kick out of putting the cast into unusual versions of themselves, in an evil persona."

Indeed, the cast seemed to rise to the occasion. Spock's mirror has a Van Dyke beard and a desire to dodge any bullets ("I do not desire the captaincy. I much prefer my scientific duties, and I am frankly content to be a lesser target"). "Mirror Mirror" gives the entire cast a chance to shine, from a craven alternate Chekhov to the scarred and scurrilous Mr. Sulu. "I was fine with that, because I loved every one of them," Bixby says of the show's cast. "I was also very impressed with BarBara Luna as Marlena Moreau, the Captain's Woman. I thought she was the best guest actress on the series."

NO REFLECTION

"William Shatner was a card, he was always a real kick to be around. I have a wonderful anecdote about how he scared the bejesus out of a stage-hand," laughs Bixby, "He had his pet Dobermans on the set one time and they were beautifully trained. Bill liked to show off, so the poor stage-hand walked about 100 feet down to the other side of the sound-stage and Bill simply pointed at him and said 'Kill.' Those Doberman Pinschers took off, like their breeds do, and they were about a third of the way down, heading straight for the poor guy, when Bill said 'Stop'. The Dobermans immediately skidded to a stop. Bill said 'Come' and they did, they came right back to him."

Bixby was also fond of Leonard Nimoy, who was quite different to his co-star, "I liked Leonard Nimoy. He was into folk music and his main interest seemed to be teaching an acting class; an all-around beautiful guy. I thought Nimoy did a great job in 'Mirror Mirror'; I liked that even in the Mirror Universe, Mr. Spock is guided by logic."

Years later, Bixby pitched a "Mirror Mirror" sequel for *Star Trek: The Next Generation.* "Picard would have been dealing with the Mirror Universe Mr. Spock. They would have had to bring back Leonard Nimoy, which I think scuppered the episode," recounts Bixby with some regret, "Eventually, Nimoy did return as Spock for a couple episodes ("Unification" parts one and two), but I think mine would have been more interesting for him."

Although *The Next Generation* crew would never make an on-screen trip to Bixby's twisted dimension, it would be further explored in various *Star Trek* novelizations and episodes of both *Deep Space Nine* and *Enterprise* (see boxout). After the writer passed away in 1998, the *Deep Space Nine* episode "The Emperor's New Cloak" was dedicated to his memory, and his inspired creation still influences the various realities of *Star Trek* today.

THROUGH THE LOOKING GLASS

Jerome Bixby may have created the Mirror Universe, but many screenwriters, authors and comic book scribes have followed in his reflective footsteps.

- Following on from the original series' "Mirror Mirror," *Deep Space Nine* would revisit the Mirror Universe no less than five times, in the episodes "Crossover," "Through the Looking Glass," "Shattered Mirror," "Resurrection," and "The Emperor's New Cloak." Prequel series *Enterprise* also took a spin with "In a Mirror, Darkly," featuring particularly ruthless versions of Archer's usually indomitable crew.

"In a Mirror Darkly"

"Crossover"

- There have been 35 novels, four comic book series (not including IDW's recent Alternate Timeline tale set in an even more mirrored Mirror Universe...) and even an official Role Playing Game traversing through this parallel reality, each bringing new dimensions to an increasingly rich – if violent and unwelcoming – re-imagining of *Star Trek*.

Kira's dark side, in "Crossover"

MORE RE-MA

IN THE CONCLUDING PART OF OUR RETROSPECTIVE ON THE MAJOR *STAR TREK REMASTERED* PROJECT, LARRY NEMECEK GUIDES THE TEAM THROUGH MORE OF THEIR FAVORITE SCENES...

The Remastered era of classic *Star Trek* is now all on the record – lacking only a special showing of the original pilot "The Cage," set for May 2009. Still largely unknown, though, is what was behind the decisions – the when and how to make upgrades to the original film.

All went beyond simply making the picture, sound and music as good as a first airing on "Living Color" NBC in the 1960s. The old opticals just wouldn't hold up in the new high-definition TV and DVDs to come so a CBS Digital team tackled the project for both TV airing and retail DVDs, headed up by Niel Wray, with longtime *Star Trek* staffers – and true fans – Dave Rossi and Mike and Denise Okuda on board as producers.

While fans know that trio well, Wray was a newcomer on the *Trek* stage, but he too boasted a lifelong love of Gene Roddenberry's universe as well. "For me, *Star Trek* was one of the things that got me into this work," Wray says. "Oh yeah! – I watched these as a kid, and I was in college when *The Next Generation* first started up; I was addicted to it. I watched all of it, and almost all of the newer series: I watched a lot of *DS9*, all of *Voyager*. *Enterprise* I didn't watch, but I've since watched it."

In fact, one of the roads not taken was Wray's pet idea, somewhere in the third season, to "update" the *Enterprise* a bit so as to start matching the components seen in the refit ship of *Star Trek: The Motion Picture*! "Ultimately, by the time I'd thought of that we had already done one or two from the late third season, so we just couldn't do it," he says.

STILL SURPRISES: "SPACE SEED"

Dave Rossi: We suddenly realized we needed to address the problem of tractor beam / no beam: In Kirk's time, phaser beams are visible, but transporter beams aren't. But *TNG* showed tractor beams; should we follow their lead? Ultimately, none of us were very fond of the idea of a *TNG*-style beam and in fact the more we discussed it, the more I realized I didn't like the idea of a beam at all, as I think we all did. The nagging question for me was: how to make tractor beams dynamic even though they were invisible?

We knew we wanted the *Enterprise* to find the *Botany Bay* tumbling slowly in space, helpless and seemingly harmless, and it struck me that when Khan releases the *BB* later in the episode, that was our chance. I remember talking to Mike, Denise and Niel somewhat excitedly about the idea that when the *BB* is released from the invisible clutches of the tractor beam, it should continue its sad, obsolete existence of tumbling through the black emptiness of space. You immediately see it released without ever seeing a beam, and I think it's a very powerful shot. It remains one of my favorites.

STERPIECES

THE "REAL" *FESARIUS*: "THE CORBOMITE MANUEVER"

Niel Wray: Even as a kid when I was watching the original show, that scene of the *Fesarius* was always laughable to me – even though I understand now those effects crews were under extremely limited resources, and all that. But I like what we did to make the *Fesarius* feel massive; I think it now has a lot better scale to it, the texturing and details, so that when this thing comes up you *believe* it's something that is 100 or a 1,000 times bigger than the *Enterprise*.

I liked the challenge to respect the original design intent of this ship, but change it in such a way that it tells the story better. I think we came up with a pretty successful solution; it's still basically the same shape and design, just now you can see all the detailing and facets.

WHEN TO LEAVE IT ALONE: "WHERE NO MAN HAS GONE BEFORE"

Denise Okuda: Regarding Kirk's "blooper" tombstone being unchanged – I know that a lot of fans wanted us to change the initial "R" to a "T." I was willing to go along with it, but I was not-so-secretly pleased when scheduling issues made it impossible to change all those shots.

KOLOS' NEW TRANSPORT: "IS THERE IN TRUTH NO BEAUTY?"

Niel Wray: My design thought on that was that the Medusans were beings without any physical form, so the ship should be designed in such a way that it accommodates that. So while it has the general shape of a Federation ship, the whole habitation/living section is just basically a bit round ball – which I guess is also a throwback, to that one interim Jefferies design for the *Enterprise*. We never gave it a name or a number – which now that I think about it, would have been a great call!

ONE LITTLE ROCK: "THE DOOMSDAY MACHINE"

Dave Rossi: I wanted to get across just how helpless the *Constellation* was. While the amazing damage to the ship's exterior (mapped out brilliantly by Mike) was certainly impactful, I really wanted the universe to kick the *Constellation* in the shin one more time while she was down, and make the audience say "Wow, that's messed up!" There's something woefully sad about a starship, once so beautiful and majestic, being peppered by space junk like that. While the show is packed full of amazing effects, that bit still sits high as a moment for me.

SIMPLE BEAUTY: "I, MUDD"

Denise Okuda: I love the ringed planet. I just wish we could have seen more of it!

THE FIRST REMASTERED LANDMARK: "THE TROUBLE WITH TRIBBLES"

Niel Wray: We had a crazed pace when we started up, and in our first eight episodes we used an older CGI model *Enterprise*. But I remember it was "The Trouble With Tribbles" when we got to debut the new model that we had tweaked and modified a lot on its features – especially the nacelle caps! And it was really the first time we got to do multiple ships in one shot – the effects crews on the original series rarely got the time or money to have multiple ships. Everything we did was to honor Gene and to honor the fans, and all the guys on our team took it to heart. This was *Star Trek*, after all!!

THE ORIGINAL BRIDGE PEEK: "THE MENAGERIE"

Mike Okuda: This was unquestionably the most difficult single effects shot – not only for the original series, but also for the Remastered effects team as well. One of the challenges was that for this episode, we did not have access to the raw film elements. Because of this, the CBS Digital team had to build a 3D model of the bridge, complete with animated crew figures, and they had to seamlessly match this model to the live-action footage of Pike and crew on the bridge. The original, by the Howard Anderson Company, speaks highly of the audacious "can do" spirit of everyone who worked on the original series' effects, which were absolutely cutting edge at the time. I think that CBS Digital captured the spirit of the original, while honoring Roddenberry's desire to show, instantly, how big his magnificent starship was.

Looking back at it all, Mike shares one way of judging the whole *Remastered* team and its progress...

"Imagine someone who really liked *Star Trek* back in the 1960s or 1970s, but who hasn't seen the show since – someone who enjoyed the show, but is a fairly average viewer and isn't fluent in the language of visual effects, " he posits. "Imagine that this person happened to stumble across a Remastered episode after all that time, but that he or she doesn't know about the Remastered effects. Ideally, I'd like this person to smile and say, 'Gee, the show – and the effects – looks just as good as I remember it.' I'd be delighted if this hypothetical viewer believed that this was what they saw and enjoyed so long ago. It's surprisingly easy to add just a little too much glitz, to the point where you're distracting from the story. Of course, there are many different opinions as to exactly where this point is, but for the most part, I think we were pretty successful."

TIME'S ARROW

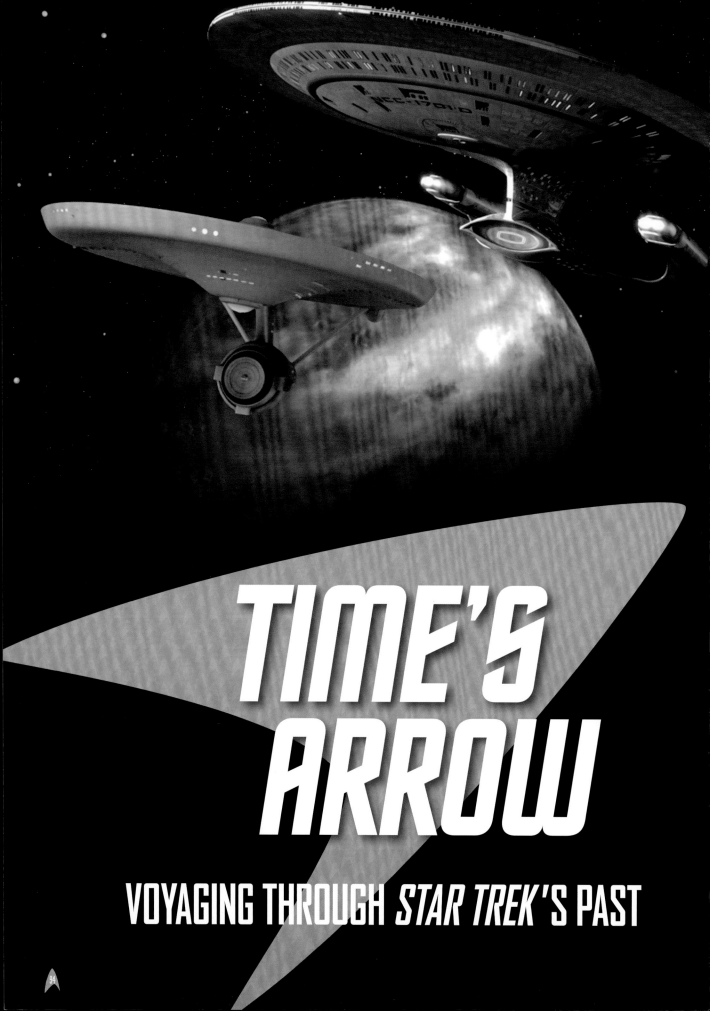

VOYAGING THROUGH *STAR TREK*'S PAST

The *Enterprise* arrives at the planet Psi 2000

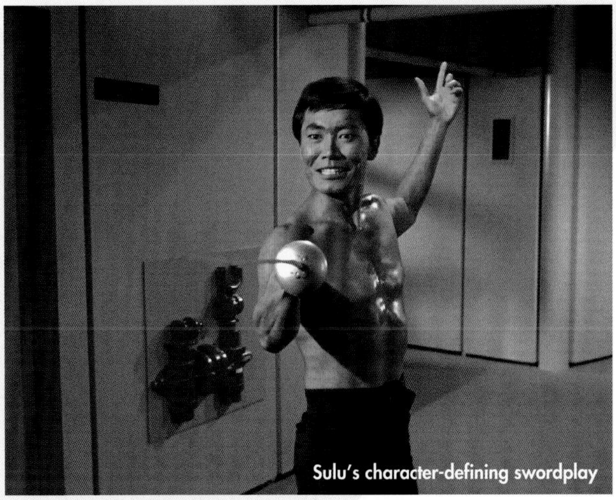

Sulu's character-defining swordplay

REDRESSED TO IMPRESS

In its freshman year, *Star Trek: The Next Generation* looked towards the mothership for inspiration, with mixed results. Brian J. Robb re-examines "The Naked Time" and "The Naked Now" – two episodes which got under the skins of *Star Trek*'s characters like no other!

One way of getting to know characters in a long-running television drama is to have them act 'out-of-character'. A virtuous guy turns evil, a demure woman revels in her sexuality, a selfish man becomes a generous gift-giver. The television series episode in which main characters act against their core attributes is now something of a cliché, alongside the boxing episode, the Native American episode, and the episode set entirely on an aeroplane.

However, when *Star Trek* engaged this narrative device, in both the original series episode "The Naked Time" and *The Next Generation*'s "The Naked Now", it was a relatively unexplored trope, and our heroes were acting 'out-of-character' at a point in each series where we barely knew them.

A broad synopsis for both episodes might suggest similar storylines, but the episodes are very different in their approach and ambition, and arguably it is the later episode which takes a more simplistic path.

While "The Naked Now" tells us little about the new *Enterprise*-D crew, the Psi 2000 virus of "The Naked Time" reveals the essential core of the original's primary characters, their hidden, interior selves that those around them rarely see.

GETTING 'NAKED'

According to episode director Marc Daniels, when they made "The Naked Time" the *Star Trek* production as a whole was just getting to grips with what kind of people the crew of the *Enterprise* actually were. 'The characters were falling into place, we began to get into the workings of Kirk's mind, Spock's powers.'

Just four episodes into this brand new space series, viewers had not had enough time to get to know these characters well, so having them act out of character would not have had the maximum effect. The three preceding episodes had been an odd bunch to launch any series. "The Man Trap" was essentially a monster show after the model of *The Outer Limits*, with third

Spock makes a chilling discovery in the DJ booth...

...while Geordi is unimpressed by the party atmosphere

Riley contracts the Psi2000 virus

Nurse Chapel only has eyes for Mr.Spock

"I am in control of my emotions."

stringer Dr McCoy getting the lion's share of character development rather than the Captain or Spock. "Charlie X" and the successful second pilot "Where No Man Has Gone Before" were showcases for William Shatner's Captain Kirk. The fourth episode, "The Naked Time", offered a chance for the ensemble cast to explore their characters, although the bulk of the focus inevitably still fell on the leads.

It can be hard to tell exactly when Kirk becomes infected, but his panic when he confronts Spock is the first clear indication that something strange has happened to the Captain. His monologue about his relationship with his ship is not an aberrant moment for this Captain but a stripping-bare of his true nature - the 'naked' of the title, perhaps? 'This vessel. I give, she takes.' Kirk laments. 'She won't permit me my life. I've got to live hers.'

At this moment, of course, the ship is in dire jeopardy, having lost helm control and engine power. The time remaining to the ship is approximately the remaining running time of the episode, making this something of a real-time situation for the crew and the viewers. It's not just the virus that's bringing out Kirk's deeply-buried character traits, it's the danger of not only losing his own life, but of losing his ship. Upon his recovery, Kirk still seems to be talking directly to his vessel: 'Never lose you. Never.'

There is, of course, another object of the captain's delusional affections, and one which informed much of *The Next Generation* follow-up. As discipline crumbles all around him, Kirk turns his attention from his ship to a real flesh-and-blood woman – Yeoman Janice Rand. "I have a beautiful Yeoman," he says to his First Officer. 'Have you ever noticed her, Mr. Spock? You're allowed to notice her! The Captain's not permitted."

This is, of course, a deeply ironic question from the Captain, as Spock's emotional suppression would not allow him to notice Yeoman Rand or any other woman. Only that's exactly what the Vulcan is struggling to deal with as a result of the same virus. Spock is overwhelmed by his long-suppressed emotions and his failure to express his love for his parents, especially his human mother. "My mother... I could never tell her that I loved her!" he says.

Spock enacts a variety of coping strategies to overcome his predicament. First he appeals to his own discipline and self-control, which has never failed him in the past: "I am in control of my emotions." As that fails, he turns to his status on the ship and his sense of duty: "I am an officer!" However, neither rank nor duty offer sanctuary from the torrent of emotions he is feeling, so he

Does the *Enterprise* demand too much of its captain?

then seeks solace in the cold logic of mathematics and the unarguable world of numbers.

Spock speculates that the virus the *Enterprise* has encountered reveals 'hidden personality traits' and perhaps exposes hidden feelings, but in the cases of Kirk and Spock it seems to simply exaggerate already-existing (if usually hidden or disguised) deep characteristics: the Captain's attachment to his vessel, and the First Officer's refuge in the suppression of emotion.

TIME'S UP

Minor characters, such as Joe Tormolen - who dies early in the episode - and the supposedly amusing, but deeply annoying cultural stereotype, Riley, become infected with the virus, though as we don't learn much about either, it's difficult for us to care what happens to them. Others are given moments to shine, and in the process become instant fan favorites, such as the much celebrated swordplay of the bare-chested helmsman Sulu. Interestingly, it is his sense of mischief and desire to abandon his post that comes to the fore, rather than any deeper characteristics, yet somehow it made him more 'real'. We also learn that Nurse Chapel is an ardent reader of ancient Mills and Boon texts, which can surely be the only explanation for her soap opera style 'love' for the unattainable Spock.

There is another intriguing possibility lurking in the sub-text of this episode. Tormolen is driven by the effects of the virus to question mankind's right to be this far out in space, to be 'out here' in what Spock calls the 'infinite unknown'. Could this be a virus with a purpose, causing sentient creatures to fear their own expansive natures and so retreat back to their places of origin? If so, this is not the narrative thread that was picked up 20 years later.

THE TIME IS NOW

In recreating the supposedly out-of-character antics of "The Naked Time", *The Next Generation*'s "The Naked Now" suffered from the same problem of transmitting early in the new show's run, being the first regular episode to follow the feature length opener, "Encounter at Farpoint". While "The Naked Time" was the fourth episode of the original series to air, allowing viewers to get some kind of handle on their new space-faring heroes, in 1987, viewers had barely seen 90 minutes of Picard, Riker, and Data in action. It was not a lot to go on.

From the first sultry message from the *S.S. Tsiolkovsky*, it is clear that this late-80s take on the same material is to be a more sexual (or sensual) experience. While Picard initially puts

DATACORE
"THE NAKED TIME"

The *Enterprise* faces destruction when her crew contract a deadly virus and begin to act out their deepest fantasies - and also reveal their repressed fears...

FIRST AIRED:	SEPTEMBER 29, 1966
EPISODE ORDER:	4TH AIRED, 7TH PRODUCED
WRITTEN BY:	JOHN D.F. BLACK
DIRECTED BY:	MARC DANIELS

- Originally planned as a two-part storyline, the episode was to end on a cliffhanger that sent the *Enterprise* back in time. The planned second part of the story was developed into the stand-alone episode "Tomorrow is Yesterday".
- George Takei was allowed to choose his own weapon for his dramatic 'berserker' scene. On offer were a Samurai sword or a simpler fencing foil. Playing against his character's suggested ethnic background, Takei chose the fencing foil, thus establishing a character trait that runs right through to John Cho's take on the character in the 2009 *Star Trek* re-boot movie.
- Leonard Nimoy contributed heavily to the scene in which Spock breaks down and is torn between his human emotions and Vulcan stoicism. The scene was shot at the end of a fraught day, with only enough time for a single, unscripted take.
- Created as a money-saving 'bottle show' using only standing sets and with very few guest stars, "The Naked Time" was also a chance to try out two new characters (Tormolen and Riley) who may have become regulars. As it was, this was Tormolen's only episode, while Bruce Hyde's rather annoying Riley appeared on one other occasion in 'The Conscience of the King'.
- As well as the follow-up episode "The Naked Now" on *The Next Generation*, the events of this episode are referred to in the episode 'Relics'.
- In his autobiography, *To The Stars*, Sulu actor George Takei declared "The Naked Now" to be his favorite *Star Trek* episode of all time. Writer John D. F. Black – also the show's earliest story editor – has also nominated this episode as his favorite.

Wesley only makes matters worse

Tasha Yar and Data wonder if he has an app for that...

History repeats itself when the *Enterprise*-D comes to the aid of the *SS Tsiolkovsky*

the irrational actions of the crews of both the *Tsiolkovsy* and the *Enterprise* down to "madness, mass hysteria, delusion", it becomes clear that temptation is the main danger. The moral of the story, according to Picard, is for his crew to "avoid temptation".

Here the virus expands and emphasizes the senses, with Geordi longing for 'proper' (if, technically, less adequate) sight, and Tasha initially exploring her sensual nature through Troi's 'off-duty' clothing options. Sight and touch (and appearance, in Tasha's case) are the first manifestations of the virus. It is clear that this is a television drama made in the 1980s, the self-absorbed decade of 'yuppies', designer suits, and conspicuous wealth. As things move on, Geordi even descends into something close to self-centered self-pity about his condition, even though technology has given him better vision than most of the un-augmented humans around him.

Unlike the 1960s version, there is a monotonous similarity about the character changes enacted on this *Enterprise* crew. Tasha, Troi, and Crusher all become sexually awakened and pursue the males around them: Data, 'Bill' Riker, and Picard. It's a depiction of aggressive female sexuality that had become much more acceptable in the 1980s, and a million light years away from Chapel's loved-up pursuit of a non-responsive Mr Spock. While the 1960s is often depicted as a 'swinging' decade of sexual liberation, this was not often reflected on contemporary television drama. In the 1980s, however, standards and practices had changed, making the discussion and depiction of such issues easier (and a more common ratings-grabbing gambit).

Most infamously, "The Naked Now" features Tasha and Data's "fully functional" encounter. Fun though this scene undoubtedly is, there is something rather uncomfortable about the way it is introduced through Tasha's description of her childhood sexual trauma. It seems unlikely that such a scene would be scripted in this way today.

What are we to make of the 'transformations' of Wesley Crusher and engineering assistant Shimoda? In stark contrast to the changes in the women, both of these supposedly intelligent men become noticeably more childish, especially the adult Shimoda. While Wesley becomes even more annoying (perhaps that's his essential character trait that the virus expands upon?), Shimoda regresses to some kind of toddler-like state, playing with the ship's vital isolinear chips as if they were building blocks. In contrast, Riker seems little affected by his

Picard gives Beverly some advice on her bedside manner

DATACORE

"THE NAKED NOW"

The *Enterprise* faces destruction when her crew contract a deadly virus and begin to act out their deepest fantasies – and... You get the general idea!

FIRST AIRED:	OCTOBER 5, 1987
EPISODE ORDER:	2ND AIRED, 2ND PRODUCED
WRITTEN BY:	J. MICHAEL BINGHAM
DIRECTED BY:	PAUL LYNCH

- Although based on John D. F. Black's episode from *Star Trek* (he has a story credit), "The Naked Now" was written by D.C. Fontana under the pen name 'J. Michael Bingham'.
- *TNG* producer Rick Berman called "The Naked Now" an 'homage' to the previous episode, with characters referring back to the events that struck Captain Kirk and his crew, although Picard's awareness of their solution to the problem turns out to be of no help to him.
- The *S.S. Tsiolkovsky* is revealed – in a briefly seen dedication plaque – to have been created in the USSR. Unfortunately, that nation fell apart just four years after this episode was broadcast, following the emergence of 'glasnost' and the collapse of the Berlin Wall.

- In contrast to George Takei's feeling about his episode, Jonathan Frakes was reported to regard "The Naked Now" as one of the worst episodes of *The Next Generation*, while Wil Wheaton also had a low opinion of the episode, seeing it as not the best way to introduce a group of new characters to the audience.

exposure (just as McCoy seemingly avoided infection altogether in "The Naked Time"), employing Spock's self-control technique to keep himself focused, while the usually uptight Picard becomes visibly hot-and-bothered by Dr. Crusher's brazen advances. It's a very 1980s approach to sexualize the women while simultaneously infantilizing the men.

In exploring the essential nature of core characters like Kirk and Spock, "The Naked Time" had laid down the basic templates of the people whose adventures we would avidly follow over the next three years. "The Naked Now", the 1980s take on the same situation, didn't have quite the same effect, with its 'sexual sophistication' dating terribly by the 21st Century in a way that does not apply to the original 60s episode's exploration of its core characters.

ERA DEFINING

These two dramatically different takes on the same storyline offer a chance to examine how *Star Trek*, television, society, and culture had changed between the "The Naked Time" and the "The Naked Now".

Those who created and featured in *Star Trek* in the 1960s had lived through the Second World War, so ideas of honor and loyalty, as displayed by Kirk and Spock, were central to their lives and the society they'd grown up in. Yet those very ideas were being questioned by the new generation of young people that this 'far out' new show was aiming to appeal to.

As the 1970s' 'Me' generation took the reins of society, giving rise to the phenomenon of 'yuppies' – wealthy professionals without the responsibility of children, it could be argued that people in the 1980s had become more self-centered, and this cultural shift is evident in *The Next Generation*'s retelling. Although the 'new' *Enterprise* has children on board, their main representative is teenager Wesley, and the command deck crew are a career-orientated bunch, having no children or family connections (though this changed in later seasons). Tasha Yar, in particular, represents a kind of liberated 1980s woman who is very comfortable exploring her own pleasure, often at the expense of others, such as the naïve Data.

Taken in isolation, neither episode truly represents their respective series, but when viewed with the benefit of hindsight, they illustrate the remarkable shifts that society can undergo in just a few decades. Perhaps we can therefore conclude that the social change required to fulfil Gene Rodenberry's vision of the future really is an achievable aspiration...

INTERVIEW

THIS SIDE OF PARADISE

ONE OF THE STAR TREK *FRANCHISE'S MOST INFLUENTIAL WRITERS,* **D.C. FONTANA** *WAS INSTRUMENTAL TO THE SERIES' SUCCESS, AS WELL AS THE SPIN-OFFS* STAR TREK: THE ANIMATED SERIES *AND* STAR TREK: THE NEXT GENERATION. *DAVID BASSOM ASKS FONTANA ABOUT HER LEGENDARY CONTRIBUTION TO THE FRANCHISE...*

Tomorrow must feel like yesterday for Dorothy Fontana. A staggering four decades after she wrote her final episode of *Star Trek: The Original Series*, the prolific screenwriter is preparing to launch viewers on a brand-new live-action adventure with Captain James T. Kirk and the crew of the Starship Enterprise. Entitled *To Serve All My Days*, Fontana's latest tale is the third installment of the fan-produced *Star Trek: New Voyages* Internet series and is set to premiere on the 40th anniversary of the franchise's screen debut, on September 8 2006.

"It was great to return to the original series universe and deal with those characters again for *New Voyages*," says Fontana of her latest *Star Trek* offering. "The idea behind *New Voyages* is that it's set after the end of the original series' third season – they want to complete the five-year mission – so it was a lot of fun to pick up from where we left off. It was a bit like getting into a time machine and traveling back to 1969! But the project also presented some interesting new challenges, since we had to find ways to do *Star Trek* within this medium that were affordable and still tell what I think is a great story.

"The wonderful thing about returning to the original series is that there are always new aspects of those characters to explore," she continues. "I really love those characters. I probably love them more than the characters of all the other iterations of *Star Trek*. They were just wonderful. They were fresh and new when we made the original series and when I go back to them now, I still find freshness and great possibilities for storytelling and character growth."

To Serve All My Days sees the Starship Enterprise's young navigator, Pavel Chekov, encountering a radiation burst that causes him to rapidly age, in a plotline that allows original series star Walter Koenig to reprise the role. As one of the franchise's most renowned writers, Fontana was enlisted by Koenig himself to script the episode.

"It was an interesting invitation," Fontana recalls. "I wasn't aware of *New Voyages* until Walter approached me. He got me a DVD of their second episode. I thought it would be an interesting and fun thing to write for. Walter then told me what he wanted to accomplish with the episode and I came up with what I think is a pretty good story. The plot takes a young Chekov and winds up with Walter Koenig. We see Chekov gain those years and it's not a trick – the plot point refers to the original series episode *The*

> **"*The Original Series* deals with themes and questions that continue to be relevant today and most of the stories we told were of an extremely high quality; they're complex stories that have validity, a message and a lot action, and are just well done."**

Deadly Years, so there is a basis in canon for it.

"I've got a good feeling about how it's going to turn out," she adds. "I know Walter is very, very happy with it and that's a very good sign. I think the fans are going to like it."

Ironically, *New Voyages* isn't the only new *Star Trek*-related project Fontana is currently involved with. On the contrary, she is presently working on the scripts for two new *Star Trek* videogames, *Star Trek: Tactical Assault* and *Star Trek: Legacy*, and is one of the authors of *Boarding the Enterprise*, an upcoming collection of essays on *Star Trek* from Benbella Books. She also recently penned an afterword for a new, 40th anniversary re-release of her classic 1989 *Star Trek* novel *Vulcan's Way*.

"I always seem to be involved with something that's related to *Star Trek*," Fontana notes with a smile. "It keeps coming back. It's funny, because *Star Trek* is just one thing I've written for. I've written episodes of *Bonanza*, *Lonesome Dove*, *Dallas*, *The Streets of San Francisco*, *Babylon 5*... a wide array of shows. I have a number of projects in development that have nothing to do with *Star Trek*; for instance, I'm working on a family science fiction adventure series with Allison Hock. I also teach at the American Film Institute. Yet *Star Trek* is the thing that stands out in most people's minds...

"A cartoon was once done by the late artists Bill Rotsler for me of a woman who has a manacle around one of her ankles. The manacle has a little chain coming from it, which has a small *Enterprise* at the end of it. The caption read: 'It keeps following me around!'" she reveals with a chuckle. "I'm happy with that. *Star Trek* is a good thing to be associated with."

Boldly Going...

Fontana's long association with *Star Trek* actually pre-dates the 40th anniversary of the franchise's screen debut by a couple of years. She first encountered the revolutionary space western in the spring of 1964, when she was supplementing her screenwriting career by working as a production secretary for franchise creator Gene Roddenberry.

"Gene called me in his office one day and handed me a series treatment that was about 10 or 11 pages long and asked me what I thought of it," Fontana recalls. "It was the bare bones of what *Star Trek* would ultimately become. The ship was the USS Yorktown, not the *Enterprise*; it was commanded by Captain Robert T. April and Mr Spock was a Martian, not a Vulcan. The five-year mission was sketchily spelled out – it talked about the ship, the mission and the characters, April and Spock principally.

"After I read it, I went back to Gene and told him, 'I really like this. This is going to be fun if someone wants to make it. Who's going to play Mr Spock?'" she continues with a laugh. "Gene pushed a picture across the desk to me of Leonard Nimoy and I was thrilled about that, because I knew Leonard from way back. So I was really excited about *Star Trek* from the start. I loved the idea and series like *The Twilight Zone* and *The Outer Limits* had shown it was possible to do some very creative and far-ranging stories on a decent budget."

Following the completion of two different pilots, *Star Trek* entered production as a weekly series on Tuesday, May 24 1966. Fontana scripted two of the series' early episodes, *Charlie X* and *Tomorrow is Yesterday*, before being offered the post of story editor on the strength of her successful rewrite of *This Side of Paradise*. She continued in that crucial role until the end of the show's second season.

"I loved working on the original *Star Trek*," says Fontana. "I have a lot of very pleasant memories of that time. The show provided my first opportunity to be on-staff as a story editor and it gave me a lot of opportunities to write and express myself, as well as become a full-time writer, which had been my ambition. The atmosphere on the show was also very good; morale was high and everyone working on the series seemed enthusiastic about what they were doing. It wasn't just a job for most people.

Series on the Edge of Forever

D.C. FONTANA ponders what fate might have held for *Star Trek* if its original pilot, *The Cage*, had been picked up as a series...

"It's hard to know for sure, but I think *Star Trek* would have succeeded if *The Cage* had led to a series," says Fontana, who observed every aspect of the original pilot's production as Gene Roddenberry's production secretary. "Jeffrey Hunter would have been a good Captain [as Christopher Pike]. He wouldn't have been Captain Kirk; his approach would have been very different, but I think he would have been perfectly fine. The whole show would have been different, but I think it could have been a success – because of the stories, the mission, the universe, the other characters, the guest stars. There were a lot of factors about why *Star Trek* caught on; it wasn't just down to the Captain."

"Everyone was committed to telling the best stories we could, the best way we could, and you can see that in the finished product," she notes. "The original series deals with themes and questions that continue to be relevant today and most of the stories we told were of an extremely high quality; they're complex stories that have validity, a message and a lot of action, and are just well done. We had a few clinkers – you always do – but on the whole I think we did a very good job."

Reflecting on the original series episodes she personally scripted or devised the storylines for, Fontana points to the ever-popular Spock-centric season two installment *Journey to Babel* as her personal favorite, followed by *This Side of Paradise*. At the other end of the scale, she selects the two episodes she employed her 'Michael Richards' pseudonym on – season three's *The Way to Eden* and *That Which Survives* – as her two biggest *Star Trek* disappointments.

"Those episode just didn't turn out the way I would have liked," she explains. "I've never actually seen the finished version of *The Way to Eden*. I did see *That Which Survives* and I thought it was okay, but I was still very disappointed by the way it came out."

Getting Animated

Fontana's disappointment at the way her scripts for *The Way to Eden* and *That Which Survives* were brought to the screen extends to much of *Star Trek*'s third season. Widely considered the show's weakest year, season three clearly suffered from both Fontana's absence as the series' story editor and the reduced involvement of Gene Roddenberry.

"The series started to turn into a monster-of-the-week show in season three," she notes. "I'm not sure the people who came in knew or really understood the show. I didn't actually watch much of the third season myself. I watched one or two episodes and was disgusted, and then bailed out!"

Of course, *Star Trek*'s cancellation at the end of its third season was just the beginning for the franchise. The saga was first revived in 1973, when NBC joined forces with Filmation to produce *Star Trek: The Animated Series*. Intrigued by the possibilities presented by an animated incarnation of *Star Trek*, Fontana accepted Roddenberry's invitation to serve as the show's story editor and associate producer.

"The key thing about the animated series was that we didn't want to do a kids' cartoon show, we wanted to do *Star Trek*," says Fontana. "We tried to keep it true to the original stories, the original characters and the original mission. The drawback was that we only had a storytelling frame of 21 minutes, so we had to do mini-*Star Treks*. But the advantage was that we had a lot more scope in terms of aliens, planets, environments and spaceships – they could all be drawn. That was a nice freedom.

"I remember the fans were very skeptical about it at first, but once they saw it was *Star Trek*, it won them over. Overall, I thought it was a good animated series that told fairly complex stories. I don't think Saturday morning was the best time for the show [to air] – it might have done better if it aired in the evening – but I think the popularity of the show on video and laserdisc has proved we did a good job. I'm looking forward to the DVD release."

Aided by a writers' strike that prevented US scribes from scripting live-action episodes, Fontana was able to successfully recruit a rich line-up of writers (including many *Star Trek: The Original Series* veterans) to work on the animated series. She points to Samuel A. Peeples' *Beyond the Farthest Star*, David Gerrold's *More Tribbles, More Trouble* and *Bem*, and Larry Brody's *The Magicks Of Megas-Tu* as obvious highlights of the series' two-season run. Fontana is also rightfully proud of her work as the writer of *Yesteryear*, the acclaimed episode in which Spock revisits his past to save his young self and restore the timeline – at the cost of his pet sehlat.

"NBC was nervous about that episode," Fontana recalls. "The storyline involved the euthanasia of a pet and said it's better to end a creature's suffering than keep it alive for your own sake. But Gene told the network they could trust me and, in the end, they didn't receive one letter of complaint."

No Man Becomes No One

Twelve years after the animated series completed its run on American television, Fontana was invited back to *Star Trek* to serve as an associate producer on *Star Trek: The Next Generation*. While many – including, most famously, Leonard Nimoy – initially balked at the viability of a *Star Trek* sequel series, Fontana sensed its potential from the start.

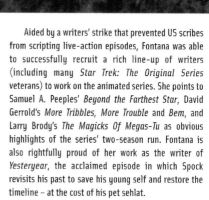

New Frontiers

D.C. FONTANA on the proposed new *Star Trek* movie from J.J. Abrams...

"The success of the new *Star Trek* film will all depend on how it's done," says Fontana of *Lost* and *Alias* creator J.J. Abrams' planned revival. "*Variety* reported that the movie's story would be about Starfleet Academy. There's been suggestions this would involve Kirk and Spock's first meeting at Starfleet Academy. I'm concerned because that's not canon and would be rewriting history; I'm not sure that would work or if the fans would accept it. But J.J. Abrams is a good storyteller and it's certainly going to be interesting to see what he comes up with."

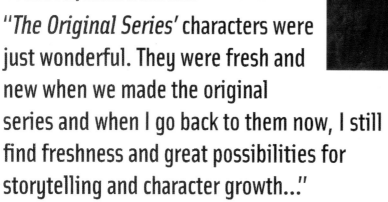

"*The Original Series'* characters were just wonderful. They were fresh and new when we made the original series and when I go back to them now, I still find freshness and great possibilities for storytelling and character growth..."

"I always thought it had a very good chance of success, because it was 'the next generation' of *Star Trek* – the show was jumping ahead and taking advantage of new things we knew about planets and technology, and had new characters who were played by very good actors. Sure, the fans could have rejected it *en masse* and simply said they didn't want it, but I think its success was largely due to the fact that we were taking [the best of] old *Star Trek* and making a new *Star Trek*, with new characters, new stories and new directions."

Fontana's first duties on *Star Trek: The Next Generation* included scripting the series' pilot, *Encounter at Farpoint*, and its first standard episode, *The Naked Now*. Sadly, her experiences on both tasks proved less than fulfilling.

"I did the story and the first draft for the pilot, but after that the script was taken out of my hands and it was totally rewritten by Gene," she explains. "The changes he made were basically the introduction of Q, because my part of it was the mystery of Farpoint station. Gene inserted the whole Q storyline, which I felt didn't fit with the other storyline.

"*The Naked Now* was very soundly related to the original series episode *The Naked Time*, and I shared the story credit with that episode's writer, John D.F. Black, while I had screenplay credit. But in the end we both used pseudonyms on *The Naked Now*, because of the way Roddenberry rewrote it. I thought the things that were added in that case were far too blatantly sexual for the time slot we had and I didn't want my name associated with them.

"Gene was a genius most of the time, but he was also a human being – he made mistakes, just like all of us," Fontana notes. "I think he made some poor

decisions on *Next Generation*, largely due to illness. But he was also a very talented person and the things he has given us in the form of entertainment were wonderful."

One of Roddenberry's rules on *Star Trek: The Next Generation* was that the show's protagonists would not have any character flaws. While this decision reflected Roddenberry's idealism, it also inevitably limited the series' potential for drama.

"That was a concern of mine," Fontana acknowledges," but it wasn't voiced much at the time, because Gene was in charge and that was what he wanted to do. He was the executive producer, he was in full control and those were the stories he wanted to tell. I think the series evolved later to have much more complex characters and stories."

"After I read the original treatment for *Star Trek*, I went back to Gene Roddenberry and told him, 'I really like this. This is going to be fun if someone wants to make it. Who's going to play Mr Spock?'"

Continuing Mission

Following *Encounter at Farpoint* and *The Naked Now*, Fontana penned two further *Star Trek: The Next Generation* episodes – *Lonely Among Us* and *Too Short a Season* – and provided the storyline for *Heart of Glory* before quitting the show to pursue other projects. Five years later, however, she was invited back to the final frontier once again, this time to script *Dax*, an early first-season episode of the second spin-off series, *Star Trek: Deep Space Nine*.

"I had a fun experience on *Deep Space Nine*," she notes. "I enjoyed working with [supervising producer] Ira Behr and [co-creator/executive producer] Michael Piller, and it was interesting to come in and work on a *Star Trek* I had not been associated with from the start. I had a good time writing the episode and I thought it turned out well."

While Fontana says that she enjoyed watching *Star Trek: Deep Space Nine* and particularly liked the show's characters, she admits she was far less impressed by the subsequent two *Star Trek* spin-off shows. "I watched a few episodes of *Voyager* when it started and, to be honest, I just found myself thinking, 'We did that!' So I decided that since I felt I had seen the episodes already, there was no point in my watching.

"I didn't watch *Enterprise* at all. I wasn't interested in the prequel concept; I had the sense that history was being changed and I didn't want to see that."

Despite her personal indifference to the last two *Star Trek* spin-off shows, D.C. Fontana remains thrilled by the success and longevity of the franchise. And she's quick to credit that longevity to the franchise's fans.

"When we said goodbye to *Star Trek* in 1969, who would have thought that the fan love for it would spur the animated series, the movies, *The Next Gen*, *Deep Space Nine*, *Voyager*, the novels and everything else?" she notes.

"If there was no fan demand and acceptance of it, it wouldn't be here. The love of the fans keeps the iterations and the original series coming back and back and back.

"I'm looking forward to more *Star Trek* in the future," she declares with a chuckle. "The enduring appeal of the franchise is just amazing."

A MATTER OF LIFE & DEATH*

(*and temporal mechanics, subspace inversions, and alien data probes...)

"It's life, Jim – but not as we know it." Even if McCoy never actually uttered those words, *Star Trek* loved to offer its characters new perspectives on their lives and the universe – usually against their will... By Rich Matthews

Star Trek is true science fiction because it deals with Big Ideas™. Life, death, time, eternity, humanity, religion – all have been explored many times since Gene Roddenberry got serious with space in 1966. And it was the five-year mission of Kirk, Spock and the original *U.S.S. Enterprise NCC-1701* that most wore its allegorical heart on its sleeve. Sometimes its use of metaphor can make *Star Trek* of the 60s seem a bit clunky and crude, but that is always counter-balanced by its insight, heart and bold concepts. The same devices became subtler and more finessed as we moved into the *Next Generation* and *Deep Space Nine* era, but the approach remained grand.

Perhaps the most indicative trope to emerge of this kind was the parallel-life device. Now, we don't mean the goatee beards and growly frowns of the Mirror Universe, or the more prescriptive time-traveling antics that were deployed to great effect throughout the franchise. No, we mean the episodes where a key character not only gets a glimpse of what their life *could* have been like, but actually *lives* some of it for a while. It allows an exploration of character like no other, and leaves that person forever changed – or at least the audience's perception of that individual is brought into a new clarity.

Many key characters have experienced smaller variations on this theme – usually in the form of "madness" episodes, such as Riker's loony bin moment in "Frame Of Mind" – but Kirk, Picard and Jake Sisko went through three of the most epic alternate timelines in *Star Trek* history. Admittedly, Kirk's is the shortest foray, but in many ways it's also the most tragic. So, come with us on a journey through time – and feel free to pick your Macguffin of choice: an ancient stone portal; an alien probe containing the history of a whole civilization in its memory banks; or a subspace temporal inversion caused by a wormhole. Well, technically, *the* wormhole,

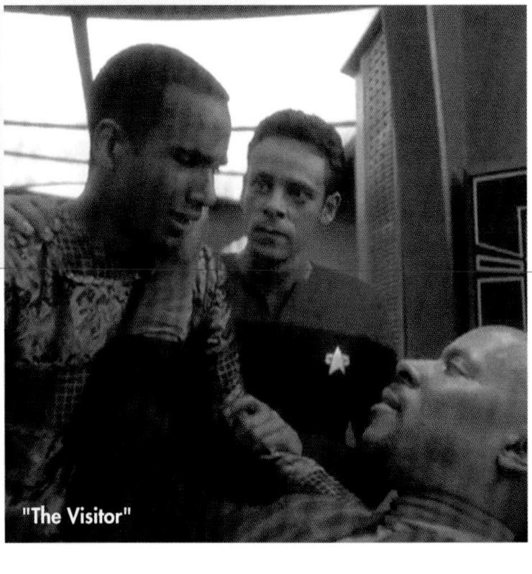

"The Visitor"

"Inner Light"

DATACORE

"THE CITY ON THE EDGE OF FOREVER"

While attending to an injured Sulu, McCoy accidentally injects himself with an overdose of cordrazine when the ship is buffeted from outside. The deranged doctor beams himself down to the planet below, where the *Enterprise* has arrived on a mission to investigate temporal distortions. McCoy finds the source – the Guardian of Forever – and travels back in time to the Great Depression in the 1930s, jeopardizing the current timeline. Kirk and Spock follow him back, but discover that the price of restoring their future is very high indeed.

FIRST AIRED:	6 APRIL 1967
EPISODE ORDER:	28 OF 80
WRITTEN BY:	HARLAN ELLISON
DIRECTED BY:	JOSEPH PEVNEY

- Although credited to renowned science fiction writer Harlan Ellison, both of his drafts were deemed "unusable" by the production team, and went through a series of rewrites by staff writers, including story editor Steven W. Carabatsos, producer Gene L. Coon, DC Fontana and, finally, Gene Roddenberry. Apparently most of the final shooting script was Fontana's, with only two lines of dialogue surviving from Ellison's drafts, both from the Guardian of Forever: "Since before your sun burned hot in space, since before your race was born", and "Time has resumed its shape". Ellison's original version saw Kirk and Spock visiting 20th Century Chicago instead of New York, and McCoy didn't feature (instead, a drug-dealing crewman "Beckwith" went back in time). Ellison actually asked to be credited as "Cordwainer Bird", which Roddenberry objected to, as he claimed it was a known mark of Ellison being dissatisfied with the final episode. Even after all this, Roddenberry listed "City..." as one of his 10 favorite *Star Trek* episodes, and it's worth noting that Ellison's key concept remained intact, in what has become one of the century's great science fiction parables.
- Asked in 1992 whether the episode's anti-Vietnam War subtext was intentional, Associate Producer Robert Justman was quick to reply, "Of course!"
- Other than the two pilots, "The City On The Edge Of Forever" was the most expensive episode of the original series filmed. It also went over schedule, shooting for eight days instead of the customary seven.
- The episode is one of the few times an expletive was uttered in the original series, with Kirk's final line being, "Let's get the hell out of here." The network wanted it changed but the production stood their ground, and it is a reflection of just how much the events rocked Kirk.
- There was no stardate for the episode, although Bjo Trimble attributed it to 3134, based on Ellison's original draft. Also, there is a sign in the 1930s showing a fallout shelter, even though nuclear weapons hadn't been invented at that time.

Too many late nights, Bones?

if you're being picky. Ever notice how the deus ex machina got more complicated as time went on...?

ALL THAT YOU KNEW IS GONE

Would you be willing to let the person you love die in order to save the rest of humanity? Poor old Jim Kirk doesn't half get some doozy decisions to make – poor soul – with his personal dilemma in "The City on the Edge of Forever" perhaps one of his hardest. No wonder he ended up loving his ship (and his Vulcan best buddy) more than any romantic partner. Kirk's experiences are often more black-and-white than Picard and Sisko's (a reflection of TV of the era more than anything else), so while his future is changed, he doesn't experience that aspect, somehow protected from being wiped from existence by proximity to the Guardian (along with Spock, Scotty, Uhura and a gaggle of red shirts – who all live!). His experience of an alternate life is only a glimpse compared to what his franchise successors would be put through, but that snapshot was of true love found... and lost. That's a cruel thing to dangle then take away. Kirk's womanizing is something of a cliché in *Trek* lore, so it's not a surprise

A love lost for Kirk

DATACORE

"THE INNER LIGHT"

The *Enterprise*-D encounters an alien probe, which promptly fires an energy beam that hits Picard, rendering him unconscious. The captain wakes up on the planet Kataan, where the local residents know him as Kamin. While Kamin lives his (long) life on the planet, fighting accusations of delusions about being a starship captain, the crew of the *Enterprise* fight to free Picard from the probe's control.

FIRST AIRED:	1 JUNE 1992
EPISODE ORDER:	124 OF 176
WRITTEN BY:	MORGAN GENDEL AND PETER ALLAN FIELDS
DIRECTED BY:	PETER LAURITSON

A mysterious probe

This is no time for a nap

An elderly Kamin takes stock

- The episode's most iconic image – the Ressikan flute – was chosen because it didn't have to be played in front of the actor's face. Composer Jay Chattaway wrote the flute solo, which has become one of the most requested pieces in the Paramount Pictures library. Chattaway expanded the composition to a six-minute full orchestral suite for *The Best Of Star Trek: Volume One* album release. The flute is seen in Picard's quarters again in a deleted scene from "*Star Trek Nemesis*".

- Kamin's son on Kataan, Batai, is played by Patrick Stewart's real-life son, Daniel.

- Stewart's old-age make-up for the final scenes on Kataan saw the actor arrive on set at 1am for a 7am filming start. He had to leave his home at midnight. Stewart has cited the episode as being the greatest acting challenge he faced in the series' entire run.

- Producer Michael Piller said that this episode is one of his favorites, because of its "remarkable emotional impact – they genuinely explored the human condition, which this franchise does better than any other." Ronald D. Moore has also said that his only regret about this fan favorite is that they didn't properly consider the impact it would have on Picard's character: "It would have been the most profound experience in Picard's life, and changed him irrevocably. We were after a good hour of TV, and the larger implications didn't hit home until later – that's sometimes a danger on TV."

The Pie(car)d Piper of Kataan

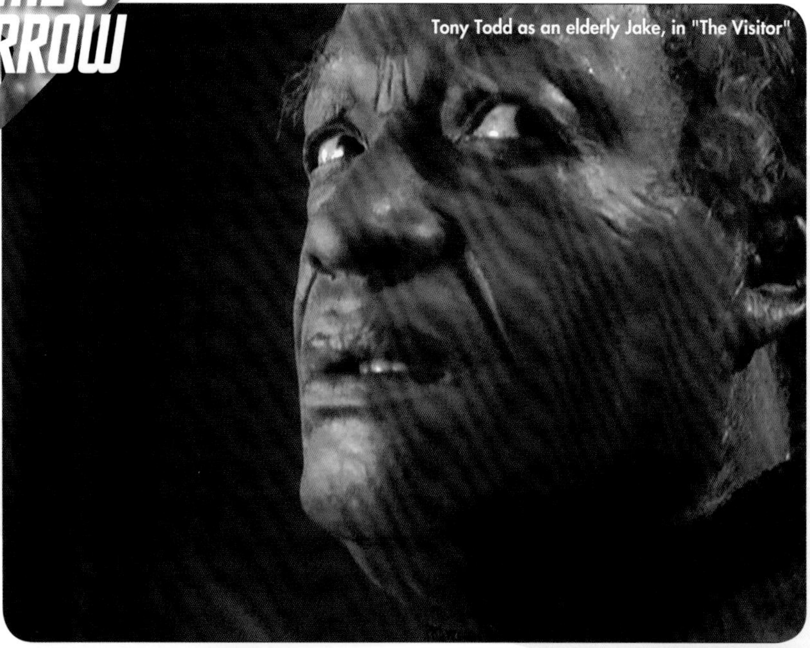
Tony Todd as an elderly Jake, in "The Visitor"

A freak accident claims Sisko Snr.

The Prophets didn't see that one coming!

that he sets his explorative eye on Joan Collins' ethereal dreamer, Edith Keeler, but we shouldn't be dismissive of how he ends up feeling about her. We may only be with them in the Great Depression for half an hour of viewing time, but Kirk and Spock are there for more than a week while they await the arrival of the deranged Dr. McCoy – more than enough time for Kirk to become fully smitten. In terms of impact, for Kirk, Keeler is up there with Carol Marcus, and her legacy is that he had to let her die. After all, the needs of the many outweigh the needs of the few or the one. So, Kirk doesn't live through an alternate timeline (like Jake) or experience a facsimile of a whole lifetime in the blink of an eye (like Picard) – no, what he experiences is real but equally as unattainable. If he saved her and lived his life with her, his idyllic future would be gone forever – then he would have been living in the ultimate alternate timeline. "City" set the template for this kind of contemplative episode, even into other shows beyond *Star Trek*, with Harlan Ellison's concept getting right to the heart of the human condition, where life is as much defined by death as it is by time. All three are linked and enmeshed, and great wonders and tragedies lie within.

LIFE IS A DREAM

How would you feel if you woke up this very moment to discover your whole life had been an illusion, beamed into your mind by an alien spacecraft? Captain Kirk may have encountered more than enough moral dilemmas for the rest of *Star Trek* put together, but it was Picard who suffered through some transformative existential experiences that would have crushed a lesser mortal. Not content with assimilating Jean-Luc into the Borg and then ripping him out of its collective, Rick Berman and co. chose to make him live the kind of loving, domestic life he could never have while serving in Starfleet – and then have it all be a simulcra, projected into his mind by a probe loaded with an entire extinct civilisation's memories. In "The Inner Light", Picard lives half a lifetime in just 25 minutes (of his time, not our viewing time). Hmm. That could really mess with a man's mind.

But that isn't the main takeaway from this episode – what you're left with as a viewer is a sense of beauty, of grace. This is because Picard's experience as Kamin on Kataan is of a species of great spirit and generosity, who maintain their humor and dignity, even in the face of unavoidable extinction. And it revealed a lot about Picard, who could easily have lost his marbles instead of adapting to his situation and surroundings, opening his mind and heart to the possibilities of this land-locked life being laid out before him. This is neatly represented by his adoption of the flute. By the time he's released and revived back on the *Enterprise*, he is now a master of the instrument, which he feels like he's been playing for decades – and because the probe contains the very flute he "played", he has a talisman of his experiences, so he will never forget. Which was the point of the probe, it turns out. The big question here is how much we're defined by memory – did time appear to slow for Picard so he lived Kamin's life, or were the 25 minutes simply spent downloading the information, and now he remembers them as if they actually happened? And that question cuts to the heart of who we are as people, how we experience the world and how memory defines us. And by the end, you love Picard even more – if that's even possible. Not bad for a TV show, eh?

A SECOND CHANCE

Would you pay the ultimate price to get your father back? Jake Sisko was often a shiftless character, an unfocused young man searching for a role outside the epic militaristic and theological path of his "Chosen One" Starfleet dad. Unlike someone like Wesley Crusher – who was both an eager cadet AND a chosen one, precocious scallywag – Jake rarely had a place or a defined role in (or on) *Deep Space Nine*. The great irony of his alternate timeline in "The Visitor" is that the removal of Benjamin from his son's life ultimately consumed Jake. In the end, the younger Sisko sacrifices his own life to get his dad back (admittedly when he's already reached his dotage), to get a second roll of the dice, because he realizes that he is the reason that Ben cannot get out of his subspace purgatory – Jake anchors Benjamin to his prison. In the *DS9* timeline we know and love, the roles are actually reversed – Ben is usually the existential anchor for Jake, holding him on *Deep Space 9*, making this episode the very embodiment of "the grass is always greener". It is also a potent study of grief, of the inability to let go, of denial and obsession. One thing is clear, though – *Star Trek* writers must have all watched Frank Capra's "It's A Wonderful Life" a lot when they were growing up.

Jake ultimately gets his father back, and has no memory of his other life, but big Benjamin does – although it's clear that he feels like he was only in the subspace rift for a short period of time, shown snapshots of Jake aging. So, even though it's Jake who lives the alternate timeline, it's Benjamin who is left carrying its legacy, it's meaning. What is that meaning? Live for now, because you never know what lies around the corner – hardly an uncommon sentiment, but one that is absolutely at the heart of all of our lives, whether we realize it or not. Father and son relationships are often fraught, even in the 24th Century, and *Deep Space Nine* has by far the most in-depth examination of that key part of life than any other science fiction series. Hell, more than most TV series, period. *Star Trek* just gives writers a bigger toolbox to play with. It also gives an amazing actor like Tony Todd the chance to swap Klingon prosthetics (from his recurring role as Kurn) for some old-age make-up, and put in a blistering performance that truly makes us feel for the older Jake, leaving us with a profound sense that we should love those close to us as hard as we can, every day.

DATACORE

"THE VISITOR"

An aging Jake Sisko explains to aspiring-writer Melanie how the disappearance of his father, Benjamin, during an accident aboard the *Defiant* while observing the 50-year Wormhole inversion, resulted in him stopping writing. It transpires that Ben is trapped in subspace by a temporal subversion – he reappears over the years, with time not passing for him. The elderly Jake has worked out that he is the anchor, keeping his father trapped, and knows what he must to do to restore the timeline...

FIRST AIRED:	9 OCTOBER 1995
EPISODE ORDER:	73 OF 173
WRITTEN BY:	MICHAEL TAYLOR
DIRECTED BY:	DAVID LIVINGSTON

- The alternate timeline didn't include the Dominion War, and Jadzia Dax wasn't killed. The latter however was most likely due to actress Terry Farrell's series exit not yet being on the radar.
- The concept for the episode was inspired by *Catcher In The Rye* author J.D. Salinger, who was interviewed by a high-school wannabe writer who turned up on his doorstep in 1980. Salinger hadn't written for years.
- Tony Todd discovered the benefit of wearing Klingon make-up as Worf's brother Kurn, as he was able to also play the adult, parallel-universe Sisko during the same season (he was seen as Kurn in "Sons Of Mogh"). Also, Rachel the aspiring scribe is played by Rachel Robinson, the daughter of Garek actor Andrew. Finally, Odo actor Rene Auberjonois was set to direct this episode, but a scheduling wrinkle involving Colm Meaney meant it was swapped with the following episode, "Hippocratic Oath", in the production order. The director timetable remained unchanged, so David Livingston got to direct it instead.
- Kira (Nana Visitor) got a new uniform in this episode that would be used throughout the remainder of the show's run. While Visitor loved it, there was a fan petition to reinstate her original uniform, for fear of sexualizing the Major. Also, "future" Starfleet uniforms and insignia were recycled from *The Next Generation* series finale "All Good Things".

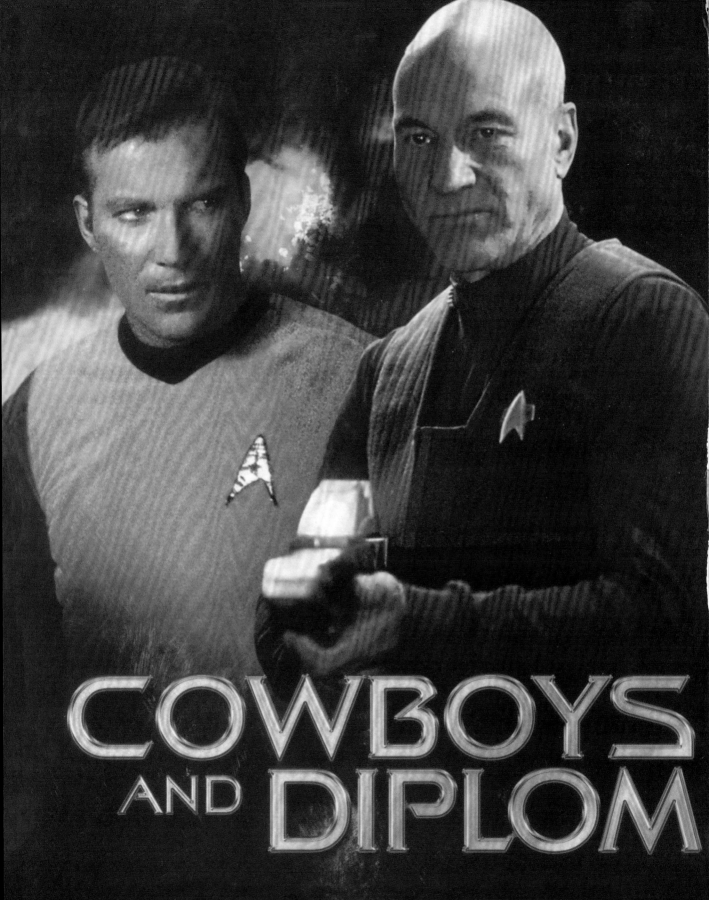

COWBOYS AND DIPLOM

David R. George III examines the differing styles of Captains Kirk and Picard and wonders whether they deserve their reputation of fighter and thinker...

Torn from his life without warning, the Enterprise *captain suddenly found himself no longer on the bridge of his vessel. In the blink of an eye, and with no hint of method, mechanism, or motive, he had been whisked from the starship he commanded and unceremoniously deposited in a small, nondescript circular room. Blank, seamless metal walls surrounded him. Dim illumination emanated from lighting panels in a ceiling three meters overhead, and a dark, featureless floor lay beneath his feet.*

Clearly the captain had been abducted, but by whom and for what purpose, he could not say. His concerns reached beyond his own prospective fate, though, to that of his ship and crew. Yes, he had been seized by some unseen and obviously powerful force, but the matter foremost in his mind remained, as always, the safety of the hundreds of lives aboard the U.S.S. Enterprise.

The captain quickly checked for anything that might have accompanied him from the ship: phaser, communicator, tricorder. Only his uniform had come with him. Escape, it seemed, would not come easily.

He moved to the wall, which felt cool to his touch. He cautiously ran his fingers across the smooth metallic surface, searching for a break of some kind, a control, anything. He'd traversed a quarter of the perimeter when he heard the footsteps behind him.

The captain whirled to see a human-looking man standing before an opening in the wall. Beyond him, a featureless corridor stretched into the distance. An unfamiliar handheld device sat perched on his hip.

"I'm Captain...-"

"I know who you are," the man interrupted. "Which is why I've brought you here. Before the end of your life, which is now only moments away, you're going to give me something."

The Enterprise *captain took two steps toward his captor and...*

And what? What would the commanding officer of the starship *Enterprise* do next? Would he attempt to elicit more information, to negotiate with his abductor and would-be killer, or would he take more direct, more *physical* action? Maybe it would depend on just which *Enterprise* captain had been stolen away from his ship.

Captain Picard took two steps toward his captor and said, "Can we not discuss this like civilized people? What is it that you need? Perhaps I can be of willing assistance to you."

Captain Kirk took two steps toward his captor and then lunged forward, throwing a fist into the man's face while at the same time reaching for the device at his hip.

ATS

For some, both within the ranks of *Star Trek* fandom and among the general populace, these portrayals ring true. You've undoubtedly encountered such opinions of the two iconic characters, perhaps even hold to them yourself. Jim Kirk cuts a brazen figure, bold and intense, prone to throw a punch or fire a phaser first and ask questions later: Captain Courageous.

Jean-Luc Picard, by contrast, appears a pensive leader, decisive but calm, with a bent for cooperation and negotiation: Captain Loquacious. But are those characterizations completely accurate? Is Kirk bellicose? Is Picard garrulous, even complacent?

Certainly distinctions can be drawn between the two *Enterprise* commanders. Even a casual pass through the three seasons of *The Original Series* and the seven of *Star Trek: The Next Generation* reveals more frequent fisticuffs, phasers, and photon torpedoes for Kirk than for Picard. The real-world reasons for this seem plain. Through the 1960s, the decade of *Star Trek's* first run, male film and television heroes often displayed an overt machismo. Think of Joe Mannix, James Bond, and Lawrence of Arabia. Twenty years later, when *TNG* premiered, another type of masculine hero had emerged – sensitive, contemplative, nonviolent – personified by such men as Hawkeye Pierce, Mohandas Gandhi, and even Michael Keaton's *Mr. Mom*. This is not to claim that physical male protagonists did not exist on TV and in the movies after the 1960s – they did and they do – or that thoughtful male protagonists did not exist in those media prior to the 1980s (they did) but to suggest that Captains Kirk and Picard generally fit in to the times in which they were created.

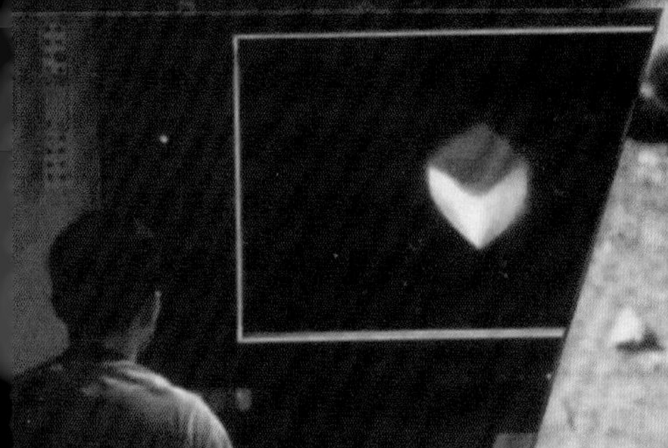

But if James T. Kirk and Jean-Luc Picard in some regard represent the eras of the shows in which they appear, does that reveal them as stereotypes, the former as the rough-and-tumble action hero, the latter as the strong but sensitive male lead? The notions of Kirk as fighter and Picard as talker frequently manifest as criticisms: the earlier captain of the *Enterprise* resorts too quickly to violence, the later captain, delays too long in taking action. From an in-universe perspective, this contention fails prima facie. From his first appearance in "Where No Man Has Gone Before" to his last in *Star Trek Generations*, Jim Kirk conducted a wildly successful career as a starship captain, just as Jean-Luc Picard did from "Encounter at Farpoint" (and even prior to that, given his long stint commanding the *Stargazer*) through *Star Trek Nemesis*. Whatever their command styles, they worked.

And what of those styles, really? During the period in which Kirk captained the *Enterprise*, Starfleet apparently maintained no policy prohibiting, or even discouraging, the commanding officers of its starships from participating in landing parties. By Picard's time, though, such admonitions had become accepted. Because of this, Captain Kirk had far more opportunities to leave the ship on away missions than did his 24th Century counterpart – opportunities of which he often availed himself. As a consequence, Kirk marched into personally dangerous situations far more often than did Picard, and thus put himself in many more situations in which he might need to draw a weapon or land a punch.

Additionally, Captain Picard, during his command of the *Enterprise* during the run of *ST:TNG*, lived into his 60s. In contrast, Captain Kirk spent the years of his *Enterprise*'s mission in *The Original Series* in his middle 30s. Clearly, the younger man would likely be in better physical shape to engage in hand-to-hand combat, while it could be argued that the older man, through experience and the attainment of wisdom, might be more inclined to avoid such fighting.

But all of these reasons for why Jim Kirk might have been more prone than Jean-Luc Picard to employ fists and phasers presuppose that viewers more often saw Kirk take up some form of arms than they did Picard. These arguments do not, however, admit that Captain Kirk *preferred* to use violent means to achieve the goals of a mission, or that Captain Picard eschewed such methods to a fault. In fact, the simple question of who actually struck more enemies or launched more photon torpedoes does not adequately address these issues.

In "The Corbomite Maneuver," the first regular season *Star Trek* episode ever produced, when an automated buoy prevents the *Enterprise* from proceeding, Kirk's first reaction is not to blast it into non-existence, but to wait to see what happens. Only after the ship has hung motionless in space for 18 hours does he attempt to pull away from it. When the buoy then begins emitting radiation and closing on the *Enterprise*, Kirk still does not fire on the potentially deadly object, but tries to retreat from it. Only after two full minutes, and only after the radiation has entered lethal range, does Kirk order phasers fired upon the device.

In *ST:TNG*'s first episode, "Encounter at Farpoint," when what appears to be an alien vessel approaches Deneb IV and begins firing on a city, Picard orders the *Enterprise*'s shields raised and its weapons armed. Rather than firing upon the alien craft, though, he decides on defensive action, choosing to interpose the *Enterprise* between the attacker and its target. Prepared for battle, Picard manages to avoid fighting.

With regard to Kirk and Picard, the telling issue is not who takes physical action more or who talks more, but whether they act appropriately in all – or at least most – circumstances. One does not thread a needle with a sledgehammer, nor move a boulder with a feather. In the two sets of circumstances just cited – circumstances completely typical for the two series – both men ready for combat, but they also strive to avoid it, if possible. In this way, Captain Kirk and Captain Picard are entirely similar in their approaches. During the courses of the two series, the situations Kirk encounters simply force him to fight more often than the situations Picard encounters. They each do what they must, and not only do the impressive Starfleet records of the two captains imply that both men frequently, if not always, choose the right course, but copious evidence exists to refute the belief that Kirk takes up arms too easily, and that Picard does not do so quickly enough.

Witness the *TOS* episode "Balance of Terror," in which a Romulan ship, outfitted with a new piece of equipment, a cloaking device, attacks and destroys several Federation outposts. Captain Kirk must decide how to respond, and

he does not do so immediately. Instead, he seeks advice from his officers, at one point questioning Spock's counsel: "Are you suggesting we fight to prevent a fight?" Later, in his quarters, he confides to Dr. McCoy that he worries about making the wrong decision. In choosing to engage the Romulan ship militarily, Kirk acts with caution and forethought; there is nothing rash about his actions.

Returning to "The Corbomite Maneuver," Kirk opts not to destroy or even abandon Balok's small, damaged ship, even though the alien threatened to destroy the *Enterprise* and its crew. Instead, the captain intends to transport over to render aid to Balok. When questioned about such a course, Kirk asks what the mission of their vessel is, then provides the answer: "To seek out and contact alien life and an opportunity to demonstrate what our high-sounding words mean."

Again and again, Kirk shows that he truly believes in those "high-sounding words," and displays his reluctance to use violence. In "The Conscience of the King," he does not kill the unmasked Kodos the Executioner. In "Arena," he refuses to kill the Gorn commander or allow its ship and crew to be destroyed. In "Spectre of the Gun," he does not shoot Wyatt Earp. In "The Devil in the Dark," although the Horta has taken the lives of miners and of an *Enterprise* officer on Janus VI, and even though Kirk had ordered it killed, he refuses to do so when he at last encounters it himself. In "By Any Other Name," even after the Kelvans have taken over the ship and reduced most of the crew to motionless shapes, Kirk offers not an epic battle, but an olive branch.

On the other hand, Picard fights, and even kills, when the situation warrants it. In "Conspiracy," he and Riker fire phasers into Lieutenant Commander Remmick, a Starfleet officer who had been taken over by the mother creature of a group of neural parasites, and in so doing, kill both Remmick and the creatures. When faced with the brutality of the Borg in "Q Who," Picard orders whatever force necessary to break his ship free. In "Starship Mine," he physically thwarts a plan by a band of mercenaries to steal dangerous trilithium resin from the *Enterprise*, with several of them being killed as a result. In *Generations*, Picard struggles to thwart Tolian Soran's attempts to redirect the Nexus, ultimately bringing about the death of the El-Aurian scientist. In *Star Trek: First Contact*, Picard once more battles the Borg, killing many of them. And in *Nemesis*, he takes on Shinzon and his starship *Scimitar*.

In the end, Captain Kirk and Captain Picard commanded their *Starships Enterprise* in different eras (both within their respective series and in the real world) and at different times of their lives. They projected distinct personalities, conducted themselves with their own styles, and carried with them their own strengths and weaknesses, some of them similar, some them not so. But while one might have thrown more punches or fired more weapons during their periods of command, the two men shared the same sensibility. They thought of themselves as explorers first, and diplomats and soldiers second. They took their ships and crews out into the galaxy in peace, and they both avoided violence as much as possible. When necessary, though, they forcefully defended themselves, their ships and crews, Starfleet, and the United Federation of Planets.

Kirk and Picard, cowboys and diplomats both, as needed – and in that way, exactly the same as one another.

The Savage Curtain

CLOAKED AND DAGGER

No culture on *Star Trek* has clashed more with other races than the sneaky Romulans. In many ways they best reveal how the franchise has handled inter-species interactions across the decades – especially its treatment of villains. Rich Matthews selects three key glimpses of life behind the Romulan curtain...

No one is better at a pithy summary than that most obsequious of Vorta, Weyoun: "Romulans. So predictably treacherous." True. But this is *Star Trek*, and Gene Roddenberry's ode to humanity always looks for the best in any race, color or creed. Even The Founders and Khan Noonien Singh have their reasons for being so unpleasant, and what sets *Trek* apart is a willingness to show and explore the "villains'" motivations, often to even make us identify with them and feel pity or sympathy for them. But the species we know least about remains the Romulans.

By now, most of us could recite some Bajoran war poetry or sing a Klingon operetta or two, but an air of mystery still hangs over the Vulcan's biological cousins – even when they are more fully explored in something like *Star Trek Nemesis*, the real Romulan Star Empire still feels elusive, out of reach.

A quick recap: in the 4th Century, Surak, the father of Vulcan philosophy, espoused abandoning emotion for an existence of pure logic. Some rejected this notion, protesting under the banner of the raptor (later to become the emblem of the Romulan Star Empire). They eventually fled Vulcan, settling numerous planets, but most famously the twin worlds of Romulus and Remus. Class M Romulus became the seat of the Empire, while inhospitable Remus, with one side of the planet in perpetual darkness, was used primarily as an abundant source of indispensable dilithium crystals, populated by a (possibly indigenous) slave underclass, the reptilian, bat-like Remans (who don't like light much).

Romulans are known throughout the Alpha Quadrant as conquerors rather than explorers. Their xenophobic politics are a frightening cross between the aggression of the Klingons and the cold calculations of the Cardassians. That's not a pleasant combination – imagine a painfully intelligent Klingon warrior who didn't care about honor. In a Beatles-style mop-top hairdo.

There are very few true villains in *Star Trek* (the Borg and the Dominion spring to mind) but the Romulans come close. They've been treated fairly onscreen but never seem to pass up the chance to stab someone – *anyone* – in the back. They are antagonists first and foremost. After all, it takes a lot to be the race that the Klingons hate above all others.

Star Trek is a model of pitch perfect allegory and the Romulans' natural, insidious thirst for subterfuge made them an ideal vessel for exploring our own socio-political problems at the final frontier.

A battle of wills, in "Balance of Terror"

BALANCE OF TERROR

It may have been inspired by a World War II ship versus U-boat story, but "Balance Of Terror" is pure 60s Cold War/Cuban Missile Crisis allegory. In the same way that both the Americans and Russians had to demonstrate some clandestine mutual understanding to avoid mutual annihilation in 1962, so Kirk and an unnamed Romulan *Bird of Prey* commander had to find a cautious, grudging respect for each other in the 23rd Century, and, by proxy, their respective races, to prevent a resurgence of the destructive Earth-Romulan War (see boxout).

As such, Roddenberry and Romulan creator Paul Schneider didn't paint them as out-and-out villains – they at least exhibited loyalty to their praetor and their mission to test a new weapon (although it was the cloaking device that really caught our collective imagination). The Romulan commander was gifted with some nobility and honor (not in a Klingon shouty way) that made him a mirror of Kirk, which was reflected by the *Bird of Prey*'s crew referring to the *Enterprise* literally as their "mirror" as it shadowed the cloaked Romulan vessel's course. Casting Mark Lenard as the commander helped – a naturally reserved but warm actor, it's clear to see what Roddenberry saw in his performance that led to his "promotion" to play Spock's father, Sarek. As it turned out, this commander was the best of his breed, not exhibiting the chronic treachery that typified his species.

The episode is about the Federation reacting to an encroachment by the Romulans into their territory (the Soviet Union putting missiles into Cuba), backing whatever action Kirk decides to take, so putting their fate in the captain's hands (Kirk and John F. Kennedy are certainly cut from the same charismatic, ladies-man cloth). Kirk decides he must do anything he can to protect the treaty and keep the Neutral Zone intact (the Cold War détente) to save both sides from a devastating conflict. The only real difference is that conventional drama dictated that Kirk actually defeat the Romulans.

Even if, like Schneider claims, the 60s political parallels weren't the intent of the episode, it's a great example of how real-world issues cannot help but inform *Trek*. It would take a jump of 25 years for the Romulans to get another equally sympathetic crack at redemption.

The enemy ship

THE EARTH-ROMULAN WAR

AKA. The Romulan War – 2156 to 2160
Combatants: United Earth, Vulcan, Tellar and Andoria vs. the Romulan Star Empire

The diplomatic efforts of the *U.S.S. Enterprise NX-01*, captained by Jonathan Archer, brought relative peace between Humans, Vulcans, Andorians, and Tellarites. Naturally, the Romulans set about sneakily ruining it for everyone. Throughout the war, which Spock claims involved atomic weapons, no one saw the Romulans – they were literally a faceless enemy to the nascent Federation, embodied only by their "primitive" starships emblazoned with birds of prey. The Battle of Cheron brought the war to a close with the Star Empire humiliated. The legacy was the Neutral Zone, violation of which by either side was an act of war. It remained intact until the mid-23rd Century. Guess who was involved when it was tested? Rhymes with "smirk"...

DATACORE
"BALANCE OF TERROR"

When Federation outposts along the Neutral Zone send out distress calls, Captain James T. Kirk and the crew of the *Enterprise* are sent to intercept. They encounter the first Romulan vessel sighted since the Zone was established. Caught up in a game of starship cat-and-mouse, the *Enterprise* discovers that the Romulans have developed a cloaking device and that they share lineage with Vulcans.

FIRST AIRED:	DECEMBER 15 1966
EPISODE ORDER:	9 OF 80
WRITTEN BY:	PAUL SCHNEIDER
DIRECTED BY:	VINCENT MCEVEETY

- Paul Schneider is credited with creating the Romulans: "It was a matter of creating a good Romanesque set of admirable antagonists that were worthy of Kirk," the writer said.
- The episode was directly based on 1957 film *The Enemy Below*, about an American destroyer battling a German U-boat.
- The helmets worn by the Romulan crew were designed to cover the actors' ears to save the cost and time of creating more prosthetic ears.
- At the wedding ceremony in the episode's teaser, the bride genuflects at the altar in the *Enterprise*'s chapel, implying she could have been Catholic. This was a big deal in the 1960s because of existing anti-Catholic sentiment – another example of *Trek*'s willingness to confront taboos.

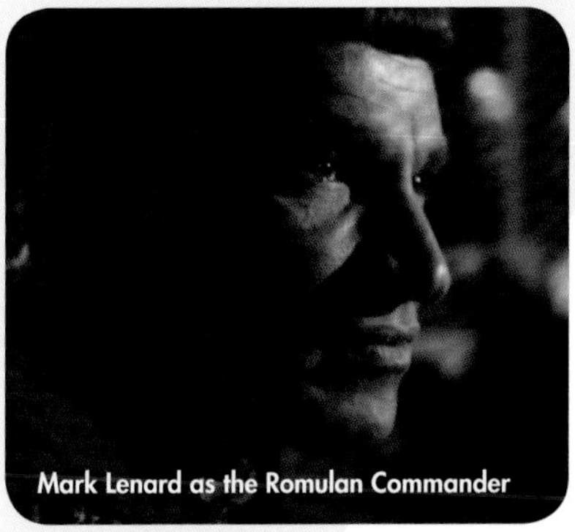

Mark Lenard as the Romulan Commander

UNIFICATION I & II

In 1991, the Soviet Union had fallen and Russia was in chaos, while East and West Germany were fusing back together. The Cold War had thawed then melted, so interstellar Glasnost seemed a natural course for both 23rd and 24th Century humans too, and the only real candidates at the time were the Klingons and the Romulans. With Leonard Nimoy instrumental in the story of *Star Trek VI: The Undiscovered Country*, the movies baggsied the Klingons to stand in for Russia, so *TNG* opted to filter Germany's unification through the Romulans. The show managed to get Nimoy on board as a piece of cross-franchise self-promotion.

Spock and Picard go undercover

ROMULANS vs. VULCANS

As distant cousins of the Vulcans, onscreen Romulans first looked identical to their genetic stable mates – swept back eyebrows, pointy ears, a little bit of blue eye shadow. This look remained consistent throughout the original series, right up to *Star Trek VI: The Undiscovered Country*. In parallel to the last two Kirk era films, the *Next Generation* were busy changing the look of their Romulans. Straddling the original style and the gnarled foreheads of the Klingons, *TNG*'s 24th Century Romulans all sported a ridged V-shaped forehead and a black or grey v-cut bob haircut. This was maintained past the Picard crew's last appearance in *Star Trek Nemesis* into prequel series *Enterprise*, causing a continuity anomaly. Finally, in *Star Trek* (2009) we only get to see the crew of the Narada, who all sported bald heads, nose appliances, tattoos and a slightly exaggerated forehead – and writers Alex Kurtzman and Roberto Orci have admitted the baldness was for practical reasons and that most Romulans probably didn't sport the same look. Unlike the Klingons, no in-universe explanation has ever been given, but various creative personnel have speculated about genetic differences, mingled species and even ritual scarring as possible explanations. There have been moments when the difference "under the hood" has been touched on, notably with Chekov being able to use sensors to find Spock among Romulans in "The Enterprise Incident", and Dr Crusher being unable to treat a disguised Romulan using Vulcan methods. There's even an implication that they share genetic material with the Klingons, which would explain the bumpy noggins. Best thing is probably to just ignore it. And those gigantic shoulder pads, too.

The ailing Sarek (Mark Lenard)

Denise Crosby returns as Sela

DATACORE
THE NEXT GENERATION "UNIFICATION I & II"

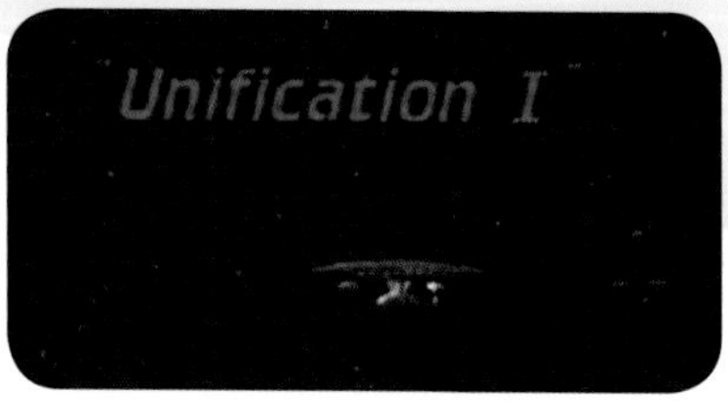

Starfleet send Captain Jean-Luc Picard on a covert mission to Romulus to investigate a possible defection from the Federation... by Ambassador Spock. However, the venerable Vulcan has far loftier and noble intentions – the reunification of Romulus with Vulcan.

FIRST AIRED:	NOVEMBER 4 1991; NOVEMBER 11 1991
EPISODE ORDER:	106 AND 107 OF 176
WRITTEN BY:	JERI TAYLOR; MICHAEL PILLER
DIRECTED BY:	LES LANDAU; CLIFF BOLE

- The two-parter was actually filmed in reverse order to work around Leonard Nimoy's schedule. They were released in reverse order on VHS in the US as a result.
- The episodes were designed to tie in with and promote *Star Trek VI: The Undiscovered Country*, which was released a month after "Unification" aired.
- Actor Malachi Throne, who played Senator Pardek in "Unification", also voiced The Keeper in original *Trek* pilot "The Cage" and played Commodore Jose Mendez in "The Menagerie, Part I".
- The episodes marked the last appearance for Denise Crosby as Romulan Sela – but the actress did pop again up again in series finale "All Good Things...", as her original character Tasha Yar.

Malachi Throne

The narrative link is the duplicitous Pardek, the former Romulan senator Spock met at Khitomer during *Star Trek VI*, who is operating under a typical Romulan web of lies and betrayal – namely luring Spock to Romulus under the pretense of reuniting his planet with Vulcan (though if I were a Romulan, I think I would have found Spock's self-declared mission extremely patronizing).

Once again, the Romulans spurn any potential to show a better side by subverting Spock's noble efforts into a cloak for a Federation invasion. To top it off, in one of *The Next Generation*'s biggest "ta-da!" moments, the mastermind behind this devilish plot is revealed as none other than Sela, the half-Romulan daughter of "Yesterday's Enterprise" alternate Tasha Yar – who blurs the cross-species politics even more. In a way, "Unification" and its treatment of Romulan/Vulcan/Klingon/Human shenanigans is a facet of the humanoid multi-planet DNA seeding later explored in sixth season *Next Generation* episode "The Chase".

Crosses and double-crosses ensue, resulting in the Romulan fleet cynically destroying their own invasion force to protect their tactical advantage, leaving the audience, like the Federation, half wondering whether it wouldn't just be better to have a war and be done with it.

Fortunately for everyone in the Alpha Quadrant, tensions were still sufficiently taught when alliances were required to fight the Dominion – and let's face it, like the Cardassians, who knew for sure which side the Romulans would fight on? Luckily, their distaste at the idea of being conquered outweighed their natural treachery.

NEMESIS

By the time Picard, Riker, Data and co. were taking their final cinematic bow, we lived in a time of global terrorism, constantly looking over our shoulders for threats from within our own ranks. In the 2002 film *Star Trek Nemesis*, the Romulans were led by Shinzon, a human clone of Picard raised on Remus and backed by insurgent Remans tired of existing under the yolk of Romulan power. It starts with a terrorist coup d'état on the Romulan Senate that wipes out the political upper tier, allowing Shinzon to become the new Praetor of the Star Empire. Then things get personal, when Shinzon makes overtures of peace to the Federation and reveals himself to Picard (the Federation's envoy) – as the heroic captain's clone!

Themes of attack from within proliferate – Picard by his own DNA in the form of genetic clone Shinzon, Data by his mirror image, and the Romulan Empire by its slave class and frustrated, power-hungry "patriots". Choosing the Romulans as the movie's bad guys was a clever move because it's difficult for the audience to have any empathy for them, establishing Shinzon's ruthless cruelty while allowing us to view his atrocities somewhat dispassionately. We don't really care what happens to the Romulans or the Remans, as they are so clearly signposted as the black hats in this intergalactic western, leaving us free to concentrate on Picard's internal struggle.

Fans would most certainly have been unimpressed if the same trick had been pulled on the Klingons, while species like the Cardassians weren't mainstream enough for a mass audience, who at worst might mistake the Romulans for Vulcans with heavy frowns. The Romulans were a perfect fit – important and notorious enough in *Trek* lore to set up the main villain's cunning and power, but hardly beloved enough not to take liberties with for the sake of the movie's plot. The same could be said for Romulus' ultimate fate in *Star Trek* (2009), which was more about Spock than the Romulans in the end (see boxout). In *Nemesis*, the Romulans are, ironically, pawns in Shinzon's power play and are effectively sidelined by their own deceit. They got what they deserved.

As vile and duplicitous as they have often been portrayed, however, you can rely on the Romulans for one thing – they can always be trusted to play the villain.

DATACORE
STAR TREK NEMESIS

STAR TREK NEMESIS

Captain Jean-Luc Picard must literally face up to himself when a mysterious human, Shinzon, assumes power of the Romulan Empire and the *Enterprise* is sent to broker a new peace. Shinzon hails from Romulus' dark sister world Remus, and has a more insidious agenda than anyone in the Federation suspects.

FIRST AIRED:	DECEMBER 13 2002
EPISODE ORDER:	10 OF 12
WRITTEN BY:	JOHN LOGAN (STORY BY LOGAN, RICK BERMAN & BRENT SPINER)
DIRECTED BY:	STUART BAIRD

- The *U.S.S. Bellerophon* beat the *Enterprise*-E to the privilege of being the first Starfleet vessel to visit Romulus in *Deep Space Nine* episode "Inter Arma Enim Silent Leges".
- Deanna Troi gets to take the helm for the first time since crashing the *Enterprise*-D in *Generations*. She crashes it again!
- *Nemesis* is the only *Next Generation* feature film not to show the Mintakan tapestry from "Who Watches The Watchers" in Picard's quarters.
- The filming overlapped with the first season of *Enterprise*, so many of the props and costumes popped up in the show, such as Reman outfits becoming Xindi uniforms or a new captain's chair deleted from the end of the film became Archer's center seat in season four of *Enterprise*. Also, the Romulan vessel *IRW Valdore* gave its name to 22nd Century Romulan senator Valdore.

DIE QUICK AND GO EXTINCT

For a species so mired in secrecy and subterfuge, it must really irritate them that their planet's final fate was publicly shown in J.J. Abrams' *Star Trek* (2009). Their star went supernova – revealed via old Spock's mind meld with alternate reality Kirk – and Romulus was caught up in the blast before Ambassador Spock could save it with his black-hole-swallowing red matter. Interestingly, part of the decision to use Romulans was because the film could then continue Spock's story from "Unification" – and because no one in Starfleet had seen a Romulan at all up to that point in the chronology. Whether or not events of the new *Trek* movie universe will see Romulus saved from the interstellar scrapyard remains to be seen, but in the current canon, which birthed the alternate timeline, Romulus doesn't see past the 24th Century.

Picard's cloned nemesis Shinzon

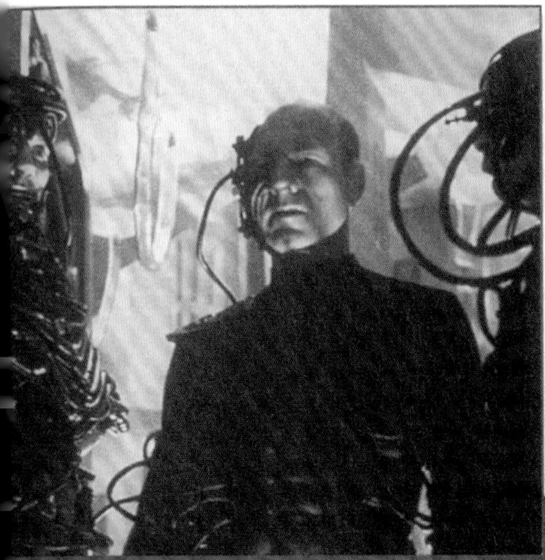

FLASH

THE BEST OF

Frank Garcia reveals the making of the story voted most popular *Star Trek: The Next Generation* story in *STAR TREK Magazine*'s recent poll

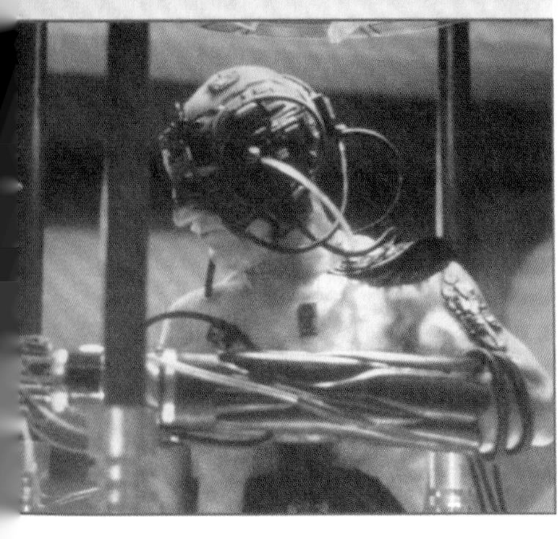

THE STORY

When the *U.S.S. Enterprise* NCC-1701-D discovers that the Borg have destroyed a Federation colony, Lt. Commander Shelby joins Picard and his crew to find a workable defence strategy. But Shelby also has a hidden agenda: She's after Commander Riker's job because he's been offered a starship command. Admiral Hanson encourages Picard to prod his first officer to finally graduate from the *U.S.S. Enterprise*.

While en route to investigate the disappearance of a starship, the *U.S.S. Enterprise* engages a Borg Cube and manages to elude them, hiding inside a nebula. When Shelby goes over Riker's head and talks to Captain Picard about their combat strategy, professional sparks fly and Shelby declares that Riker has lost his edge – and she wants his job after he accepts the command of the *U.S.S. Melbourne*. But Riker bristles at her assumptions of his decision-making.

As the *U.S.S. Enterprise* leaves the nebula, the Borg Cube follows in pursuit and three drones beam onto the Bridge and kidnaps Captain Picard. Worf reveals that the Cube is now on a direct course for Earth.

To attack the Borg Cube, Geordi says that they must first disable and slow it down to impulse speed. When that's accomplished, Riker is quick to assign himself as the leader of the Away Team to beam aboard and retrieve the Captain. But Counselor Troi reminds him that he's now in command and must stay behind, and it's Shelby who must take on the task. Aboard the Cube, the Away Team only locates Picard's discarded uniform. They're forced to leave quickly, and, as they return to the Bridge, Data tells Riker, "Captain Picard has been altered by the Borg!"

"Altered?!" replies a startled Riker.

"He *is* a Borg!" growls Worf.

On the viewscreen, the Borg speak, and reveal that Picard has indeed been re-made as a Borg drone, Locutus. Their former captain declares that he will now serve as the speaker when the Borg proceeds with their "assimilation" of Earth's population.

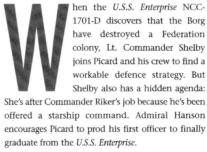

BACK

BOTH WORLDS

"I thought that for the first time, in a long time in my career, and I've directed hundreds of episodes of television, it looked like everything, all the ducks were in a row." – director Cliff Bole

BEST OF BOTH WORLDS MINUTIAE

- Created by writer/producer Maurice Hurley for the second season episode *Q Who?*, the Borg appeared in three episodes of *Star Trek: The Next Generation* after *Best of Both Worlds*: *I, Borg*, and *Descent Parts I and II*. They went on to feature heavily in later seasons of *Star Trek: Voyager* and in the feature film, *Star Trek: First Contact*.

- Patrick Stewart has previously indicated that he would have loved to have been Locutus for several episodes, wreaking havoc upon the galaxy before being rescued. "I had hopes that Picard would go on being a Borg a bit longer. I thought it would be a lot of fun for Picard to be marauding around the galaxy for several episodes, destroying everything and beating up the universe. "The Borg experience changed Picard in some ways," says Stewart, who feels he tried to acknowledge those changes in certain episodes when the Borg returned. "For me, the Borg episodes were not as dramatic as they were for our audience. I can think of other episodes where the characters are expanding, developing and learning much more than in that one. It principally for me was a way of finding out how to make a Borg character work."

- In the original version of the story, both Picard and Data were supposed to be assimilated by the Borg and be combined as one unit.

- George Murdock, who played Admiral J. P. Hanson, has several genre credits including *The X-Files* and the original *Battlestar Galactica* – and he played "God" in *Star Trek V: The Final Frontier*.

- *The Best of Both Worlds* was originally supposed to be a three-part episode, and include scenes of the battle at Wolf 359 – eventually seen, at least in part, in the *Star Trek: Deep Space Nine* premiere, *Emissary*. Budget concerns forced producers to edit the story down to a two-parter.

- Michael Piller, who wrote the story, felt very strongly that there ought to be a third episode where Picard recuperates emotionally from his Borg experience, and fought hard to convince Rick Berman into doing *Family*, where Jean-Luc returns home to France, and visits his brother. At the time, it was considered controversial to serialise episodes.

With no other option available to them, Riker gives the order for Worf to fire upon the Cube with their converted deflector dish, re-tooled to emit a one-off massive pulse of energy in a last ditch effort to disable the Cube. In Part II, the weapon is fired but, to everyone's surprise, fails. Now that Picard is a drone, the Borg Collective knows everything that he does and are able to generate a defence to the weapon's energies. This knowledge also serves to assist them in their attack against Earth.

With Picard now their most dangerous enemy, Admiral Hanson grants Riker a field promotion to Captain and declares that Starfleet will make their stand against the Borg at the Wolf 359 planetary system. Riker selects Shelby as his new first officer.

Arriving at Wolf 359, the *U.S.S. Enterprise* crew are shocked to discover that the Borg have ploughed their way through all the starships attempting to hold the Cube back, destroying their final line of defence. Riker conjures up a radical plan of attack, ordering a saucer separation. As the two sections of the *U.S.S. Enterprise* bombard the Borg with quantum torpedoes, Data and Worf beam aboard the Cube and succeed in recapturing Picard.

Riker plans to defeat the Borg using Picard's connection with the Collective. In their attempt to electronically "interface" with Picard's Borg implants, Data, Doctor Crusher and Troi make a breakthrough. Just as Riker is about to order Wesley Crusher to ram into the Borg Cube at warp speed, Data transmits a command that sends the Borg "to sleep" and saves the Earth from Borg domination.

Later, after the Cube is destroyed in an explosion, Dr. Crusher restores Picard to his normal self. Riker decides to stay aboard the *U.S.S. Enterprise* as First Officer, while Shelby is reassigned to rebuild the Federation fleet that was destroyed at Wolf 359.

THE PRODUCTION

The Best of Both Worlds continues to be a fan favourite – but just why does it continue to attract such devotion and applause among *Star Trek* fans? Director Cliff Bole has a simple and straightforward answer. "It was Picard being turned around and becoming a Borg," he says. "It intrigued the audience. I think seeing Picard [as Locutus] and not knowing what was going to happen," was the nature of the show's appeal. Part one, after all, was the third season cliffhanger. *Star Trek* fans had the summer to bite their nails and wait for months to find out how the story would play out.

Bole reveals that the chilling cliffhanger shot of the transformed Picard with a head-mounted laser beaming straight into camera was not wholly his idea. "[Make-up Designer] Mike Westmore called me up one night and said, 'I've got this idea for a laser' and I said 'Jesus Christ, that sounds great! Do it! Do it! Do it!' He said, 'Where do you want to put it?' And I said, 'Right here, on the side of his head – and every time he looks in the camera it's there.'"

Many fans speculated whether the cliffhanger was a clever set-up because Patrick Stewart's contract with the show was up for renewal. Would he sign on again? If not, Picard could have been killed in part two as a means of writing the actor out of the show and elevating Commander Riker to Captain.

In fact, executive producer Michael Piller, who wrote part one and was assigned to continue the story with part two, confessed at the time that even he didn't know how the story would end. He had the luxury of having a summer break to consider the possibilities.

"He was a marvelous writer," declares Bole. "He had a little thinking time, a little room to work rather than having the pressure to come up with the story in seven days. We split it up during the hiatus.

We did the last show and then did the other part after the hiatus."

Bole is one of Hollywood's most experienced TV directors. His professional credits stretches all the way back to the 1970s, including such popular prime-time entertainment as *The X-Files*, *The Six Million Dollar Man*, *Emergency!*, *Charlie's Angels*, *Fantasy Island* and *The Amazing Spider-Man*. In the 1980s, he directed *T.J. Hooker*, *V* and *MacGyver*. Consequently, in 1987, when *ST:TNG* started up, Bole's name was on the directors list. He even had a *Star Trek* race named after him – the blue-skinned Bolians.

When Piller's script for part one landed in his lap, Bole was already familiar with everyone on the *Star Trek* team. He had already directed nine episodes, beginning with the first season's *Lonely Among Us* and including *Hide and Q*, *Conspiracy* and others. By series end, Bole was one of the most prolific directors, having helmed 24 *ST:TNG* episodes.

For Bole, *The Best of Both Worlds* was a rare treat in his directing career. "I thought that for the first time, in a long time in my career," he smiles. "And I've directed hundreds of episodes of television, it looked like everything, all the ducks were in a row. Rick Berman had masterminded a great two-parter. Michael Piller wrote two great scripts. Everything just came together.

> "This was the first time I'd been with a crew that was organized and creative, and they had a great new cameraman with [director of photography] Marvin Rush. He came to task on that one and did an excellent job." – Cliff Bole

"This was the first time I'd been with a crew that was organised *and* creative," he reveals. "And they had a great new cameraman with [director of photography] Marvin Rush. He came to task on that one and did an excellent job."

Bole says that he liked that the Borg were zombie-like and didn't have dialogue, but also notes that Michael Westmore's intricately designed prosthetics make-up was very time-consuming. "It was a lot of make-up and facial appliances. Michael Westmore had a great team."

In addition to presenting an exciting story, these two episodes introduced a strong female guest star, Elizabeth Dennehy. It so happens that she is actor Brian Dennehy's daughter, and was new to the film business at the time. "I don't think her father wanted her to be in the business," Bole chuckles. "That's what usually happens with parents who say, 'Don't go into the film business!' She did a great job for a first-timer."

It was exciting, says Bole, to watch Patrick Stewart walk on the stage, for the first time, as Locutus in complete Borg make-up. "When he walked on stage for the first time, it was quite

EPISODE STATS

"They were almost robots, and in a sense, maybe they were. The fact that Picard still had most of his faculties, that he could still communicate, gave him an edge." - Cliff Bole

EPISODE: *The Best of Both Worlds, Parts I and II*
SERIES: *Star Trek: The Next Generation*
SEASON: Three and Four
PRODUCTION NUMBER: 174/175
FIRST U.S. TRANSMISSION: 18 June 1990/ 24 September 1990

CAST
Patrick Stewart – Captain Jean-Luc Picard
Jonathan Frakes – Commander William Riker
Brent Spiner – Data
LeVar Burton – Geordi La Forge
Michael Dorn – Worf
Gates McFadden – Doctor Crusher
Marina Sirtis – Deanna Troi
Wil Wheaton – Wesley Crusher

GUEST CAST
Whoopi Goldberg – Guinan
Colm Meaney – Chief O'Brien
Elizabeth Dennehy – Lt. Commander Shelby
George Murdock – Admiral J. P. Hanson

CREW
Director: Cliff Bole
Writer: Michael Piller

breathtaking. It was unique. If I'm not mistaken, and we're going back here 15 years, this was probably one of his first big [make-up] appliances on his face. It took a lot of time and I think he just ate it up.

"After seeing him in his Starfleet outfit for a couple of years, this was unreal. I think he loved it. He's a true performer, being a stage actor. He loved getting out of the normal Captain routine. I'm sure it was a challenge for him and I'm sure a breather, to jump into that character. He really stepped out on this one."

Bole says he's very pleased that the Borg were popular with *Star Trek* audiences. He tackled them in a different way than other villains on the series. "I approached it like a Marine who can't talk," he says. "They were very militaristic, obviously. They were not very animated. They were almost robots, and in a sense, maybe they were. The fact that Picard still had most of his faculties, that he could still communicate, gave him an edge."

Bole also pulled one of the oldest film-making tricks in the books – making sets look bigger than they really are, thus fully utilising the Borg set designed by Richard James. This, combined with the intricate, claustrophobic look of all Borg hardware, and the work of Marvin Rush and the crack lighting team, plus the visual effects magicians supervised by Robert Legato, made the set look immense in the final episode. But to deliver that illusion, a few cinematography sleights of hand were employed. When the camera pointed down one particular hallway, they would light it a certain way and place the camera in a certain angle. And to make that same hallway look different, they needed only to change the lighting and the camera angle, and perhaps some walls as well.

"The Borg set was actually relatively small, Bole reveals, "only about 40x60 feet in size. We turned it around a couple of times and [the viewer] doesn't even know it."

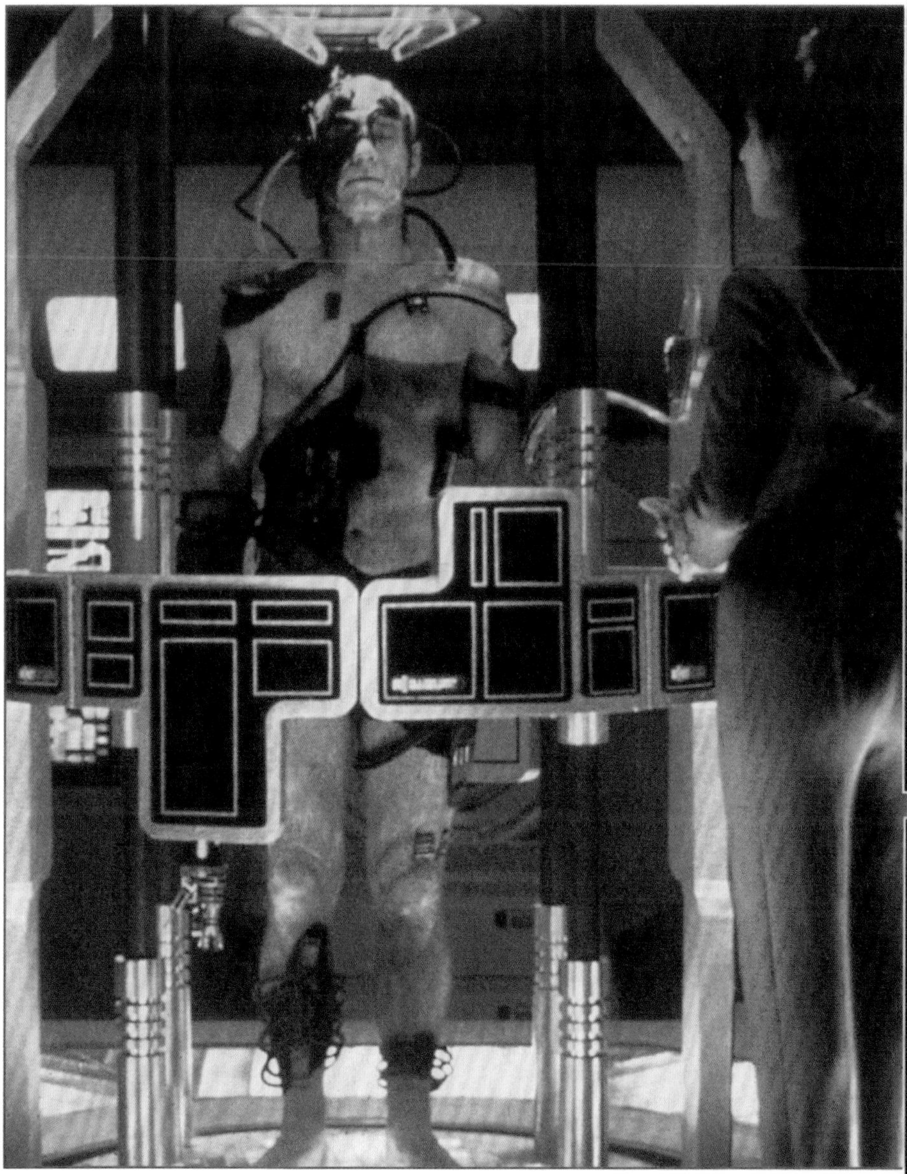

Bole's favourite shot of the two episodes was that spine-tingling moment when, viewed from the *U.S.S. Enterprise* bridge, Captain Picard turned around and was revealed as a member of the Borg Collective. "That was tough to beat!"

Looking back at his encounter with the Borg 15 years ago, Bole appears satisfied, "It was one of my more enjoyable experiences in directing. The actors are a great ensemble. There wasn't a lot of personality problems or anything like that. It was just a real fun two episodes. We made a movie! I've done a lot of great shows, but this one is tough to beat. I'm really proud of it. Everyone feels the same way. It sticks in my mind more than a lot of episodes that I've done since. It was one of my best efforts." ■

"I'm really proud of it. Everyone feels the same way. It sticks in my mind more than a lot of episodes that I've done since. It was one of my best efforts."
- Cliff Bole

"I am now once again a resident of the UK, but be warned that all of those well-worn jokes about being a 'resident alien' are not funny any more..."

AT THE CAPTAIN'S TABLE

Just before addressing 1000 eager fans at this year's *SF Ball*, Patrick Stewart took time out to talk exclusively to Nick Joy about the future of the *Star Trek* franchise, his upcoming work, rejected movie ideas, and just why he's not getting involved with *Doctor Who*!

Ask a group of *Star Trek* fans to name which actors they would most like to meet in person, and, invariably, it'll be the captains. And of those captains, you'll probably find an even split between Picard and Kirk. But there's no doubt today as to whom the throng of convention-goers at the SF Ball have travelled to see, and it's this degree of enthusiasm extended towards Patrick Stewart that means he has to be smuggled incognito into the Green Room at this Bournemouth hotel. Removing his baseball cap, which might at least disguise him from the most casual of observers, Stewart is immediately recognisable as *Star Trek: The Next Generation*'s valiant Captain, even if his suede jacket is strictly non-Starfleet attire.

Squeezing past a coffee table, Stewart reclines on a settee and graciously chats with the convention staff in this rest period before embarking on his marathon autograph session. "Could I ask for a cup of coffee?" he smiles at one of the assistants in the room. What, not tea? Earl Grey? Hot? He later tells his audience that, "When the subject of the tea first came up in *Encounter at Farpoint*, I actually suggested it should be Lapsang Souchong, but the Producer said, 'What's that?' So we settled for something a little less sophisticated. Earl Grey. Combined with English breakfast, it's delicious."

Stewart's face clearly lights up when I tell him that Jonathan Frakes made his entrance at yesterday's guest talk by hiding behind a life-size cut-out of Jean-Luc Picard, complete with phoney British accent. "Oh he did, did he?" he counters, smiling into space. "That man really is quite incorrigible," he chuckles. I add that during the same guest talk Frakes made the comment that in his opinion Picard is *the* best *Star Trek* captain. While clearly flattered by the remark, Patrick replies matter-of-factly. "Yes, and if it was Avery Brooks appearing on stage today then Sisko would be the best captain," Stewart laughs. "Jonathan's very pragmatic. He's also aware that I'm meeting him for lunch next week, and these things *do* get back to me."

Since *Star Trek Nemesis*, Stewart has been Golden Globe-nominated for his portrayal of King Henry II to Glenn Close's Eleanor of Aquitaine in *The Wind and the Lion* and relocated himself permanently to England. "I am now once again a resident of the UK, but be warned that all of those well-worn jokes about being a 'resident alien' are not funny any more," he stresses.

PATRICK STEWART PROFILE

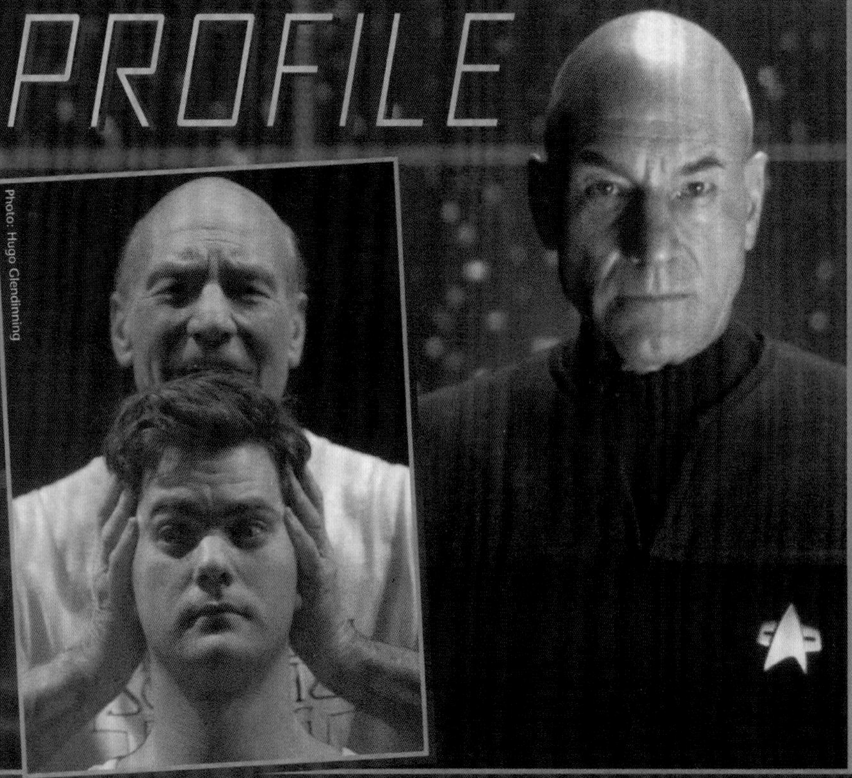

Photo: Hugo Glendinning

BIRTHDAY: 13 July
***STAR TREK* CHARACTER:** Captain Jean Luc-Picard, Captain of the *USS Enterprise NCC-1701-D* and *USS Enterprise NCC-1701-E*

FIRST *STAR TREK* APPEARANCE:
Encounter at Farpoint

WHERE IS HE NOW:
Patrick has just completed a run of David Mamet's play *Life in the Theatre* at the Apollo, London. He's scheduled to begin filming *X-Men 3* in June, which will be released next year.

The youngest of three brothers, Patrick Stewart was born in Mirfield, Yorkshire, the son of a regimental Sergeant and a mill worker. He worked as a junior reporter on a local paper, the *Dewsbury and District Reporter*, after leaving school at 15, but left after the Editor told him he was spending too much time at the theatre and not enough working. (Recently, Stewart revealed he might have become an athlete but the acting profession claimed him instead).

Stewart saved some money for a year working as a furniture salesman to attend drama school and was accepted by the prestigious Bristol Old Vic Theatre School in 1957. He made his professional debut in 1959 and has never looked back, joining the Royal Shakespeare Company in 1966, and staying with them for 27 years.

In the 1970s and early 80s, in addition to his stage work, Stewart was seen in numerous BBC dramas including *I, Claudius, Tinker, Tailor, Soldier, Spy* and *Smiley's People.*

During his time with the RSC, Patrick became one of the founding directors of ACTER (A Centre for Theatre Education and Research). It was during an ACTER visit to the US that he first came to the attention of *Star Trek* producer Bob Justman and was cast as Picard in *Star Trek: The Next Generation.*

Since *ST:TNG*, Stewart has had several film roles, including reprising Picard for the *Star Trek* feature films and as Professor X for the *X-Men* franchise, and plenty of theatre work on both sides of the Atlantic. He continues to be an active supporter of the work of Amnesty International (sponsoring the Patrick Stewart Human Rights Scholarship which offers students a unique opportunity to gain practical experience in the field of human rights) as well as a spokesperson for London's bid for the 2012 Olympics. He is a lifelong supporter of Huddersfield Town Football Club.

Memorable Character Quote:
"Things are only impossible until they are not." – *When the Bough Breaks*

Web Links
Official Fun Club: www.patrickstewart.org
Amnesty International: www.amnesty.org

After an impressive run on Broadway in Harold Pinter's *The Birthday Party* he is once again treading the boards of the West End theatre.

"I'm loving every moment," he gleams. "*The Master Builder* [adapted by *Nemesis* writer John Logan] was a grand experience last year, and my new play [*A Life in the Theatre* by David Mamet] is going really well. I'm hoping to encourage a lot of my fans here today to come up to London to see it." The 1977 play centres around the rivalry between two bad actors, with critics making the observation that, "Patrick's really good at being a really bad actor, darling" and that, "There is something disconcerting about watching Patrick Stewart play a second-rate actor, but no mistaking his enjoyment in doing so."

Stewart shares the two-man play with former *Dawson's Creek* actor Joshua Jackson, and Jonathan Frakes made the observation the previous day that, "I believe this is his best work since *A Christmas Carol*."

"The theatre offered me this play just hours after another one fell through after nearly a year of negotiating," Stewart explains. "I'm hoping that more plays will follow and that producers are waking up to the reality that I'm now living in England and looking for work."

Surely Patrick Stewart, Shakespearean actor and film star, isn't struggling for work? "Oh yes, I went through a very lean period in the spring/summer," he reveals. "After I relocated, I naively thought that they'd be fighting one another to employ me, but that really didn't happen. So, I was initially a bit dismayed, but I guess it takes time for people to get used to my being here – they just assume I'm living in the States." Looking forward, the work offers seem more promising. "There's the possibility of a television series in the spring," he continues, "and X-*Men 3*, which is absolutely certain, is booked to begin filming in Vancouver in June/July or July/August until the end of the year. I also have some very exciting plans for 2006 which I am not permitted to talk about, but they are very exciting for me."

Regardless of the project he's in, *Star Trek* fans support Stewart, and he is delighted to see them at the stage door. "Sometimes it's hard to determine which fans are Joshua's and which are mine – he has quite a following of young women," says Stewart. "He wanted to know why he wasn't invited to the

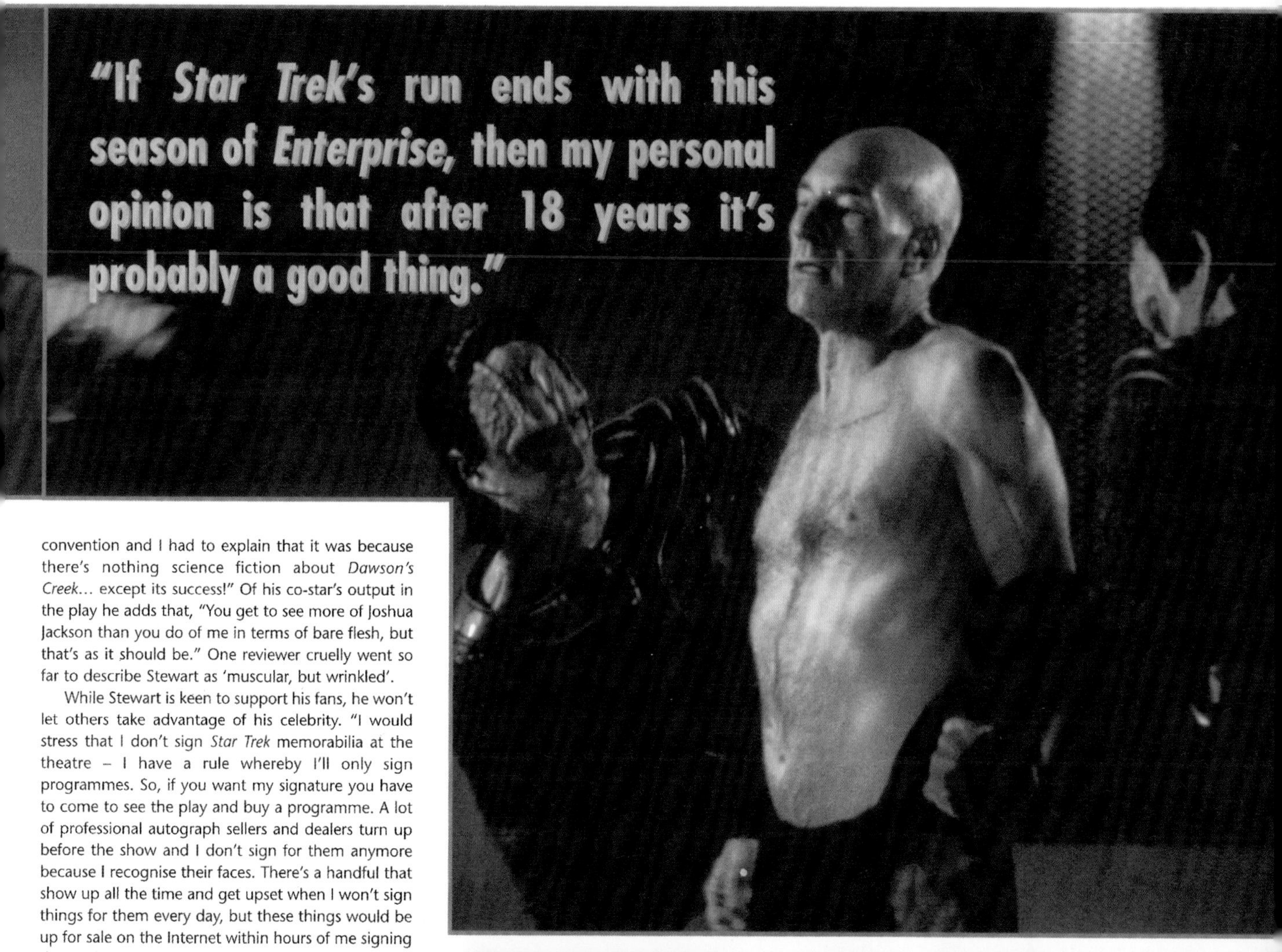

> **"If *Star Trek's* run ends with this season of *Enterprise*, then my personal opinion is that after 18 years it's probably a good thing."**

convention and I had to explain that it was because there's nothing science fiction about *Dawson's Creek*... except its success!" Of his co-star's output in the play he adds that, "You get to see more of Joshua Jackson than you do of me in terms of bare flesh, but that's as it should be." One reviewer cruelly went so far to describe Stewart as 'muscular, but wrinkled'.

While Stewart is keen to support his fans, he won't let others take advantage of his celebrity. "I would stress that I don't sign *Star Trek* memorabilia at the theatre – I have a rule whereby I'll only sign programmes. So, if you want my signature you have to come to see the play and buy a programme. A lot of professional autograph sellers and dealers turn up before the show and I don't sign for them anymore because I recognise their faces. There's a handful that show up all the time and get upset when I won't sign things for them every day, but these things would be up for sale on the Internet within hours of me signing them. These aren't fans."

Indeed, Stewart continues to discover the real fans in the most unlikely of places. "There are a huge number of fans who continue to make their presence felt. In the last 12 months I've travelled to 13 countries round the world and there are still things that take my breath away. I first played Picard *18* years ago, and I still get surprised by the reactions I get. Nine months ago I went to the Philippines and thought, 'Here's somewhere I can go unnoticed,' but as we were approaching immigration the chap at the desk said, 'I can't believe it, Captain Picard in my country!' You really can't escape from it.

"From rural towns in Thailand to parks on the outskirts of Tokyo, people get sight of me and then follow me around," he continues. "I was in Thailand at the invitation of Hallmark Television and Kyle McLachlan [his co-star in *Dune*] to play Captain Nemo in a new version of Jules Verne's *Mysterious Island*. I was there for almost a month and got to know a lot of the people very well, so what happened over Christmas [the earthquake and ensuing tsunami] was horrific because it involved tragedy for a lot of my new friends..." He pauses. To lighten the tone I mention that apparently *ST:TNG* is currently big in the Balkans. "Really? I look forward to an invitation to go to Serbia or Montenegro," he smiles. "I'd love it!"

One of the hot subjects on the fans' minds this

"I first played Picard 18 years ago, and I still get surprised by the reactions I get."

weekend is the future of *Star Trek,* following the confirmation of *Star Trek: Enterprise*'s cancellation. Considering his lengthy involvement with the franchise, Stewart is an ideal spokesperson to discuss the implications of no new *Star Trek* product being in development or production either for television or movie theatres.

"You know, I'm absolutely out of touch with what's going on with *Star Trek,*" he admits. "I only got a phone call from Marina [Sirtis] last week saying that she and Jonathan were going to do the last episode of *Star Trek: Enterprise.* And how do I feel now that the show has been cancelled? Frankly, I'm indifferent. I know that must sound awful, but *Star Trek: Enterprise* meant nothing much to me, and this latest run of *Star Trek* has been running for 18 years. How many other series can boast that sort of longevity?" he poses.

"If *Star Trek*'s run ends with this season of *Star Trek: Enterprise,* then my personal opinion is that after 18 years it's probably a good thing," Stewart feels. "It's obviously not a good thing if you are a fan. If you are a fan, I imagine it's horrible, but I personally don't see how they've managed to keep it going for so long. I don't know how the production team led by Rick Berman have managed to achieve such a run. When I last saw Rick he said that he'd produced 600 hours of television. That's 600 stories! I'm surprised that he's not out of his mind by now."

And while *Star Trek: Enterprise* marks the end of the *Star Trek*'s TV incarnation, Stewart also stresses that there will be no more *ST:TNG* movies. In fact, it was a close call that he even made *Star Trek Nemesis.* "You know," he reveals, "all of us in the cast have always had the same conversation – 'Should we really be doing this film?' It didn't look like *Star Trek Nemesis* was going to happen, but then it did. After *Star Trek Nemesis.* we decided that we really did want to do another one – a final one. Brent Spiner and John Logan, a superb writer who I hope gets rewarded at the Oscars for his screenplay of *The Aviator,* had a scenario for the final movie, which was wonderful. It would have brought all the captains and all the principal casts together into one movie. It would have been a winner, but the studio decided that that was it," he shrugs. "It wasn't that they weren't making money from the franchise, it was they weren't making *enough* money to justify the spend on that size of project," Stewart asserts. "Their phrase was 'franchise fatigue'. They weren't interested, and so our movies came to an end."

One project that Stewart won't be associated with, contrary to Internet and news report rumours, is the narration of a BBC Radio 2 documentary about *Doctor Who.* "I was asked to do it, but I declined. *Star Trek* has been a great blessing to me, but it carries with it a weight too, which is identification exclusively with science fiction." Add to that Stewart's pre-Picard appearances in *Dune* and *Lifeforce* and he's something of a genre stalwart. "And since Picard I've also played Charles Xavier and inherited the 'curse of the *X-Men*'.

"While both are wonderful franchises, and I'm very proud of them," Stewart explains, "when someone says, 'We want you to narrate a programme about *Doctor Who*', you just have to say 'No, no, no. Ask me to narrate anything but more sci-fi or fantasy." He pauses. "I wonder how you knew that I was asked to do that programme? It must be the Internet. You know, I'm discovering that people truly know more about me than I do."

Break over, Stewart rises from the table and slips out to meet his public. This is a man who absolutely commands your respect, but at the same time he is warm and easy-going. He makes the point "I truly no longer know where Captain Picard begins and Patrick Stewart leaves off." So, how does one address him when saying goodbye? 'Pat'? 'Patrick'? 'Mr Stewart'? I settle with 'Sir'. I'm sure that the Captain would approve. ■

Forty-five episodes and 18 months after the unremarkable Okona boarded the ship, the *Enterprise-D* finally carried its crew into the heights of mainstream acclaim, with the *Star Trek: The Next Generation* episode, "The Best Of Both Worlds."

STAR TREK 45s

THE BEST OF BOTH WORLDS

"The Best of Both Worlds" was born out of producer Michael Piller's uncertainty over whether he would stay in charge of the show for the following season. He wrote a cliffhanger to reflect his own situation, mirroring his own predicament in Riker's uncertainty over whether to take command of the *Melbourne*, but Picard's abduction by the Borg fits the situation as well. As Piller ran the show, so Picard ran the ship.

The heart of the episode is Riker's relationship with newcomer Elizabeth Shelby, allowing us to identify with Riker and his choices, and to see how he'd fare under different circumstances. Shelby's ambitions versus Riker's settled attitudes echo Decker's pushing of Kirk in *The Motion Picture*. Here, however, Shelby gets her way, and Elizabeth Dennehy's smile belies her admitted unfamiliarity and uncertainty about her role intruding among a regular set of characters.

The similarity to the Kirk/Decker antagonism isn't the only familiar element here. The admiral's ship alongside the *Enterprise* is a reuse of the shot of the *U.S.S. Hood* with the *Enterprise* from "Encounter At Farpoint." Hiding from the enemy in a nebula harkens back to *The Wrath Of Khan*, and actually uses footage of the nebula shot from that film.

The secondary focus is on Picard and his nemesis, the Borg. Where Riker is merely contemplating his career, Picard faces having possibly met his match. His tour of the ship, and conversation with Guinan about his people's future at the hands of the Borg, are masterpieces of intimate cinematography, direction and acting.

We can see here that so many things have changed in the past 45 episodes. The most obvious difference, at first glance, is that the crew now has proper two-piece uniforms to replace the romper suits. Gates McFadden is back in the opening titles, and Chief O'Brien is now settled in as the regular transporter chief.

Back at the time of "The Outrageous Okona," the show looked rather flat and two-dimensional, with the same kind of picture quality that you often saw in US sitcoms. Here, the look has changed for the better, with the transfer to film for editing allowing much greater depth of field, and color contrasts.

Other visual efforts have also improved,

such as the Planet Hell set, in this case portraying Jouret IV. The switch to using matte paintings for backgrounds means that the effect is better than the cyclorama used previously, though it still appears artificial. The interior of the Borg ship also gets a new, more detailed, matte-painted interior, as well as reusing shots from "Q Who," while the *Enterprise* herself is new in some scenes, a more detailed four-foot model having been built for the third season by Greg Jein.

In-universe, things were changing just as radically from this episode. In only their second appearance, the Borg's whole ethos and *raison d'etre* changes – although this won't actually be acknowledged until afterward. Previously, they were only interested in assimilating technology, but this changes from hereon in. From now on, they assimilate *people*, because that makes them a scarier enemy. An enemy who just wants to incorporate your iPod into his life is one thing, but an enemy who wants to make you his zombie slave is far more frightening.

Something that doesn't change is *Trek*'s

"THE BEST OF BOTH WORLDS"

Writer: Michael Piller
Director: Cliff Bole
Broadcast number: 180
Production code: 40273-174
Stardate: 43989.1
Novelization: None, although the Myriad Universe story "The Embrace of Cold Architects" charts an alternate series of events following this episode.
First broadcast: June 18, 1990

On the same day, recently freed South African political prisoner Nelson Mandela addressed the Canadian Parliament as part of an international campaign to end apartheid in his homeland.

Earlier in the month, U.S. President George H.W. Bush and Soviet leader Mikhail Gorbachev signed a treaty to end chemical weapons production and begin destroying their respective stockpiles.

Three days after the broadcast, a 7.3-magnitude earthquake killed 40,000 people in Iran.

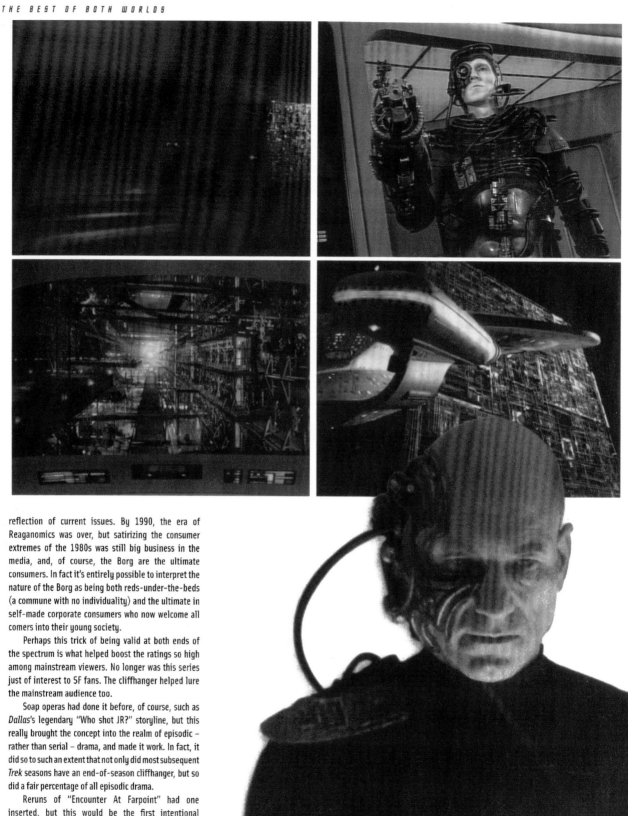

reflection of current issues. By 1990, the era of Reaganomics was over, but satirizing the consumer extremes of the 1980s was still big business in the media, and, of course, the Borg are the ultimate consumers. In fact it's entirely possible to interpret the nature of the Borg as being both reds-under-the-beds (a commune with no individuality) and the ultimate in self-made corporate consumers who now welcome all comers into their young society.

Perhaps this trick of being valid at both ends of the spectrum is what helped boost the ratings so high among mainstream viewers. No longer was this series just of interest to SF fans. The cliffhanger helped lure the mainstream audience too.

Soap operas had done it before, of course, such as *Dallas*'s legendary "Who shot JR?" storyline, but this really brought the concept into the realm of episodic – rather than serial – drama, and made it work. In fact, it did so to such an extent that not only did most subsequent *Trek* seasons have an end-of-season cliffhanger, but so did a fair percentage of all episodic drama.

Reruns of "Encounter At Farpoint" had one inserted, but this would be the first intentional cliffhanger since *Star Trek*'s "The Menagerie," more than 20 years earlier. Although the series budget was always relatively tight, the crew was allowed a little more leeway for this episode, as it was recognized that the first half of a cliffhanger needed to do something a little extra, to work as both a big finale, and to lure viewers to tune in a few months later. This budget increase could still never have enabled the original concept – Picard and Data merged into one cyborg – to be realized effectively, but it was enough to make a lasting impression.

READERS' MEMORIES:

Commander Shelby is an important character to me. I frequently wish that Riker had taken his promotion and gone off to explore strange new worlds on another show. No offense to Jonathan Frakes, who is both an excellent actor and director, but I must admit that I never cared for Riker. In fact he is my least favorite main character in the franchise.

"The Best of Both Worlds" introduces Shelby, a strong female character with ambition, and a desire to rise through the ranks by gaining experience from the captain of Starfleet's flagship. These were pretty much Riker's goals when we see him in "Encounter at Farpoint," but since then he has turned down every offer of command because he's become too comfortable. Not only is he delaying his own career, but by refusing to move on, he's stopping other potential officers getting the same well-earned opportunity he had.

Many people find Shelby too abrupt, and don't like that she wants Riker's job, but from the perspective of someone who hates this Number One's guts, she was a headstrong officer with initiative.

Bryony Harrison

The episode also introduces the Borg's two big catchphrases: "Resistance is futile," and "...is irrelevant." The Borg themselves would return for several more cliffhangers in attempts to repeat the success of this one, and the movie *First Contact* is a direct sequel. The movie's novelization would also recap the events of the episode. Guinan's origins, Picard's relationship with her and the Borg, and Riker's career would continue to be recurring themes throughout the franchise, both on screen and in print. Riker would eventually take a command of his own, the *U.S.S. Titan*, but not for another 13 years.

One side note: you have to assume that the whole concept of a Christmas or New Year holiday or celebration must be dead by the 24th Century. Stardates represent a whole year, with the last episode being the latest Stardate of the year – and that's usually when all hell breaks loose. Starfleet Officers must be terminal cases of Seasonal Affective Disorder – 'tis the season to... be mangled and assimilated, usually.

David A McIntee

Soap operas had done it before, of course, such as *Dallas*'s legendary "Who shot JR?" storyline.

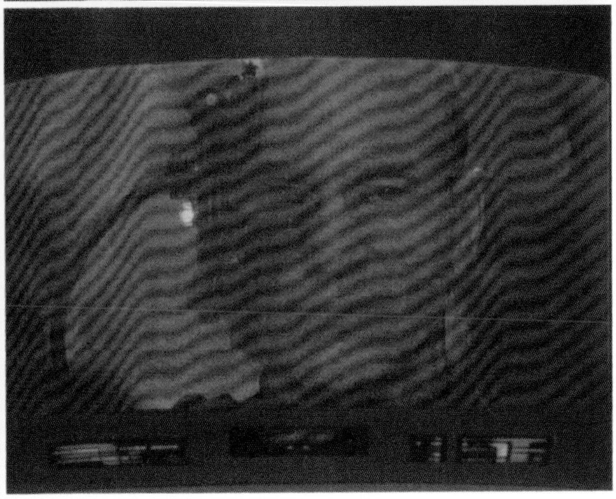

Jonathan Frakes directs *Star Trek: First Contact*

DIRECTOR ACTION!

From actor to film director, Jonathan Frakes has a unique insight on the *Star Trek* franchise – and, as Ian Spelling found out, he's not afraid to speak his mind…

Spend a couple of days on the *Star Trek: Enterprise* set and you'll see the damnedest things. Look, there's Jonathan Frakes in a chef's outfit, trading dialogue with Dominic Keating, both men cracking up as they blow take after take and crack off-colour jokes. Look, there's Frakes again, this time in an old *Star Trek: The Next Generation*-era uniform, very much in classic Riker mode. Oh, and isn't that Frakes yet again, now in a *ST:ENT*-esque MACO uniform?

Frakes, settling into his trailer during a break from shooting the *ST:ENT* series finale, *These Are the Voyages…*, laughs. "It's been a little hard to keep up with everything," he admits. "They've got me bouncing around a lot, from set to set, ship to ship, character to character." He's not kidding. A production assistant knocks on the door. He's there to check on Frakes, who's in Riker's Starfleet uniform at the moment. "So you'll be in a MACO uniform for the next scene," the production assistant informs him. Frakes smiles. "Sounds good to me," he says. "Just tell me where to go and what to wear and I'll be there."

The actor takes a bite of his lunch and proceeds to explain what's going on. Of course, as you read these words, *These Are the Voyages…* has aired already in the United States, *ST:ENT* is no more, and every last one of the show's sets and costumes and props have been stored away. But for the sake of this piece, we'll stay in the moment. "Riker is struggling with a moral dilemma that's got him thinking about a lot of things," explains Frakes, who's looking trim and healthy and believably Riker-like. "The episode and, actually, the moral dilemma are based on the *ST:TNG* episode, *The Pegasus*. That was a wonderful episode with Terry O'Quinn as my old captain. In the episode he was an admiral. I had been sworn to secrecy about a situation. We'd been testing the cloaking device and, for *These Are the Voyages…*, they came up with more back story about Riker's decision about whether or not to tell Picard [Patrick Stewart, who did not appear in *These Are the Voyages…*] about what's happened. And so, in trying to make the

Frakes as a MACO in *These Are the Voyages...*

ship to ship, char[illegible]
to character."

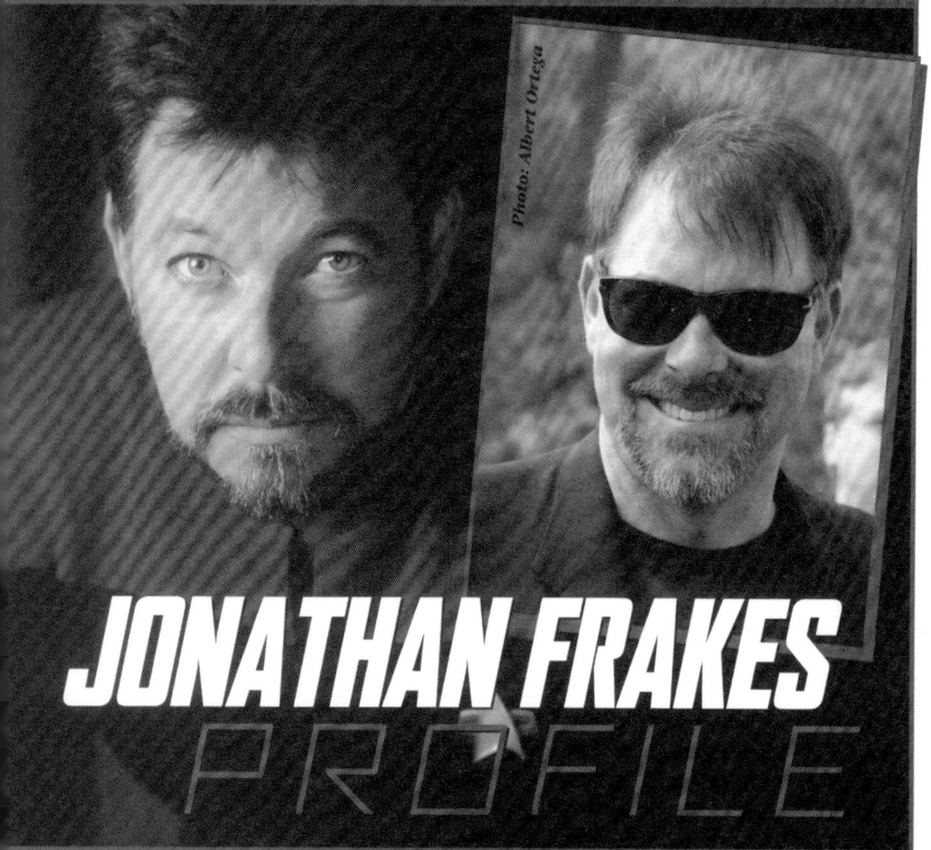

JONATHAN FRAKES PROFILE

Frakes and Marina Sirtis between takes on *These Are the Voyages...*

"Riker is struggling with a moral dilemma that's got him thinking about a lot of things..."

BIRTHDAY: 19 August
***STAR TREK* CHARACTER:** William Riker
FIRST *STAR TREK* APPEARANCE: *Encounter at Farpoint*

Now largely directing rather than acting, Jonathan Frakes, who was born in Bellefonte, central Pennsylvania, started acting in a local theatre while at Pennsylvania State University. The experience moved him to change his degree from psychology to theatre arts, graduating in 1974. Moving to New York he took on various jobs to supplement acting (such as a role in the Broadway musical *Shenandoah*), including playing Captain America for Marvel Comics.

Frakes moved to Los Angeles in 1978, guest-starring on shows such as *Charlie's Angels* and *The Waltons* before gaining a starring role in the soap, *Bare Essence*, in 1983. Although that was unsuccessful, it meant a return to guest star roles, and, while working on the American Civil War mini-series *North and South*, he met Genie Francis, who he finally married in 1988. Before that happy event, it was Genie and her family who persuaded him to audition for the role of William Riker in *Star Trek: The Next Generation*.

Frakes (who, like his on-screen character, can play a trombone) began directing while working on *ST:TNG*, starting with the Season Three episode *The Offspring*. In all, he directed eight episodes of *ST:TNG* as well as episodes of *Star Trek: Deep Space Nine* and *Star Trek: Voyager*, in addition to behind the camera work for *Diagnosis Murder* and *University Hospital*. In 1996, he moved to feature film direction for *Star Trek: First Contact*, followed by *Star Trek: Insurrection*, *Clockstoppers* and *Thunderbirds*. He also executive-produced the science fiction drama *Roswell*.

MEMORABLE CHARACTER QUOTE:
"Speak for yourself sir, I plan to live forever."
Star Trek Generations

Captain's Holiday

Contagion

decision, Counselor Troi [Marina Sirtis, who did appear in the finale] has advised Riker to go back and look at events that occurred aboard the *Enterprise* NX-01. So it's really Riker studying Trip. That's the core of it.

"So they have me going into the holodeck and calling up several of these programs, and the programs show me what happened aboard the NX-01," Frakes continues. "You see me interacting with Trip and the other characters aboard their ship. And the interesting thing they did with it is I go back and forth between being subjective and objective. It's very much a *Star Trek* episode. And it's good science fiction. In the end, it's about my finding, through other people's behaviour and their decision-making, the ability to follow my instincts. To tell Picard the truth despite the fact that Pressman [the O'Quinn character from *The Pegasus*] ranks higher than Picard and had ordered me not to and had sworn me to secrecy.

"It's been fun," Frakes reveals, "I'm playing the before-unseen chef. That was a blast. I was a chef all day yesterday and had small scenes with pretty much everyone. We've had a ball. Bakula is a delight to work with and a pro. This could have been a tough situation, but it hasn't been. And the show is filled with good actors, most of whom I hadn't worked with. I'd met John Billingsley when he did an episode of *Roswell*. So it's been great working with these people, and I always love doing anything with Marina. And, God, what, 75 per cent of the crew on *ST:ENT* I worked with on *ST:TNG*. So it's really been like coming home."

Everyone on the set has been having a good time. There's plenty of laughter and joking and even dancing, in part because the *ST:ENT* regulars have had some time already to deal with the notion that the show will not be back for a fifth season. They're already auditioning and, in between takes on *These Are the Voyages...*, some of them are even reading scripts as they hunt for their respective next gigs. Still, a certain sense of melancholy hangs over the proceedings. Each scene means the end is that much closer. Each shot on this set or with that actor may be the last such shot. And while most of the cast has publicly expressed nothing more than mild frustration, it's got to be tough on everyone that when it boils down to it, *These Are the Voyages...*, is a *ST:TNG* episode with *ST:ENT* folded into it, with the emphasis on Riker more so than on the *Enterprise* NX-01 crew.

"If I were them, if I were the cast of *ST:ENT*, my feelings would be hurt, too, I think," Frakes says diplomatically. "I understand how they feel, completely. But I know what [Executive Producers and *These Are the Voyages...* writers] Rick [Berman] and Brannon [Braga] are trying to do with this finale.

Time Squared

Contagion

"It's the valentine to the fans of *Star Trek: The Next Generation*. I see that and I like that,
and I think people can appreciate that. You have to separate it."

These Are the Voyages...

The Icarus Factor

It's the valentine to the fans of *ST:TNG*. I see that and I like that, and I think people can appreciate that. You have to separate it. You have to separate people taking it personally from the bigger picture."

The end of *ST:ENT* also represents the end, for now, of *Star Trek*. Consider this the re-boot phase, the battery recharging time. It's been oft-stated, and it's true, but the 40th anniversary of *Star Trek* next year will come and go with no current *Star Trek* television series on the air and no feature either in cinemas or, it seems, in production. "It's sad," Frakes acknowledges. "It's very sad, to be honest. But I suspect that it's not over. I always feel that *Star Trek* is never really over. There may be a longer break this time than there has been before, but *Star Trek* will be back. I don't think there's any doubt that Star Trek will be back."

So what went wrong? Why are we discussing such a sad state of affairs? "I don't know what went wrong with the franchise or with *ST:ENT*," Frakes replies. "I've been out of the country, over in England, for most of the last three years. So I've really been out of touch with what's been happening in television and with *Star Trek*. I wouldn't even try to venture a guess about the business. So far as *Star Trek*, we've talked in the past about the fact that maybe they've gone to the well one too many times. But because I've been away, because I've not be involved with *ST:ENT* as a director at all, I'm really not in a position to say what went wrong with *ST:ENT*. I think others can talk about that. Right now, all I know is that Paramount is going to give *Star Trek* a rest. How long that rest will be, how long it should be, I don't know. There's a new regime at the studio, and it's going to be a question of what [new Paramount boss] Brad Grey and others feel about the value of the franchise. I'm very curious to see what, if anything, they have in the pipeline."

With Picard in *Star Trek: First Contact*

THE PEGASUS 101

The *Star Trek: Enterprise* finale *These Are The Voyages...* is set during the Season Seven *ST:TNG* episode, *The Pegasus,* written by Ronald D. Moore and directed by LeVar Burton. That story attempted to explain why the Federation has never developed cloaking technology. As part of the Treaty of Algeron which ended the Earth-Romulan War, the Federation agreed not to develop such technology. However, it's a variant of cloaking technology – a 'phasing cloak' which enables a ship to pass through solid matter – which the *U.S.S. Pegasus* was testing under the command of now Admiral Pressman. The Admiral is determined it should not fall into Romulan hands, and equally determined that Riker does not tell Captain Picard the real reason the *U.S.S. Pegasus* came to grief.

Despite Pressman's orders, Riker finally reveals the secrets of the *Pegasus* when the *U.S.S. Enterprise* is trapped by the Romulans, risking his own career to do the right thing.

CLASSIC RIKER EPISODES

A MATTER OF HONOR
Riker becomes first mate on the Klingon cruiser *Pagh* as part of a Federation officer exchange program. A misunderstanding leads to a Klingon attack on the *U.S.S. Enterprise* NCC-1701-D and Riker must sort out his conflicting loyalties.

FIRST CONTACT
Critically wounded during a first contact mission, Riker is mistaken for a hostile alien.

SCHISMS
The *U.S.S. Enterprise* crew suffers bizarre consequences following a secret, unwelcome alien visit.

FRAME OF MIND
Trapped in an alien mental hospital, with little memory of the past, Riker is convinced he is going insane.

SECOND CHANCES
Thanks to a freak transporter accident eight years before, William Riker discovers he has a double – Thomas – who tries to rekindle his romance with Deanna Troi. Thomas eventually leaves the *U.S.S. Enterprise* to find his own path (which will eventually lead him to the Deep Space Nine space station...).

Facing danger in *Star Trek: First Contact*

Frakes has been so out of the loop of late because he and his family relocated to London while he realised the big-screen version of Gerry Anderson's Supermarionation series, *Thunderbirds*. Frakes was on board from the start and immersed himself in every element of the production. Unfortunately, the resulting film – which starred Bill Paxton, Ben Kingsley and Sophia Myles – suffered critical slings and arrows and never caught on with moviegoers upon its release last year. "There, I do know what happened," Frakes notes. "A lot of people liked the movie. I must say that Universal, to their credit, called when the movie didn't do well, and they said, 'You know what? You made the movie we wanted you to make. And we put it out at the wrong time.' They copped to it and I must say they've been very upfront about it. It came out in the summer along with *Shrek 2*, *Spider-Man 2* and *Harry Potter 3*, and that's a lot of times for parents to take their kids to the movies. It was originally intended for a March release [in the US] and, in retrospect all of us believe that would have been a much better place for it. It was not marketed as well or as effectively as it could have been.

"I always feel that *Star Trek* is never really over. There may be a longer break this time than there has been before, but *Star Trek* will be back."

"I know the film got some harsh reviews, but I missed them," says Frakes. "I heard about them, but I was in Maine. So my timing was such that I didn't really have to see the blood on the walls. I think the people who most strongly criticised the movie were comparing it to the old series. They didn't take into account that this film was a 21st Century feature made for families. But the whole experience was a real education for me. I'd never experienced anything like that before."

So what's next for Frakes?

"I just got offered something that I can't talk about yet, because I'm waiting to see if that's real," he replies. "I've been talking to Nickelodeon Films about a couple of projects. I've been talking to New Line Cinema about another project. So there are four things that are in different stages of becoming a reality, but we all know that nothing is a reality until you say 'Action' that first time. One of them is a very dark vampire-cop movie. One of them is a family movie. One of them is a family comedy. And one of them is a period family movie. So those are all projects that I'd come on to as a director for hire. There are other projects that I'm trying get moving along, a couple that I've been plugging away on for a long time, but you never know what's going to come together first."

Notice that Frakes mentioned nothing about acting or seeking out acting jobs in the paragraph above. There's a reason for that. "I guess I am a director these days," he says. "*ST:ENT* is really the first acting I've done since *Star Trek Nemesis*. I don't count my little [cameo] bit in *Thunderbirds* as acting. I was just 'Chubby Bearded Cop #2' in *Thunderbirds*. It's been good to act again [on *ST:ENT*], but I'm glad I'm not counting on it. If I held my breath waiting for acting roles I'd be in trouble. There doesn't seem to be a lot of work for aging superheroes, for guys who are attached and identified with something else – like *Star Trek*!"

Still, there's one role out there that Frakes could – and would play again. And that role, to be sure, is William Riker. "I don't think I've played Riker for the last time," Jonathan Frakes says as the conversation comes to a close. "It comes up every time I play him. 'Is this the last time?' It's a good question. It's a fair question. And the answer is I don't think so. I am eternally optimistic. Whenever *Star Trek* comes back, whether it's as a movie or as a television show, if they ask me to play Riker again, of course I'd be open to it. I'm very appreciative of the fans, very appreciative of everything that *Star Trek* has done for me. And I like the character. Just doing *ST:ENT*, while it's been bittersweet, it just reminds me how lucky we've all been to be a part of this family, how it's effectively given us all our careers, our houses. It has been a real blessing. So, they know where to find me." ■

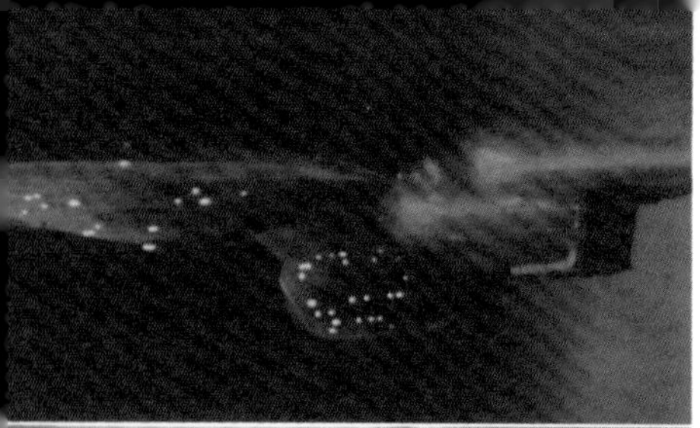

FLASH

YESTERDAY'S ENTERPRIS

Frank Garcia uncovers the origins of the classic third season episode of *Star Trek: The Next Generation*, in which a *U.S.S. Enterprise* from the past mysteriously reappears…

"We were very excited about giving everyone a death scene, to do a show that had a darker texture to it than what we were able, in the series itself, to accomplish."
IRA STEVEN BEHR, WRITER

The genesis behind *Yesterday's Enterprise* is a testament that dreams can come true if you have good ideas and if you're standing at the right place at the right time. It was for Trent Christopher Ganino and Eric Stillwell, who sold a *Star Trek* story idea that would evolve into one of the series' most celebrated episodes. These two would-be screenwriters each had their own *Star Trek* fantasies on paper, but when they met and began collaborating, their story ideas were snatched up and made into an *ST:TNG* episode. They lived a dream that thousands of fans all over the world wish was theirs.

In *Yesterday's Enterprise* the *U.S.S. Enterprise* NCC-1701-D encounters an anomalous 'rift' in space, and through it comes the *U.S.S. Enterprise* NCC-1701-C, from 22 years in the past. But in the instant the earlier starship passed through the rift, Federation history changed. The Klingons never signed a peace treaty with the Federation, and is now at war with it. Tasha Yar never died and is aboard the 1701-D. Worf is the enemy. It's a darker, bloodier world.

The alternate Picard discovers that Captain Rachel Garrett, who had fought the Romulans to defend a Klingon outpost, was on the verge of being destroyed before being thrown into the future. With dismay, Picard realises that to restore the timeline – it's Guinan who convinces him things are wrong – he has to return Garrett and the ships' crew to their time period, to certain doom. As events progress, it's Lieutenant Tasha Yar who takes the centre seat of the vessel and returns to its proper time period so that history can be put right.

In 1989, when screenwriter Michael Piller joined *ST:TNG* and took command of the writing staff, he was appalled that the production had few scripts in the pipeline. In response, he made an astonishing decision that became an industry-wide first: he arranged to have anyone, provided they were willing to sign a release form, submit scripts to the series.

"As long as I have known him, Michael Piller has always believed in giving new writers an opportunity to get their foot in the door and a chance to prove themselves," recalls Eric Stillwell, the series' script co-ordinator at the time. "He himself had once been given a similar opportunity.

"The studio agreed to allow the open submission policy providing we followed certain guidelines," Stillwell explains. "*Star Trek* became the only show in Hollywood that would allow non-professional, unrepresented writers to submit scripts. Until then, only entertainment attorneys and professional agents – those registered with the Writers Guild of America – had been allowed to submit scripts to studios."

It fell to Stillwell to sort and process the avalanche of submitted scripts by eager fans. The program attracted so much attention by would-be writers that "By the fourth or fifth season, we were literally receiving up to 5,000 speculative scripts per year," Stillwell recalls. "Over the course of Seasons Three through Seven, I would estimate that more than 15,000 speculative scripts were submitted during the *ST:TNG* tenure. Maybe as many as 20,000. And because the program overlapped with *Star Trek: Deep Space Nine* (and later *Star Trek: Voyager*), it's hard to say how many scripts were submitted exclusively with *ST:TNG* in mind, verses *ST:DS9*."

Sandwiched between all those brown envelopes, was a script titled *Yesterday's Enterprise* by Trent Christopher Ganino, submitted in April 1989. In it, an *Enterprise* from the past had accidentally travelled to the 24th Century and Picard was struck with a dilemma whether or not to return the ship and its crew to their original timeline.

In spite of some mistakes (the series guidelines urged "No time travel stories! Don't double-space to 104 pages!"), Ganino's script got read by two staffers who found enough good

EPISODE STATS

EPISODE TITLE: *Yesterday's Enterprise*
SERIES: *Star Trek: The Next Generation*
SEASON: Three
PRODUCTION NO: 163
FIRST US TRANSMISSION: 19 February 1990

CAST
Patrick Stewart – Jean-Luc Picard
Jonathan Frakes – William Thomas Riker
Brent Spiner – Data
LeVar Burton – Geordi La Forge
Michael Dorn – Worf
Gates McFadden – Beverly Crusher
Marina Sirtis – Deanna Troi
Wil Wheaton – Wesley Crusher

GUEST CAST
Whoopi Goldberg – Guinan
Denise Crosby – Natasha 'Tasha' Yar
Tricia O'Neil – Captain Rachel Garrett
Christopher McDonald – Richard Castillo

CREW
Director: David Carson
Teleplay By: Ira Steven Behr, Richard Manning, Hans Beimler and Ronald D. Moore
Story By: Trent Christopher Ganino & Eric A. Stillwell

WEB LINKS
• Eric Stillwell's Blog
http://liberalbydefinition.com

YESTERDAY'S ENTERPRISE MINUTIAE

things to push it forward until it got into Michael Piller's hands. Meanwhile, with Stillwell's help, Ganino was on the Paramount lot as an employee, the pair meeting to share their ideas for scripts to submit to *ST:TNG*.

After an encounter with actress Denise Crosby at a convention, Stillwell knew that she would be happy to return in some fashion (Lieutenant Tasha Yar had been killed by an 'oil slick monster' in the first season) and came up with a script to achieve just that, which also combined themes from two *Star Trek: The Original Series* episodes and put them into *ST:TNG*.

"What if," they proposed in *Shattered Time*, "Ambassador Sarek visited the Guardian of Forever planet and witnessed the alteration of Vulcan's distant past? And how could the damage be repaired?" Their eventual script saw Sarek going back in time and *becoming* the much-revered Vulcan Surak, thus restoring the timeline to its proper path. It was Tasha Yar's presence in this alternate timeline that would have allowed Denise Crosby to return to the show.

When Piller read Ganino's script, he asked Executive Producer Rick Berman to buy the story and have a professional write it. He wanted Tasha Yar to reappear, too, but was unaware of Stillwell and Ganino's other story with a Tasha Yar element.

At this point, Stillwell had the luxury of walking into Piller's office, and pitching "this other story that we're working on" that had the Tasha Yar component. Piller's response was "Combine the two stories for a story credit..." and that's what they did.

In their revised treatment, combining Ganino's *Yesterday's Enterprise* premise with Stillwell's *Shattered Time*, the storyline was very much as it was in its final form. However, Data's 'love' for Tasha was an element that was later excised and it is an alien probe, not Guinan's extrasensory powers, which provides information indicating history has been changed.

Once the newly revised story was struck and

BEST OF SERIES?

- *Yesterday's Enterprise* achieved ratings of 13.1 when it was first broadcast in February 1990 – the third highest ratings for the series and highest for the third season. Writer Eric Stillwell originally thought the show would be a flop
- *Starlog* magazine readers voted *Yesterday's Enterprise* as most popular episode of the series in 1993
- In 1994, in a US nationwide viewer marathon, *Yesterday's Enterprise* was voted most popular one-hour instalment of the series
- In 1996, US *TV Guide* readers voted the show as one of the top five all-time best episodes of *Star Trek* and UK viewers voted this as the all-time single most popular episode of *Star Trek* ever.
- In 2002, *TV Guide* listed *Yesterday's Enterprise* as one of the top five all-time classic episodes of *ST:TNG*.

STORY NOTES

- Captain Rachel Garrett's last name was taken from a pizzeria in writer Trent Christopher Ganino's hometown, San Jose.
- Dr Selar, seen in *The Schizoid Man*, can be heard being paged, as can Lieutenant Barrett, a tribute to Majel Barrett.
- *Yesterday's Enterprise* marks the first appearance of an *Ambassador*-class starship, and the first appearance of the *Star Trek* film uniforms in a *Star Trek* series set in the 24th Century, albeit without their undershirts and belts.
- The *U.S.S. Enterprise* NCC-1701-D was given a more intense background sound throughout the episode, to emphasise the workings of a warship, including continuous voiceovers of intercom calls in the background and bosun whistles.
- The time travel aspect of the story later enables Denise Crosby an opportunity to return to *Star Trek: The Next Generation* as Sela, a half-Romulan daughter of the alternate Tasha Yar.
- Denise Crosby may have ended her role as regular castmember Tasha Yar in *ST:TNG*'s first season, but she continued to appear as a guest in the series either as Tasha or Sela. Today, she is best known to *Star Trek* fans for her involvement in the *Trekkies* documentaries, tracking fandom across the world, but she continues to make appearances on television, in series such as *Eyes*, and *Crossing Jordan*
- A *Star Trek* fan herself, Tricia O'Neil was ecstatic to get the role of Captain Rachel Garrett. She subsequently guest-starred on *Star Trek: The Next Generation* (as the Klingon scientist, Kurak in sixth season episode *Suspicions*) and *Star Trek: Deep Space Nine* (as Korinas in Season Three's *Defiant*). She also appeared in the *Babylon 5* telefilm *In the Beginning* as the Earth Alliance president – some thing of a promotion from mere captain!
- Filming *Yesterday's Enterprise* brought back childhood memories of watching *Star Trek* for Eric Stillwell. "Of all my pilgrimages to the set, visit ing the bridge of the *Enterprise-C* was strangely eerie," he recalls. "It was the only set I visited when nobody was around. It was cast in long shadows and very quiet. This was the bridge of a starship which had sustained heavy damage at Narendra III during a battle with the Romulans... Wreckage lay strewn across the decks. Like any fan, I immediately headed for the captain's chair. I sat down and surveyed my bridge. I could almost feel the fantasy of the battle taking place around me. I imagined what it would be like to command this mighty starship – to lead my crew into battle with the Romulans. I wondered how the Captain would feel when members of her crew were injured or died in the line of duty. And like the actress who brought Captain Garrett to life on the television screen, I asked myself, 'What would Captain Kirk do in this situation?'"

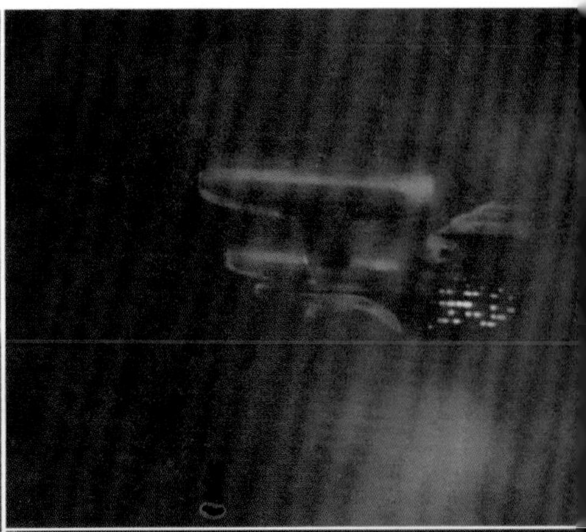

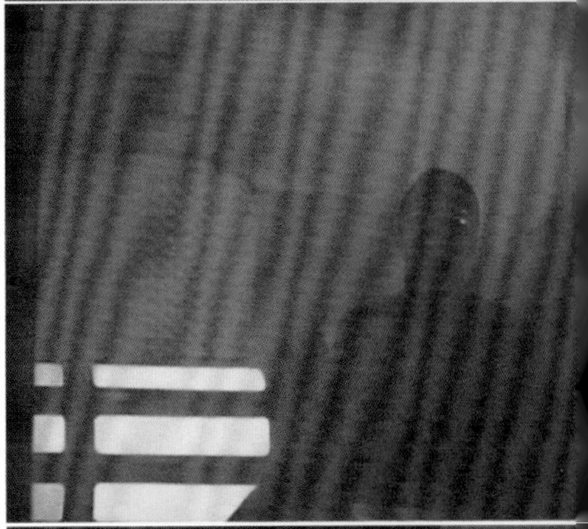

recast by Ronald D. Moore, it was up to the writing staff to turn the story into a full-blown teleplay. But there was a problem: the episode's production was moved up from January 1990 to 11 December, 1989 to accommodate Denise Crosby and Whoopi Goldberg's schedule. This meant that the script had to be written fast. How fast? Over the long American Thanksgiving holiday. So fast that, in the end, four screenwriters each took a slice of the script's acts just so the script could get out the door. Ira Steven Behr, on the writing staff at the time, called in Ronald D. Moore, Hans Beimler, and Richard Manning. (Michael Piller later contributed a 'polish' to the story, voluntarily taking his name off the credits to conform with the Writers Guild's credit limit of four names).

Recalling the moment, Behr says, "No one wanted to be there. Everyone was in a bad mood. And they blamed me. I was the good soldier. Michael asked me to do this – so get it done!

"What got us excited was that there was a lot of complaining amongst our writing staff about how much the show lacked action, tension and fun. This was a chance to go much darker than what we usually get to do." Specifically, because *Yesterday's Enterprise* was entering an alternate universe, it was an opportunity for the writers to develop 'death scenes' for the entire crew, which included Data being electrocuted, Wesley being decapitated and Riker being mutilated.

"It was a chance to see the crew fighting in a big, nasty battle," says Behr. "Ron and I were big fans of 'last stand' movies where, at the end of the movie, all your heroes are lying in the dust. It's the romantic in us, the noble sacrifice. So, it was a chance that we thought we'd never get to do with the *Star Trek* cast. We were very excited about giving everyone a death scene, to do a show that had a darker texture to it than what we were able, in the series itself, to accomplish."

Unfortunately, because of both time and money, their hopes were not realised and only Riker's death was retained in the final filmed version. "We wrote the thing in a very quick and expedient manner," says Behr. "Everyone wrote stuff beyond just the act. It was truly a group birth."

That the final product did not become a *Star Trek* embarrassment, with seven distinct writers involved, is a rare example in Hollywood. "Things like that do happen," explains Behr. "Rarely is the end product a success for obvious reasons. I thought this turned out pretty well, even though, at the last minute, Ron and I both felt betrayed that they did not film everyone's death scenes because of time and money. We wanted everyone to go down blazing. The other thing that we wanted, that we did get, was the end shot of Picard standing there, defiantly and firing away which is a direct steal from an old 1940s war movie I was a fan of – *Bataan!* starring Robert Taylor."

When the episode aired, it was a big hit among viewers. Today, 15 years after the creation of this episode, Eric Stillwell continues to work for Michael Piller at the production company Piller^2, and he is currently associate producer of USA Network's *The Dead Zone* hit TV series, having moved up the ladder from script co-ordinator. The company's new series, *Wildfire,* featuring *ST:DS9*'s Nana Visitor, launched on ABC in June. He was production associate on *ST:VOY* and the *Star Trek: Insurrection* feature film. He also supplied the story for *ST:VOY*'s first season episode, *Prime Factors.*

"*Yesterday's Enterprise*' is an achievement I am extremely proud of," says Stillwell. "It's my one small claim to fame. If I never accomplish another thing for the rest of my life, I will never be ashamed to speak proudly about the years I spent working on *Star Trek* and my small, but significant creative contributions to a beloved worldwide phenomenon.

"To this day, no matter where I travel in the world, *Yesterday's Enterprise* continues to evoke high praise and delightful feedback from fans everywhere. As a fan myself, the experience is incredibly gratifying; and to the fans, I am greatly appreciative." ■

01

CHRISTOPHER MCDONALD

LT. RICHARD CASTILLO, "YESTERDAY'S ENTERPRISE"

An actor for 40 years, Christopher McDonald has delighted audiences on stage, TV, and on the big screen, in both dramas and comedies. Remember him as Big Chuck in Kyle Newman's *Fanboys*? Or maybe the mean-spirited Wilson Croft in *Flubber*? Or you might recall his voice from a number of DC Comics animated shows – Jor-El in *Superman: The Animated Series*, Superman in *Batman Beyond* – or perhaps his role as Harry Daugherty on *Boardwalk Empire*. For *Star Trek* fans, though, it's surely for his performance as Lieutenant Richard Castillo in "Yesterday's Enterprise" – one of *Star Trek: The Next Generation*'s finest moments – that he'll always be remembered.

Words: Mark Newbold

***Star Trek Magazine*: Do you prefer playing good guys or having a meaty bad guy to get your teeth into? Or do you like both?**

Christopher McDonald: I like both, but at the same time there's nothing more fun than getting carte blanche to do a bad guy. Keep it real, keep it honest, keep it truthful, but at the same time have the time of your life. It's kind of like a get-out-of-jail-free card. It's great fun, I've done both and I love being the lead, but the bad guys are more fun, I must say.

Your character in "Yesterday's Enterprise" couldn't have been more of a good guy. Looking back, when you were offered that role and looked at the script, what were your first impressions of the character?

It's very funny you ask that because the character's original name was Manuel Castillo, and I said, "There's no way they're going to cast me, I'm Irish!" I said, "I'm going anyway because I love, love, love *Star Trek*," so I went in. I was doing a play in downtown Los Angeles, the Arthur Miller play *Death of a Salesman*, and I had a brilliant time. Philip Seymour Hoffman played Willie and I played the hell out of Biff. When the audition came up for *Star Trek: The Next Generation* I said yes. So I go and meet the director, David Carson, and he says, "The most important thing in this whole show is to bring back Tasha Yar and for her to have a significant death." I had such chemistry with her [Tasha Yar actress Denise Crosby], I think that's what really sold it.

That relationship was the cornerstone of the episode. Had you two known each other beforehand?

We knew each other socially, but she'd had a big influence on that show for years. It was the first time she'd been back in a long time. And by the way, we laughed and loved. That's the great thing about being an actor, an actor can leave his own personal life and go into the world of fantasy, which we all love, and as a character I fell in love with her. She's a doll, and that's what helps – chemistry.

When you saw the script, and the way it was going for your character – who was very much the fulcrum of everything that happened, in his willingness to make the ultimate sacrifice and go through the rift – how did you feel about that? There aren't many more heroic endings than that.

Well, you just nailed it. It's the most heroic thing in the world, to say, "I know I'm going to my death, and I'm going to say goodbye to you right now but in another world wouldn't it be great, if we could, someday I'll find you." And then she comes onboard and makes her death worthwhile rather than waste it, like Guinan says.

It was a great opportunity and I'm so glad and so honored that it's one of the most popular episodes of *TNG*.

Absolutely – whenever there's a fan poll, and given the episode is a while ago, 27 years...

Shush, don't say it out loud!

...There are a handful of *Next Generation* episodes that always come up, and "Yesterday's Enterprise" is one of those. That must make you feel pretty good.

It does. It was David Carson's first episode as well. We were on the same slippery slope, as it were, we really hit it off, and the fact that I was in *Death of a Salesman* at the time, I think that really helped me connect and lift the storyline to a higher level. There was a great camaraderie between me and Tasha Yar, but wow, to sacrifice your life, knowing you could change the next 20 years... That's pretty cool.

01 Richard Castillo and Tasha Yar.

02 Castillo ponders a bleak future.

02

"What was great about the episode was the whole timeline changed, and that's big stakes."

Stepping back to your casting in the role, Castillo was a very different character on the page compared to what we saw on screen.

They brought me in as a Hispanic character. I said, "OK, alright, I'm still going, but I'm not Hispanic. I'll try to do my thing." Kudos to David Carson for that, for saying, "No, he's perfect, he's great. We need a guy who has that kind of connection [with Tasha Yar]." In the moment, you see it. Attraction. That is universal.

We finished the timeline, fixed the past, as it were. What was great about the episode was the whole timeline changed, and that's big stakes. I love the fact that there's a lot invested on both sides. I'm going to my death, but I'm

Photo © Shutterstock

"I had such chemistry with Denise Crosby, I think that's what really sold it."

doing it for the right reasons. As actors we have to sell that, and that's why it's a popular episode.

What was it like being on the set and working with the *Next Generation* cast?
Here's the thing, as a fan of the show, I watched Michael Dorn get his face put on. That was huge! I watched Whoopi Goldberg get in the hat. And I embraced the fact that I had to get little pointy sideburns. I watched a lot of artistry going on, which was a blast, and in the very studio I got started on in *Grease 2* back in the day. It took me a few years to come back, but wow.

Most of the time, actors really kibbutz, they share stories, tell jokes, they make light. It's real fun and a rare and wonderful experience. I knew Brent [Spiner] and a couple of the other guys, it was all very friendly.

***The Next Generation* was known for working long and hard hours. You must have put in a shift and a half on that show.**
You bring up a very sore point. So, I'm doing *Death of a Salesman* and I'm playing Biff, the son. It's the quintessential American drama. One night we went into extra hours, it was probably a Friday. I couldn't make the curtain at 8pm. I got there at 9.20pm, and my understudy went on. You're giving up one of the greatest, richest parts in American theater and that hurt me a little bit to do that. It was a great experience to do the episode, but it was a heartbreaking experience because I wanted to play that part [on the stage] again for the Friday night crowd.

We've had the 50th anniversary of *Star Trek* and the 30th anniversary of *The Next Generation*. Does it surprise you that *Trek* has survived so long?
Honestly, it is loved because it's real in a fantasy world. In a fantasy world, that stuff happens. It's Patrick Stewart, it's Jonathan Frakes, it's Data, Whoopi Goldberg, they make this thing live. And you care. I'm a fan and I think it's going to go on forever.

By the way, I'd love to be in the new one.

04 Christopher McDonald in 2017.

05 The chemistry between Castillo and Yar is undeniable.

06 Guinan gazes on.

We were going to ask if you'd be interested in coming back to *Star Trek* and doing something in *Discovery* if the opportunity arose…
Absolutely, it's one of the great stories. It's generations now, 50 years. The greatest moment for me was to sit in the *Enterprise*-C chair. The captain's dead, now I'm in charge, and I say, "Full warp speed." Come on – that is a gift.

"Yesterday's Enterprise"

***Star Trek: The Next Generation*, Season 3, Episode 15**
First aired: February 19, 1990
When the *U.S.S. Enterprise*-C emerges from a temporal rift, creating a new reality where the Federation and the Klingon Empire are at war, the only person on the *Enterprise*-D who knows something is awry is Guinan. In order for the timeline to be restored, the *Enterprise*-C must return to the past – even though it means everyone onboard will die. With the ship's captain dead, it's down to the *Enterprise*-C's helmsman, Lieutenant Richard Castillo, to guide the ship and its crew back through the rift – accompanied by the *Enterprise*-D's Lieutenant Tasha Yar, determined that this time, her death should have meaning.

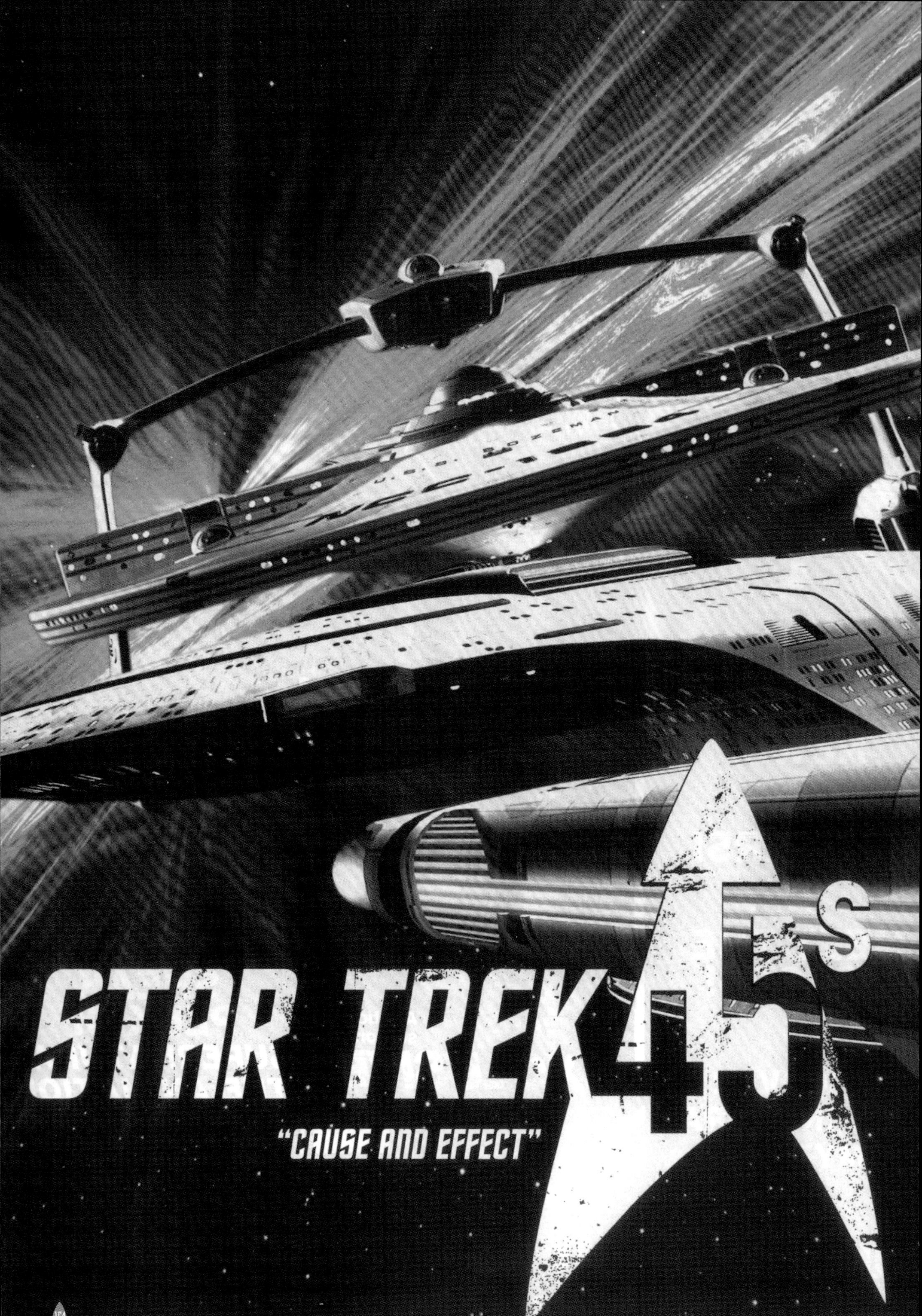
STAR TREK 45s
"CAUSE AND EFFECT"

Nearly two seasons have elapsed since our last story. The original *Enterprise* crew have sailed on their final voyage, leaving the *Enterprise*-D crew a clear field – at least for the moment – although story 225's opening does leave the audience to wonder how much longer they can survive...

It is perhaps the greatest teaser ever, starting in the middle of a catastrophe as the *Enterprise*-D tumbles out of control, venting plasma, unable to eject the warp core... then is ripped apart by multiple explosions with all hands lost. Viewers knew things would somehow be set right by the end of "Cause And Effect," but it's a scene that helped make this episode a fan favorite.

Following the credits, the ship is intact. Dr. Crusher, called away from the weekly poker game, dismisses the déjà vu she has while examining La Forge, but the *Enterprise* is soon destroyed again, trapped in a temporal causality loop. The poker game, the sickbay visit, a briefing about the Typhon Expanse, distortions in the space-time continuum, and a mystery ship suddenly appearing and colliding with the *Enterprise* – the same events rebooting and replaying. The veteran staff rose to the challenge of keeping these scenes engaging.

Although some had moved on since the third season's finale, "The Best of Both Worlds," the previous episode in our 45th anniversary review, many names in the fifth season credits are familiar, if occasionally with new titles. Michael Piller moved up from co-executive to executive producer. Ronald D. Moore has gone from story editor to co-producer. Wendy Neuss bumped up from post-production supervisor to associate producer. In front of the camera, Wil Wheaton's Wesley Crusher had left for Starfleet Academy. A new ensign, Ro Laren (Michelle Forbes), occasionally took Crusher's place at the conn, replacing his earnest goodness with some dramatic edge.

"CAUSE AND EFFECT"

Writer: Brannon Braga
Director: Jonathan Frakes
Broadcast number: 225
Production code: 40275-218
Stardate: 45652.1
Novelization: None, though Captain Morgan Bateson and the *U.S.S. Bozeman* are featured prominently in the *TNG* novel *Ship of the Line* by Diane Carey, which picks up from the final scene of the episode.
First broadcast: March 23, 1992

Earlier in the month, a Sarajevo shooting claimed the first victims of the Bosnian War. 263 people perished in Turkey's worst coal mine disaster, followed 10 days later by a 6.8 magnitude earthquake in eastern Turkey that kills over 500.

Around this time, the People's Republic of China ratified the Nuclear Nonproliferation Treaty.

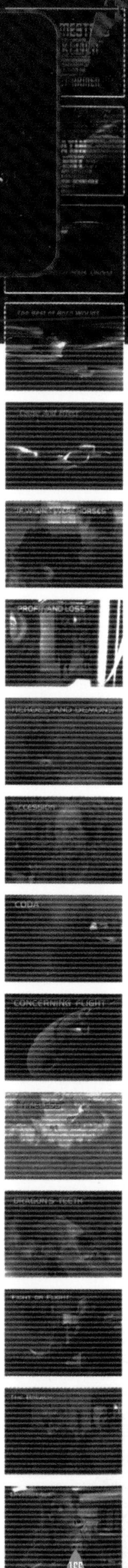

"Cause And Effect" writer Brannon Braga had come aboard in 1990 (not long after the original broadcast of "The Best of Both Worlds"), and this episode was his first solo credit. Actor Jonathan Frakes had directed three previous episodes. The cast and crew had hit their stride by the third season, and two seasons later were still at the top of their game, providing the show with continuity of style... and poker. Although the senior staff's weekly games had featured in several previous episodes as fun asides, the time-looped dealings in "Cause And Effect" were an integral plot point.

To keep repeated scenes interesting, executive producer Rick Berman told Frakes not to reuse footage. Scenes were sometimes shot with multiple cameras, capturing the same take from different angles simultaneously. This simple technique, combined with accumulating plot changes as more crewmembers experienced déjà vu and heard mysterious voices, kept viewers guessing about what would happen next in the rebooted scenes. A handy subatomic particle, a dekyon, allowed echoes from previous loops to bleed into the next iteration and provided the loophole (pardon the expression) to break the cycle by sending the "next" Data a clue to help him avoid the collision. The effects crew went the extra mile to destroy the

"My oddest memory of it isn't actually the episode, but the fact that a preacher at my church used the episode to illustrate a point in his message!"

Reader Robin Bradley

READERS' MEMORIES

"Cause And Effect" just stood out for me. It was nowhere near the first one I saw or anything like that. But I do remember it for being the first one that I felt I must own and actually sought out and bought.

To me, this was a great blend of very talented writing, acting and directing. Given the timing of commercial breaks, this was only an eight- or nine-minute story being told several times over. And yet, thanks to the direction and the actors' performances, you saw that during each iteration, the crew had a bit more awareness of the situation.

With *TNG* airings being much less frequent then than they are nowadays, I wanted to be able to watch this at any time. On a trip to visit friends in New York City, I dragged everyone down to lower Manhattan just so I could get the LaserDisc with this episode shortly after it was released! And even though I can go to my DVD shelf and pull out this episode, I still have that old 12" disc too.

Nicholas Monnito

"Cause And Effect" was the first complete *TNG* episode I ever saw. I had seen bits and pieces of other episodes here and there from channel flicking, but I never bothered to watch a whole episode until this point.

"Cause and Effect" was brilliantly directed by Jonathan Frakes. There was a risk of it becoming boring and monotonous. The directorial choices, however, prevented that from happening; in fact, we got to see some really interesting camera angles, not typical of your usual *Trek* episode. I liked the scene in which Dr. Crusher moves her wine glass, unknowingly trying to prevent it being knocked over. The fact that it still gets knocked over is rather creepy and foreboding, a mood created through the lighting and underscore.

Ironically, after discovering how much I like *TNG*, whenever I tried to catch another episode on re-runs, it was always this episode that was on...

Bryony Harrison

Enterprise, blowing up an actual model instead of doing a simple superimposed explosion. It made the scene more visceral as the ship ripped apart, pieces flying in all directions.

"One of my favorite *TNG* episodes – a great time travel riff from a fresh and new Braga. Great twists, great dialogue, I love it."

Author David A McIntee

The show's staff didn't get everything they'd wanted. The *Bozeman,* the ship that had been trapped in the loop for 90 years (and named for Braga's hometown), was originally conceived as a *Constitution*-class cruiser, like Kirk's original *Enterprise*. When the budget didn't allow building a new model, they simply remodeled the *Reliant* from *Star Trek II: The Wrath of Khan*. They had wanted Kirstie Alley to return as Saavik, joining her former *Cheers* costar Kelsey Grammer, who played the *Bozeman*'s Captain Morgan Bateson. It didn't work out – different sources cite scheduling conflicts and salary demands – which was just as well, since Saavik's disappearance in 2278 would have blatantly contradicted her appearances in *Star Trek II, III*, and *IV,* generally accepted as taking place in the mid-2280s.

Budget constraints aside, *Star Trek* was in its glory days, notwithstanding the sad loss of creator Gene Roddenberry in October 1991. *The Next Generation* was the highest-rated syndicated show of all time, and its fifth season marked the 25th anniversary of the franchise. The original cast's final bow, *Star Trek VI: The Undiscovered Country*, had opened in December 1991 to great reviews. *The Next Generation* ruled genre television, with *Quantum Leap* (starring future *Enterprise* captain Scott Bakula) the only other major hour-long genre show on the air in spring 1992.

Jeffrey Sconce, associate professor in the department of radio, television, and film at Northwestern University of Illinois, wrote that *The Next Generation* was "by far the most pivotal series in rekindling science fiction as a viable television genre," also pointing out that "in this new incarnation, *Star Trek* became an ensemble drama structured much like *Hill St. Blues* or *St. Elsewhere,*" two hit series of the time period. The show had earned the flash added to its name in the main titles for the fifth season, a three-dimensional effect receding into the starry background.

Its reputation was assured by creative episodes like "Cause And Effect." Although Grammer's Captain Bateson only appeared briefly in the final scene, the character and the episode achieved enduring popularity. *The Next Generation*'s finale, "All Good Things..." and the films *Star Trek Generations* and *Star Trek: First Contact* all name-dropped *Bozeman*. Bateson has been featured in comic books, short stories, and novels, most prominently in Diane Carey's *Ship of the Line* and most recently in David Mack's *Destiny: Lost Souls*. The Typhon Expanse became the meeting place for a group of Federation enemies, launching the Typhon Pact, a threat to the Federation recently detailed in a miniseries of four novels. All because of perhaps the greatest teaser ever, starting in the middle of a catastrophe as the *Enterprise*-D tumbles out of control, venting plasma, unable to eject the warp core...

Scott Pearson

THE MAKING OF STAR TREK: THE NEXT

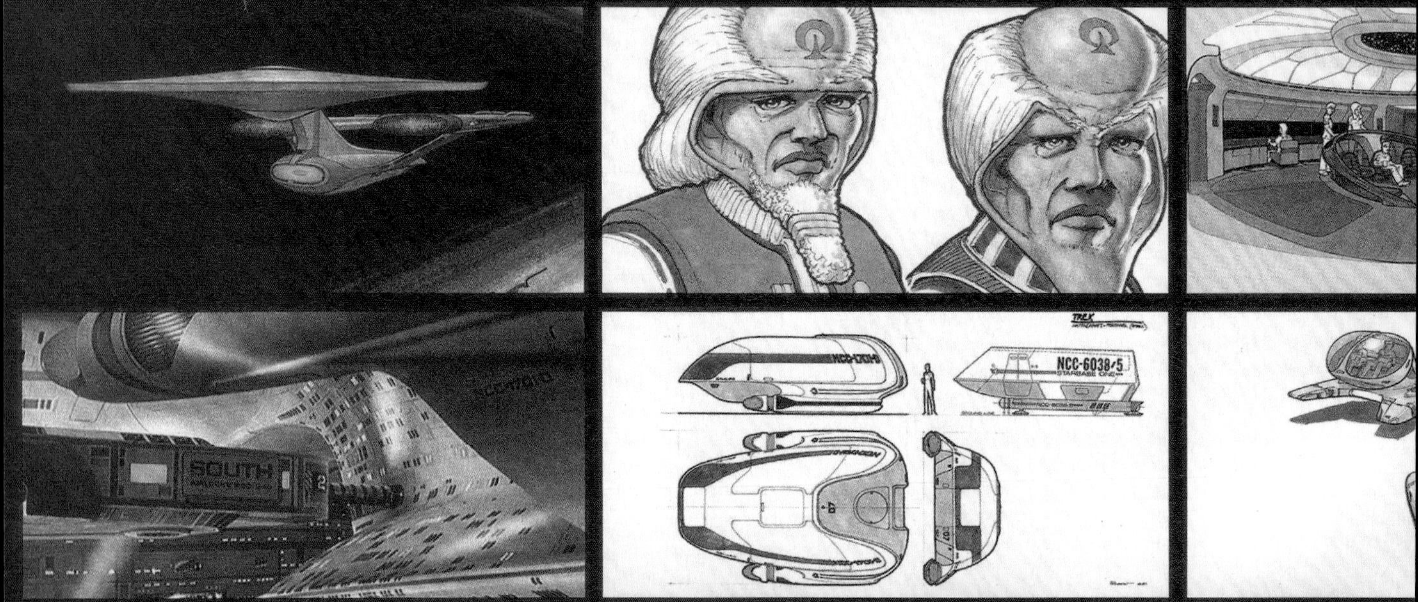

Various early designs for *Star Trek: The Next Generation*, including some that were never used, such as a very different look for the Ferengi (second picture, top) and internal cargo transports

In 1986, *Star Trek's* 20th anniversary year, the franchise was flying high, with *Star Trek IV: The Voyage Home* its biggest hit film yet, and steady ratings for episodes in syndication. Encouraged by the success of its biggest franchise, Paramount decided to launch a new *Star Trek* series. After all four networks turned down the proposal, Paramount committed to produce the new *Star Trek* itself and sell it directly to the hungry syndicated market. Although original syndicated drama was almost unheard of at that time, the risk seemed worthwhile, given the success of *Star Trek*.

Gene Roddenberry had been reduced to executive consultant on the films, but he was a seasoned and successful television producer and was wooed back by Paramount to develop the new series. His development team included *Star Trek* stalwarts Robert Justman, David Gerrold and Eddie Milkis. He also recruited Paramount executive and experienced producer Rick Berman, a complete newcomer to the *Star Trek* universe, after the two met early in the development process and struck up an instant friendship.

Rather than rehashing the original, Roddenberry insisted that everything and everyone had to be new – the time, the characters and especially the aliens. Luckily for Michael Dorn, Justman convinced Roddenberry that the *U.S.S. Enterprise* NCC 1701-D needed a Klingon officer to show that the Federation had progressed enough to embrace a former enemy race. Justman also persuaded Roddenberry (who wanted a French actor) that Patrick Stewart was the ideal man to play the new Captain. With the rest of the cast in place, production began in June, 1987.

The 90-minute pilot script, *Encounter at Farpoint*, written by *Star Trek* veteran D.C. Fontana, told the story of Farpoint Station; when Paramount decided to expand the pilot to two hours, Roddenberry added the alien trial which introduced *ST:TNG*'s favourite adversary, Q. With syndicated broadcast due to begin in September 1987, the series went directly into regular production.

ST:TNG's first year was a rough shakedown cruise in the writers' room, as the writers struggled to find the series' voice and establish a core team. The outcome was trouble, especially with the female characters, who remained so underused that Denise Crosby asked to be released from her contract, leading to Tasha's memorable demise, and Gates McFadden's contract was not renewed for the second season, though she returned in the third. Fortunately, the show's production team and the cast were solid enough to keep the ship on course, and

GENERATION

(third picture bottom).

from its first season, *ST:TNG* won wide critical recognition and a hefty audience to keep it on the air.

Many of the staff changes in those first seasons were a passing of the torch, as professionals from the original series helped launch *ST:TNG*, then moved on and were replaced by *Star Trek* newcomers who in turn became the "old guard" of the new incarnations: Michael Piller, Jeri Taylor, Ron Moore, Robert Blackman, Michael Okuda, Brannon Braga, Michael Westmore, Dan Curry and many, many others. Most important, before Gene Roddenberry passed away in 1991, his successor was already at the helm as the new Captain of the *Star Trek* franchise – Rick Berman.

Long before *ST:TNG* wrapped in the spring of 1994, it was clear to everyone that *Star Trek* would continue, with spin-off series *Star Trek: Deep Space Nine* going into a third season, and *Star Trek: Voyager* preparing for its maiden flight. But there was also no question of ending the story of the *U.S.S. Enterprise* NCC 1701-D and its crew. Production had already begun on *Star Trek Generations*, the first *Star Trek* movie that would feature members of the *ST:TNG* cast, alongside members of the original cast. Another passing of the torch was under way. ■

AWARDS AND HONOURS

Star Trek: The Next Generation *won enough to fill a shuttlecraft!*

- **Emmy Awards, Academy of Television Arts and Sciences**
  Over seven seasons, *ST:TNG*'s creative team won 17 Emmy Awards, for Sound Mixing, Sound Editing, Visual Effects, Costume Design, Hair Styling, Make-Up, Special Visual Effects and Art Direction. The series also earned 40 additional nominations, including Best Dramatic Series in its final year.

- **Hugo Awards**
  1993 Best Dramatic Presentation, *The Inner Light*

- **Saturn Awards, Academy of Science Fiction, Fantasy and Horror Films**
  - 1990 and 1991 Best Genre Television Series
  - 2003, Best DVD TV Programming Release, (for seasons one to seven)
  - 2005, Special Recognition to the *Star Trek* TV Series, 1987-2005 (with *ST:DS9*, *ST:VOY* and *Star Trek: Enterprise*)

- **ASCAP Film and Television Music Awards**
  1995, Jay Chattaway, Top TV Series; Dennis McCarthy, Top TV Series

- **CAS Awards, Cinema Audio Society**
  1994, Outstanding Achievement in Sound Mixing for a Television Series, *Descent, Part I*

- **Peabody Awards**
  1988, *The Big Good-Bye*

- **Young Artist Awards**
  1989, Best Syndicated Family Drama or Comedy Series; Best Young Actor in a Family Syndicated Show, Wil Wheaton.

The Inner Light

Q'S TIPS

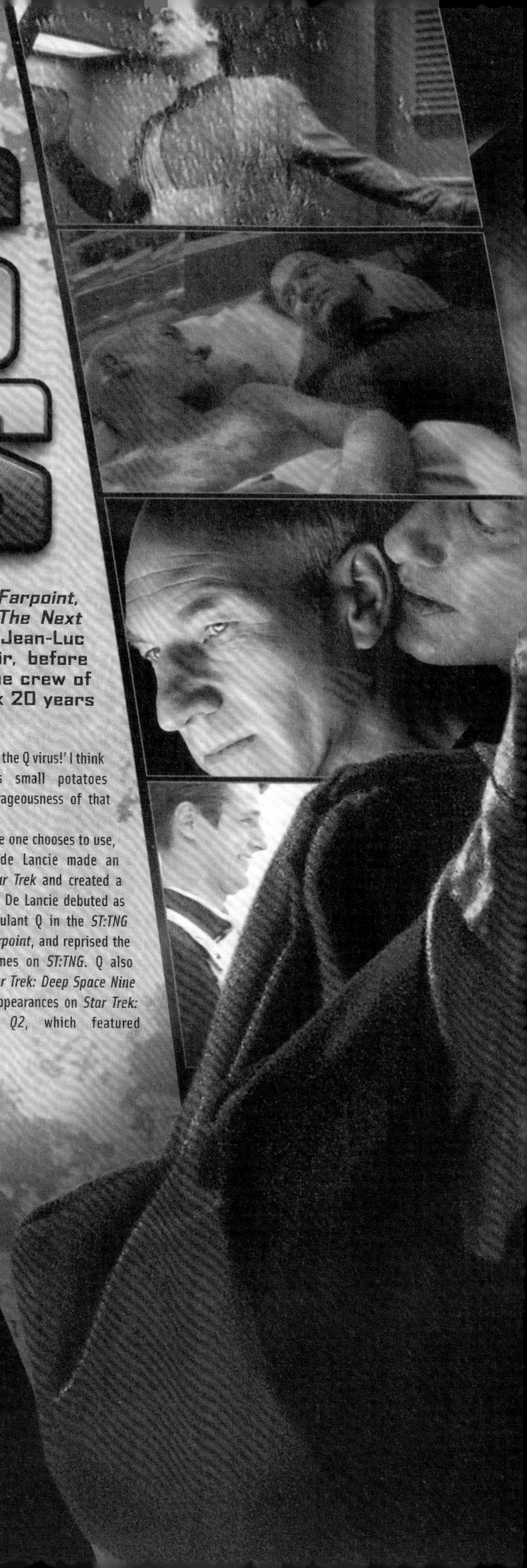

Right from the very first scenes of *Encounter at Farpoint*, John de Lancie made his mark on *Star Trek: The Next Generation*, and would go on to plague Captain Jean-Luc Picard throughout *ST:TNG*'s seven years on air, before turning his attentions to *Deep Space Nine* and the crew of the *Starship Voyager*. Ian Spelling takes him back 20 years to the start of a legend...

John de Lancie has heard and seen it all when it comes to the devotion of *Star Trek* fans. So you'll have to forgive him if he's fairly nonplussed about the fact that the judge's costume Q wore in the *Star Trek: The Next Generation* finale *All Good Things...* elicited a top bid of $10,800 (USD) – or $10,150 above the highest advance estimate – during the '40 Years of *Star Trek*' auction at Christie's in New York City last year. "It pales in comparison to the story about the guy who ran up on the stage after I'd made an appearance at a *Star Trek* convention and grabbed the glass of water I'd been drinking," de Lancie recalls, laughing as the memory comes back to him. "I walked off the stage. He grabbed the water – and I'd had a cold – and he downed it and said, 'I now have the Q virus!' I think selling costumes is small potatoes compared to the outrageousness of that particular act."

Whatever example one chooses to use, there's no denying de Lancie made an indelible mark on *Star Trek* and created a magnificent character. De Lancie debuted as the powerful and petulant Q in the *ST:TNG* pilot, *Encounter at Farpoint*, and reprised the role several more times on *ST:TNG*. Q also turned up once on *Star Trek: Deep Space Nine* and made a trio of appearances on *Star Trek: Voyager*, including *Q2*, which featured

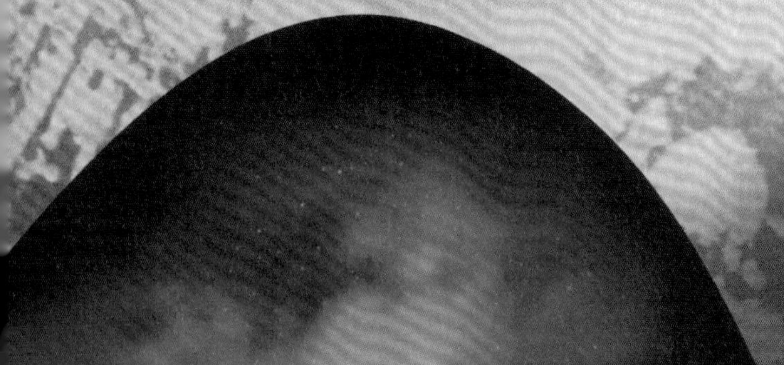

Pictures left: *Deja Q; Tapestry; Q Who; Tapestry*
Pictures right: *Q-Pid; Hide and Q; Encounter at Farpoint*

Pictures right: Q as he appeared in the *ST:TNG* comics; *Encounter at Farpoint; Deja Q; Deja Q; Deja Q; Deja Q; Q Who; Encounter at Farpoint*

de Lancie's son Keegan as Q2. The actor also provided the voice of Q in several *Star Trek* games and in two audio dramas released by Alien Voices, a company formed by de Lancie and Leonard Nimoy.

De Lancie was a busy character actor before landing the role of Q, working regularly on television, in theater and in feature films, and he's as ubiquitous as ever now. In fact, when *Star Trek Magazine* caught up with de Lancie to talk about his time as Q and *ST:TNG*'s 20th anniversary, he was riding on a tour bus with several other actors – including Ed Asner and fellow *ST:TNG* guest stars Jerry Hardin, Harry Groener and Marnie Mosiman, the last of whom is de Lancie's wife – on their way to a performance of the play *The Great Tennessee Monkey Trial* in Williamstown, Massachusetts.

"You knew that you were doing something iconic and special," recalls de Lancie of his first day on the *ST:TNG* set. "I do remember being a little horrified that the cherry picker they used to have me come into the scene moved so much. It was not one of those really clean moves they can make now or that I made in the seventh year when I zoomed in again [in *All Good Things...*]. The cherry picker was bobbing and weaving

"I WAS PARTICULARLY PLEASED WITH *ALL GOOD THINGS...* EACH SCENE WAS WRITTEN IN SUCH A WAY AND I THINK ACTED IN SUCH A WAY THAT YOU GOT A REALLY CLEAN, DEFINED, DELINEATED FACET OF THE CHARACTER..."

a little bit and I just thought, 'Oh dear, it's a little cheesy.' But I also had a sense that this was a special event and was certainly more than what you'd feel on a normal pilot."

De Lancie also discovered, during the pilot shoot, that he'd be back as Q. However, matters didn't pan out quite as he'd envisioned. "Gene Roddenberry came up to me and said, 'We're going to have you back,'" the actor says. "And then my agent got a sort of letter of intent stating that they wanted me back six or eight times, as I recall, in the first season. Then Gene, during the second show, said, 'You know what? We're not going to be able to do that. We feel that if we do that the character is flamboyant enough that the audience is going to wind up waiting for those episodes. So we're probably going to do this once a year.' I was not in a position to be happy or sad or anything about it. It just was what it was.

"Because it was just once a year it was a little bit like having to... not quite start at square one, but it was always a little bit of a jump-start," he continues. "I was always happy when the scripts were of a more philosophical nature because I thought the character could handle big philosophical issues. And, in point of fact, I think the scripts that were that way were the most successful. I was the least happy when they were of a mundane subject. I looked forward to doing the episodes. They would call and say, 'We have something.' As usual you didn't get it until five or six days beforehand and even then you weren't sure that that's what you were really going to have to learn or not. It was a television show. We're not talking about scripts that were honed over months or a year's time. So it was always a little bit by the seat of the pants, which suited the playing style, frankly. So that was nice."

All of de Lancie's performances as Q can be found on the Q-centric DVD set, *Star Trek: Q Fan Collective*. When it comes to picking favorites, de Lancie's choices echo those of the *Star Trek* fan base. "I was particularly pleased with *All Good Things...*" he notes. "I didn't have a great deal to do, but each scene was written in such a way and I think acted in such a way that you got a really clean, defined, delineated facet of the character, and so I thought that was a very good episode. When we were shooting the finale you had a sense that, by that point, this had been a successful and important run. And to be a part of it, even in a small way, was grand fun. I also thought *Tapestry* was a very good episode. I know a lot of the fans think that's actually the best episode of the whole show. And I thought *Death Wish*, the *Voyager* episode about suicide, was a very good episode. It was very well done. Those are all good episodes. Whether or not Q was in love [in *ST:TNG*'s *Q-Pid* and *ST:DS9*'s *Q-Less*], that was not what the character was really about. It just took us down a path that was really a sort of dead end."

De Lancie last portrayed Q in *Q2*. Despite a push from the Q faithful, de Lancie was not called upon to reprise the character on *Enterprise* or in a *ST:TNG* feature film. The actor hesitates for a moment when asked what, if anything, he never got to play as Q. "You know, God, if you'd asked me that 10 years ago I might have had something in mind," de Lancie explains. "But I really don't have anything in mind about it anymore. The other thing is that when you are a recurring actor, almost from a protective point of view, you shoot the episode and then you quite literally work to get it out of your mind because more often than not, in most instances, that episode you've just done will be your last episode. So to hang on to, 'Oh, the next time I'll do this...' and stuff like that is a little delusional. I have played in a lot of shows over the years and

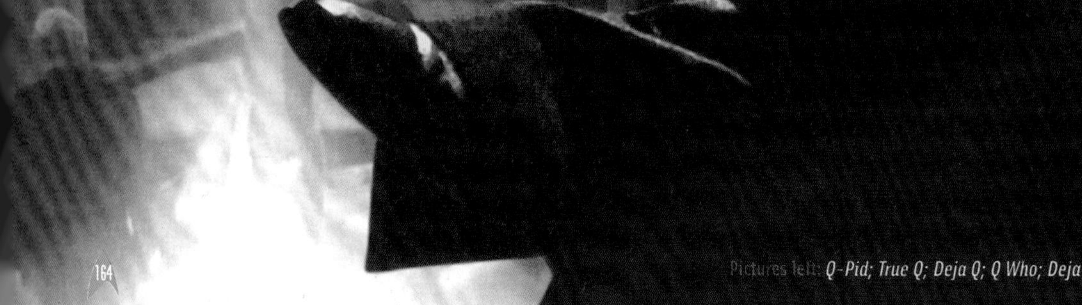

usually when I walk off the set at the end of the shooting session that's it. By a couple of days later it's out of my system and I honestly don't think about it."

For all that, Q refuses to go gently into the night. De Lancie is comfortable with the notion he'll be forever referred to as "John de Lancie, best known as Q from *Star Trek*..." Fans still recognize him on the street. He remains a favorite at *Star Trek* and sci-fi conventions worldwide. His popularity in genre circles led, directly and indirectly, to gigs in other sci-fi series, including a regular role on *Legend* (created by the late Michael Piller) and a recurring part on *Stargate SG-1*. He even co-wrote a Q novel with Peter David. And let's not forget the $10,800 someone forked over for that old Q costume. "It is probably the biggest tomato that has stuck on the wall," de Lancie says. "I was at Harvard last night, performing at the Kennedy School, and the Dean came up to me and said, 'I loved the Scopes trial show you just did,' and then he launched into Q. You just never know where it's going to come up, and it comes up all the time. Q was obviously a character that made a big impression on a lot of people. I am not in any way upset about it. It's great. I think every actor should be so lucky. Not only has it not kept from doing other things, but it's probably been one of the reasons why I've gotten to do many of the things I have done. So I'm delighted. Would I have enjoyed playing him more? Sure, but I don't know if the effect would have been that much more anyway. Would it have been that much better or different if I'd played him 19 times? I don't know. My instinct tells me it probably wouldn't have been. The effect on the public, on the fans, would not have been twice as much."

De Lancie has kept tremendously active in his post-*Star Trek* years. Since 2001, in addition to his genre TV turns, he's guest starred in everything from *The Closer* to *Without a Trace*, and featured in this year's Adam Sandler movie *Reign Over Me*. He returns to the theater whenever possible and often serves as the narrator at major orchestra performances. In 2006, he ventured into opera, directing the Atlanta Opera in *Tosca*. "I really have been lucky to always be working," de Lancie says. "The show I'm doing now, *The Great Tennessee Monkey Trial*, is basically a radio play about the Tennessee v. John Scopes Monkey Trial from 1925. However, we're using the actual transcript. So it's not *Inherit the Wind*. It is the actual trial transcript. It's very successful and very dramatic. We did it last year on the west coast and east coast, and we're doing it again now. Just before this show I finished a play called *Life Is a Dream*, a Pedro Calderon de la Barca play which was translated by Nilo Cruz, who won the Pulitzer Prize. So there was a lot of heat around that. I have another opera, *Cold Sassy Tree*, that I'm going to direct. I'll be doing *Peer Gynt* in Cleveland in the fall. I've also done a couple of independent movies [including *Teenius* and *You*]. I have done a lot of those, at least 10, and you just never know what's going to happen because it's such an uphill climb to get any of these smaller films released."

The conversation closes with de Lancie contemplating how differently his career has evolved from what he hoped or anticipated after he'd graduated from Kent State University and studied at the Juilliard School of Drama. His expectations when he started were that he'd perform Shakespeare – and only Shakespeare – in theaters across America. "Well, I did more Shakespeare in high school than I did as a professional," de Lancie says, laughing. "The theater scene is such that, while it's a nice place to have a gymnastic time stretching as an actor, it's not enough to sustain you financially. So much of what I've been doing is stuff I never thought of doing. That's why I feel I need to keep my hand in a pretty artsy-fartsy scene, because that's more of what I thought I was going to be doing. While I'm happy to do film and television, I think it's equally important to do all the theater and music work."

Pictures left: *Q-Pid; True Q; Deja Q; Q Who; Deja Q*

THE ME
OF A

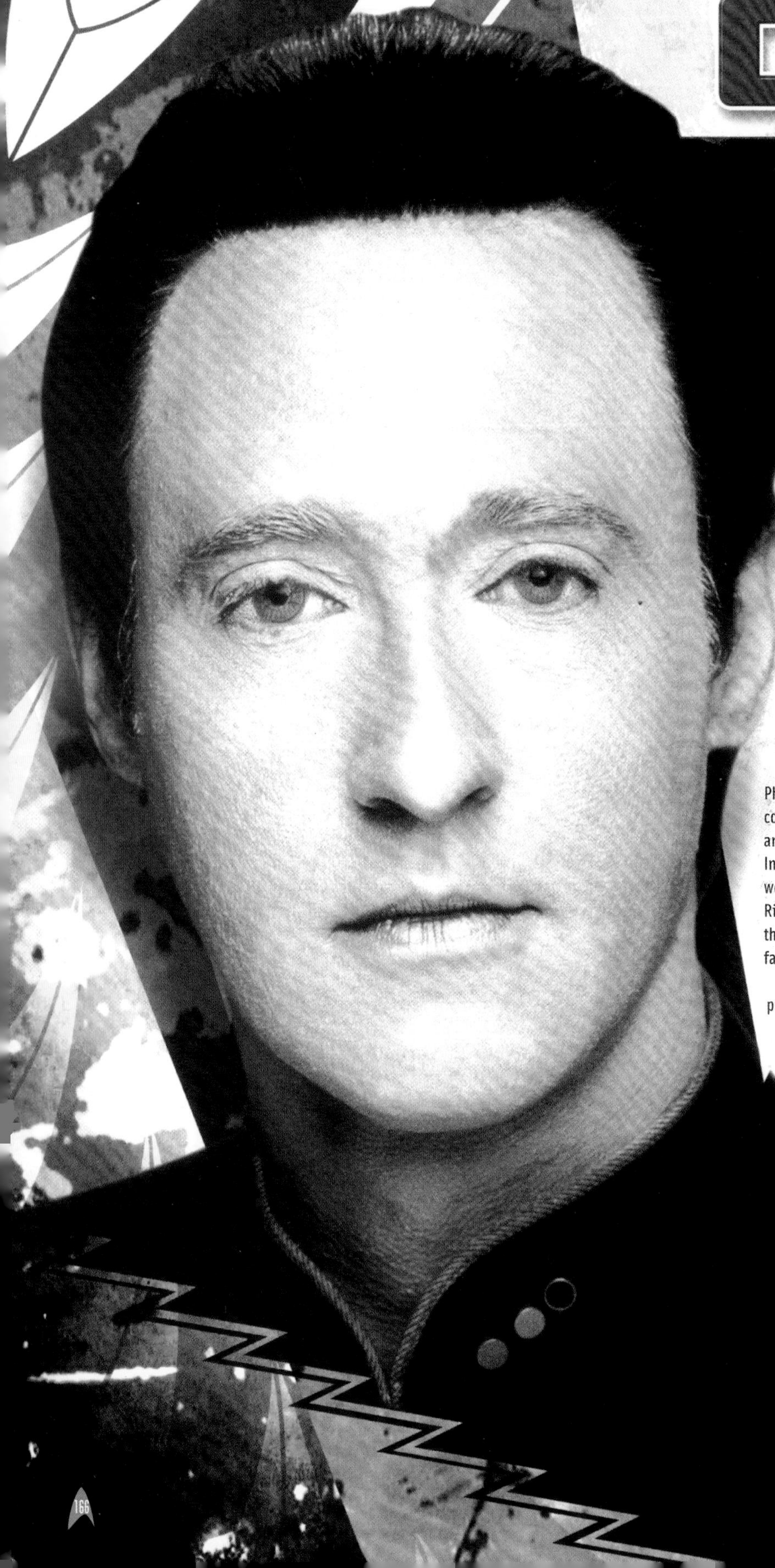

SYNOPSIS

When the *U.S.S. Enterprise* arrives at the newly established Starbase 173, Data is ordered to serve under Captain Bruce Maddox, who wishes to disassemble and study him so that more androids can be made for Starfleet's use. But after Data learns that Maddox may not be able to reassemble him, he refuses to submit to the procedure. When Captain Picard is unable to have the orders changed, Data's only option is to resign from Starfleet. His decision to resign, however, is challenged by Maddox on the basis that Data is not a person with rights, but property of the Federation.

The J.A.G. (Judge Advocate General) officer of the starbase, Phillipa Louvois, an old acquaintance of Picard, rules that Maddox's contention is supported by a 21st Century precedent. Picard announces that he will challenge that ruling at a hearing. Insufficiently staffed, Phillipa explains that as senior officer, Picard would have to defend Data, while the next most senior officer, Riker, would have to prosecute. A stickler for the law, Phillipa warns that if Riker does not give his best effort, she will summarily rule in favor of Maddox.

Faced with no other choice, Riker must contend in his prosecution that Data is simply a machine – the creation of man – and dramatically emphasizes his point by approaching Data from behind and switching him off, leaving him lifeless in his seat.

Certain of his defeat, Picard has a discussion with Guinan and she suggests that the Federation's desire to create and own a race of disposable androids is the recreation of slavery.

Making an impassioned plea for Data's freedom, Picard declares that in a sense, all beings are created but that does not necessarily make them the property of their creator. Phillipa agrees with him, asserting that Data may be a machine, but he is owned by no one and has the right to make his own decisions regarding his life.

Synopsis courtesy of startrek.com

ASURE MAN

PERSONAL LOG

COMMANDER BRUCE MADDOX: STARDATE 42522.9

The *Enterprise* will soon make her scheduled port call here at Starbase 173. Not an occurrence out of the ordinary in and of itself, even for Starfleet's flagship, but onboard that ship is one of the most remarkable achievements of mankind – Soong's android, known as Data – the object of my study and fascination throughout my entire career.

It's been almost 25 years since I first encountered it as it attempted to enter Starfleet Academy. At the time I was certain this action was likely in response to some sort of loyalty subroutine, as it was Starfleet personnel who discovered and activated it on Omicron Theta. Still, its request was reviewed as with any other applicant by Academy officials, but on that occasion they invited me to weigh in on the matter based on my experience in cybernetics. Data's performance was impressive, particularly in its incredible approximations of even the subtlest of human behaviors, but I voted to decline its admission. For all of its programmed mimicry, the android Data is just that – a device, really, an artificial construct merely designed to appear human. At that time, the notion of putting it through Academy courses seemed ludicrous, like recruiting and training a fractal algorithm or a navigational deflector. Mine was the only dissenting vote that day, and I must admit that – had my lead been followed – I may not be poised as I am to potentially change the course of Starfleet forever.

Since that first meeting, Data's complexity – its intricacy of design and suprahuman abilities – has always captivated me. In many ways, its successful implementation in Starfleet, right down to its being recognized with a number of commendations and honors, has inspired me in my own career, leading me to the Daystrom Institute and the associate chair in robotics I now hold. I've devoted a great deal of time to study and experimentation toward replicating Dr. Soong's creation in ways that will serve *all* of the Federation.

Despite my best efforts, several barriers stand between me and success, and the only way to clear them is to examine Data firsthand. Once I deconstruct and analyze it, and fully understand Soong's work, I'm sure I can replicate it and begin the construction of androids the like of which we've never seen. We're not far from a time when such devices will be standard equipment on Starfleet vessels, facilitating research in conditions dangerous to organic life and assisting in unimaginable breakthroughs in scientific discovery. The possibilities stagger me, and I'm dedicated to making this dream a reality.

I can't help thinking that Data's arrival, here and now, would seem to be a fortuitous sign of my eventual success, and the ultimate creation of Soong-type androids for every ship in the fleet.

It's an important day, indeed.

COUNTER MEASURES

VETERAN DIRECTOR ROBERT SCHEERER WAS VERY LUCKY WITH HIS FIRST SCRIPT ON *STAR TREK: THE NEXT GENERATION* – MELINDA SNODGRASS' COURTROOM DRAMA, *THE MEASURE OF A MAN*. HE TOLD LARRY NEMECEK ABOUT THE PROBLEMS HE FACED...

For director Robert Scheerer, now four years into retirement, it's easy for the recollections of projects over the years to blur together. But mention *The Measure of a Man,* and the memories are as fresh as ever. By the luck of the draw, it was his first foray ever into *Star Trek.*

"A lot of the scripts I got were [only] serviceable," says Scheerer, whose 11 episodes for *Star Trek: The Next Generation* rank him fifth highest among its directors. "But *The Measure of a Man* was one of the ones that was really a thrill to work with."

Still, that very first outing almost sent him packing, thanks to a long scene shot on the first day in the Conference Lounge for guest star Brian Brophy as Commander Maddox.

"He came in and had to do a tough scene right off the bat – a long speech, the captain and crew all around – and he just absolutely couldn't remember his lines," Scheerer says. "And it was disturbing, because it was the first scene of the first day! And it was like, 'Oh my god, we won't get this for a week!'"

In an effort to reduce the pressure on the actor, despite the clock ticking, Scheerer called a five minute break. "I just wanted to give him time to get away from it, and we walked around a little bit and chatted, not a big deal. And finally he came back... but still didn't do it. So I ended up doing it in pieces: I would do up to the point where I *knew* I had to have a cutaway, then I would do the cutaway... and do another piece, and another piece... and do the cutaways after that." However the issue, thankfully, was short-lived: Brophy was fine the next day and for the rest of the shoot, "and he was very good, finally, on the show."

Scheerer fondly mentions guest star Amanda McBroom as a great singer on Broadway, and how he enjoyed setting up an atypical, triangular courtroom for the episode – another scene with special memories. The script has Riker unhappily doing his duty as an attorney for Starfleet's case that Data is property, not a sentient being, by removing the android's arm and revealing his "off" switch.

"That moment had to be reshot, because Frakes had a look of concern on his face when he did it," Scheerer recalls. After seeing the daily film rushes executive producer Rick Berman said, "'No, no, no, no, no! He's got to do it very distant, matter-of-fact!'" The scene was refilmed the next day causing only slight delays: "I screwed up, but I fixed it," Scheerer smiles.

The Santa Barbara native had not really been a fan nor a veteran of science fiction, but he recalls not being concerned by that when he came on board *ST:TNG*. "It never occurred to me to think of that as 'science fiction,' he explains. "They were good people to work with and very professional people. And I was very impressed with their sets – lots of room for tracking shots and big scenes. But it was a little nervous-making because I hadn't done that show, and I wasn't exactly sure how far to go with stuff."

But something went right: Scheerer was asked back for many more. "I did a *DS9* and a couple of *Voyagers*, but the fun for me was *The Next Generation* – that was a good group to work with," he recalls. "The cast was great, and crew used to like me, especially, because I would get 'em out – they could get home to their families!"

Pictures left to right: Director Robert Scheerer; Robert Scheerer directing on set of *The Measure of a Man; The Measure of a Man;* Commander Riker removes Data's arm; *The Measure of a Man;The Measure of a Man*

PERSONAL LOG

COMMANDER WILLIAM T. RIKER: STARDATE 42526.8

It's been three hours since I was ordered by Captain Louvois to act as lead prosecutor in the hearing she's convened, which will determine whether Data is the property of Starfleet or if he's an individual possessing the same basic rights as any other sentient being. Using some arcane piece of law with regards to salvage rights from 300 years ago, Louvois has already issued a preliminary ruling against Data.

Captain Picard has challenged that claim, and is now acting as Data's defense counsel. Louvois' warning to me was clear: anything that makes her think I'm pulling my punches will cause her to issue a summary ruling against Data. It doesn't matter that he's a valued member of this crew, or even that he's become my close personal friend. Duty demands that I put aside all of that and do my best to prove Louvois' original assertion.

The argument Commander Maddox is putting forth is that Data is simply a machine, presumably in the custody of Starfleet since his discovery by a Starfleet away team years ago. As such, he's nothing more than a phaser or a computer console, a tool to be used by other Starfleet officers as they see fit. Officers like Maddox, who wants to take apart Data and see what makes him tick, and who doesn't seem to care that he might not be able to put Data back together once he's finished poking around.

After sitting here in one of the *Enterprise*'s computer labs and poring over Data's technical schematics, it only took me five minutes to find everything I need to prove my case. Strictly speaking, yes, Data *is* a machine. He was designed and built, the same as one might construct a tricorder or even a *Galaxy*-class starship. He even has a power switch! It doesn't get any simpler than that! The evidence is irrefutable, and I'm finding it hard to argue against Louvois, or Maddox, for that matter.

And yet, I know there's something more here. I've seen it with my own eyes.

Since I first met him, I've always known there was something special about Data, an indescribable quality that manifests itself not while he's performing his duties, but instead when he's simply taking in the world around him. Whether it's trying to whistle a tune, tell a joke, paint a picture, even learning to play poker, he never approaches these very human activities with the clinical detachment of a mere machine. If anything, he displays the same sense of wonder and – dare I say it – joy that a child might exhibit. But, does he truly feel that same excitement and joy upon learning new things, or is it simply a programmed response? I can't help thinking of that first time I met him on the holodeck and how I so casually dismissed his desire to be human as the statement of a cybernetic Pinocchio. How wrong was I then? How wrong are we all now? I honestly don't know.

It doesn't really matter what I know or don't know. What matters is what I can prove. I can prove Data's a machine. After that? All I have is my gut, and my friendship, none of which means anything in a courtroom.

All I can do is my best, and hope that Captain Picard's argument is better.

A DATE WITH DATA

BRENT SPINER, ALTER EGO OF *STAR TREK: THE NEXT GENERATION*'S LIEUTENANT COMMANDER DATA, CELEBRATES 40 YEARS OF *STAR TREK* AND REMINISCES ON HIS FORMER LIFE AS AN ANDROID WITH NICK JOY...

Pictures clockwise: *Masks; The Defector; Elementary Dear Data; All Good Things; Encounter at Farpoint; Data; Sarek*

"MUCH AS I HATED WEARING THEM, THERE WAS SOMETHING ABOUT THE YELLOW CONTACT LENSES THAT FLIPPED ME INTO THE GEAR OF PLAYING THAT CHARACTER."

"Your challenge is to come up with something that I haven't already been asked over the last few days," Brent Spiner playfully poses. He's in London at the plush Dorchester Hotel, promoting the franchise's big four zero, and inevitably some reporters have been asking the same old questions. But for someone who has been in the public eye as Data for nearly 20 years, it's hardly surprising that he has heard them all before.

"I don't tire of talking about Data though," he quickly reassures. "I mean, what would be the point? There's nothing I can do about it. This character is going to be with me for the rest of my life, one way or another. I don't feel pigeonholed by the role, and a lot of other things have happened as a result of playing it. Certainly going back to Broadway and doing the lead in a Broadway musical [John Adams in the revival of Founding Fathers musical *1776*] was as a result of the box office value that Data brought."

Spiner is enthusiastic about *Star Trek*'s birthday, but questions the year count. "Is it really 40 years? It feels like 90. Maybe I'm younger than I think! I recall it premiering like any other new show on NBC," the accomplished actor continues, "so September 8, 1966 in itself was no big deal for me. I guess that I really only got into it in the 1970s when I was at college and watched it in the afternoon during daily re-runs. All the guys I knew would come up from school to watch it."

While fans are celebrating the series' anniversary, many people are just as keen to play down the achievement, Spiner reveals. "I find it interesting that the people who don't watch *Star Trek* are always interested in telling you that they don't!" he observes. "I don't understand that. They say 'I hear you've been on *Star Trek*. I have to say that I *never* watched it.' And I say to them, '*Why* are you telling me this? I don't care what you do or don't watch, but why do you feel the need to tell me?'

"It's all about respecting people's choices, and it's a good thing that the anniversary is high profile. It's a way of showing the fans that you respect their choice to watch and support the programs. We're recognizing that their choices are valid and that it's OK to embrace this whole phenomenon."

Star Trek was a little over 20 years old when Spiner landed the role of Data, and he recalls the significance of the appointment. "Was it a big deal because I'd got a role on *Star Trek*? In all honesty, I was more excited because it was going to be regular work and a good job," he confesses. "I was just happy to be employed at that time, and because the show had been pre-sold for a

DATA FILE

"I DON'T TIRE OF TALKING ABOUT DATA. I MEAN, WHAT WOULD BE THE POINT? THERE'S NOTHING I CAN DO ABOUT IT. THIS CHARACTER IS GOING TO BE WITH ME FOR THE REST OF MY LIFE, ONE WAY OR ANOTHER."

Played by Brent Spiner in *Star Trek: The Next Generation* and the subsequent films, the android Data's desire to be more human gained ground during his years aboard the *U.S.S. Enterprise* NCC-1701-D, culminating in the fitting of an "emotion chip" built by his creator, Dr. Noonien Soong, by the time of *Star Trek Generations.*

The android served aboard the *U.S.S. Enterprise* as lieutenant and then later operations officer and second officer. In addition to his well-documented service under Captain Picard's command – including duels with android brother Lore – he also captained the *U.S.S. Sutherland* during the Klingon Civil War.

Transferring to the Sovereign-class *U.S.S. Enterprise* NCC-1701-E in 2372, Data helped Picard defeat the Borg and preserve the timeline. He met his end in 2379, sacrificing himself aboard Reman ship *Scimitar* in order to destroy the Thalaron beam generator and save the crew of *U.S.S. Enterprise.* Before his destruction, Data did however download his entire memory database into android prototype B-4, so perhaps Data lives on in it...

whole season, I knew that I was going to be working solidly for a year. I'd previously only worked in the theatre, where my longest run at that point had been three months. So, steady employment, and getting paid better than anything I'd ever had before, were important considerations to me."

The fact that Spiner took to Data immediately was also a great advantage. "I liked him as soon I'd read the pilot [*Encounter at Farpoint*]," he beams. "My agent sent me the script and said, 'Read it and see if there's a character that appeals to you.' Data appealed to me, so that's what I went after."

While the character had his attractions, there were times that Spiner considered how much easier his life would have been if he'd ended up playing Picard, Riker or La Forge. "Patrick [Stewart] could turn up a quarter of an hour before rehearsals started, but because of the extensive make-up that Data required, I'd have to be there at 4:45 every Monday morning," he recalls. "That start time got later as the week went on because they had to allow us a 12-hour turnaround between finishing the night before and starting again the next day, but Monday was always 4:45. On the positive side, it was very quiet in the make-up trailer with Michael Westmore, who was a great guy to be around at that time of the morning."

Patrick Stewart has boasted that when playing Captain Picard, he could be changed out of his 'spacesuit' and into street clothes in less than 10 minutes. "That's true," Spiner agrees. "The worst part of the make-up for me was the point at the end of a 16-hour day where everybody just changed out of their clothes, washed their faces and left, while I was just trying to get enough of the stuff off my skin so that I could go home and then *really* take it off." Regardless of how much purging he undertook, the make-up seemed to be permanent. "You know, I'm still finding gold make-up even now in places that I really shouldn't," he chuckles. "In the early days I used a product that was kerosene-based because it was the only thing that would cut through the make-up (and presumably a layer of skin). Nowadays I understand that they use something a little... kinder."

In addition to playing Data and twin brother Lore in the season four episode *Brothers*, Spiner also wore extensive prosthetics to play the aged Dr Noonien Soong. "That was a three hour make-up job," he confirms. "Wearing the make-up really helped me to find the voice and mannerisms of the character." In the same manner, Data's make-up design helped Spiner to keep focused on the android. "Much as I hated wearing them, there was something about the yellow contact lenses that flipped me into the gear of playing that character. It was something about not being able to see very well that made it easier to play an android. It wasn't so much that the lenses in themselves limited my peripheral vision, it was how the make-up reacted with them. First of all they applied a regular make-up base, which they powdered over with a thick layer of gold powder. Because powder moves, it would come off my face and go directly into my eyes, smearing the lenses. An hour into the day and I really couldn't see," he winces.

While Spiner came to terms with the demands of the make-up, he freely admits he was less successful in combating the effects of ageing. As time went by, it became increasingly apparent that the actor was getting older, while his character was not meant to age.

"Frankly, the age issue was never a problem when we started. No one could have predicted that we'd go seven years and four movies. I didn't think that the show would go beyond a year," he reveals. "I thought that we were attempting the impossible – trying

Pictures clockwise: *Nemesis; Data's Day; A Fistful of Datas; Brothers;* Data; *Descent* part II; *Datalore*

"I DO FIND IT INTERESTING THAT THE PEOPLE WHO DON'T WATCH STAR TREK ARE ALWAYS INTERESTED IN TELLING YOU THAT THEY DON'T!"

to capture lightning in a bottle for a second time; but somehow it worked."

Time did inevitably catch up with Spiner, and the writers tried to deal with the issue in the show. "They talked about the problem and decided to write it into one of the episodes [*Birthright, Part 1*]. There was a scene with LeVar [Burton] and [Alexander] Siddig – who was guesting on our show from *DS9* – where they discussed a special ageing chip. I guess they thought it through and just dropped the idea," he suggests.

The audience was forgiving, even if time wasn't, and Spiner believes that it wouldn't have been a problem if he'd landed the job while younger. "It would all have been fine if I'd got that job ten years earlier. I was 38 when we first started doing *The Next Generation*, so when I finished the series I was 45. In the last film [*Nemesis*] I was in my early 50s. One really shouldn't be playing a child-like android at that point in your life! If I'd started at 28 I could have played it for 20 years without any noticeable change."

Spiner decided to halt the ageing process when developing the storyline for *Nemesis* with John Logan by taking the ultimate action – and killing Data off. "I'd like to clarify something here," Spiner interjects. "It was my decision, but I didn't *have* to kill Data. We were all pretty much aware that this was going to be our last film and as such thought we'd go for broke.

"We worked on the story with the intention of making it for the fans," Spiner recalls of his approach to what was the final *ST:TNG* movie. "With every *Star Trek* movie prior to that we tried to find a way to bridge the gap between the fans and the general public. Even reading the latest quotes from J.J. Abrams about the next movie, it makes sense for the movie to be as inclusive as possible. With *Nemesis* we said 'Forget that! Let's make

FAST FACTS

a movie for the fans, because that's the people who actually go to see the films.' And what happened? They didn't go! Usually the films opened big, even if they had a lot of competition, but *Nemesis* didn't even do that. This was a message from the fans that they were done with us," he feels, pausing. "It was unexpected."

Debates rage as to whether *Nemesis*' box office was down to poor scheduling, *Star Trek* fatigue, or the fact that it wasn't a great movie. Spiner avoids pointing the finger of blame. "You always make compromises with movies, but I think the final film was pretty close to what I originally imagined. You always overwrite your initial drafts, knowing that they will have to be cut down for pace. *Nemesis* was directed by an editor [Stuart Baird] where pace was his number one concern. A lot of stuff that was cut out of the movie was pretty good, while some of it wasn't. Could a better movie have been made from the material that was shot? Maybe. Maybe not."

If *Nemesis* had been the box office success that Paramount wanted, it seemed likely that a further installment would follow. While Data was killed when Shinzon's ship exploded, his memory had already been transferred to his brother B-4, thus giving Spiner the chance to return to the fold, albeit in a slightly different guise. "We probably would have come back and done another one," Spiner opines. "There was enough of Data within B-4 for Data's spirit to live again through him. Data's memory was now in B-4 and, ultimately, that positronic brain was going to kick in."

To date, there's hasn't been a new *ST:TNG* film. Spiner and John Logan did present a possible treatment for a follow-up, though this was not developed. "John and I had a great story that would bring together all the captains, crews and villains together at the same time. It was the 'Justice League' of *Star Trek*, but Paramount decided it was too expensive a move to make."

Not only was a further *ST:TNG* film put on ice, but *Star Trek: Enterprise* was cancelled after four seasons, thus presenting fans with the prospect of no new *Star Trek* product in active development. Fortunately, a new movie is now being planned. "Neither the cancellation of *Enterprise* nor the announcement of the new film were a surprise to me," Spiner admits. "I think they're right to start a new movie franchise that will hopefully spawn a new series that in turn will spawn new movies. I think it was disappointing that they cancelled *Enterprise*, because I don't think that they [the viewers] ever quite 'got' it. *Enterprise* wasn't doing great numbers and they decided it wasn't cost-effective to keep it on. I disagree with their decision because I think that it was coming into its own in the fourth season. Like the other series that preceded it, it took a while to find its feet. I think they were getting good when they cancelled it. My experience on the show [as Arik Soong in three-part story *Borderland/Cold Station 12/The Augments*] was a really positive one."

Unfortunately, early cancellation was a fate that also befell Spiner's most recent TV show, the Brannon Braga-produced *Threshold*. Aside from that show, Spiner has kept a lower profile than his fans would like. "I'm just looking for my next project," he says. "I might do another CD." In 1991 he recorded *Ol' Yellow Eyes is Back*, a collection of classic songs, supported on some tracks by his *ST:TNG* co-stars. "I'm part-owner of a recording studio in Los Angeles, and one of my partners is a great engineer and producer. I suggested that we do another CD and he said 'Why not. At least we can get studio time cheap!'"

Spiner's most recent role is in teen 'chick flick' *Material Girls*, playing opposite Hilary and Haylie Duff. An opportunity arises to ask Spiner something completely new: who were scarier to act against – the Klingon Duras sisters or the Duff sisters? "Scary?" he chuckles. "I don't think that any of them were scary. The Duffs were really lovely girls and arguably they were only similar to the Duras sisters insofar as none of them had much experience with Planet Earth!"

- Data was the fifth and next-to-last model created by Noonien Soong and his then-wife Juliana on the Omicron Theta science colony.
- Doctor Soong was killed by Lore on Terlina III
- Data was activated on February 2, 2338 after he was found by members of a *U.S.S. Tripoli* away team after the Crystalline Entity had drained the life force from the 411-member colony on Omicron Theta.
- Data's interests include Sir Arthur Conan Doyle's detective Sherlock Holmes; art, theater and playing musical instruments, including the violin, guitar, oboe and flute. He can also dance and play poker and other card games.
- Data weighs 100 kg and carries a concealed master on/off switch centered just below his right shoulder blade.
- Data's body was temporarily hijacked by Dr. Ira Graves, Soong's mentor, who was seeking to cheat death.
- Data's rights as an intelligent being rather than Starfleet property were challenged and determined in his favor in 2365.
- In addition to close friendships with Captain Picard, Tasha Yar and Geordi La Forge, Data had a pet cat called Spot that survived the destruction of the *U.S.S. Enterprise NCC-1701-D*.

Pictures clockwise: *Generations;* Data playing poker; Spot; Juliana Soong; Dr Noonien Soong

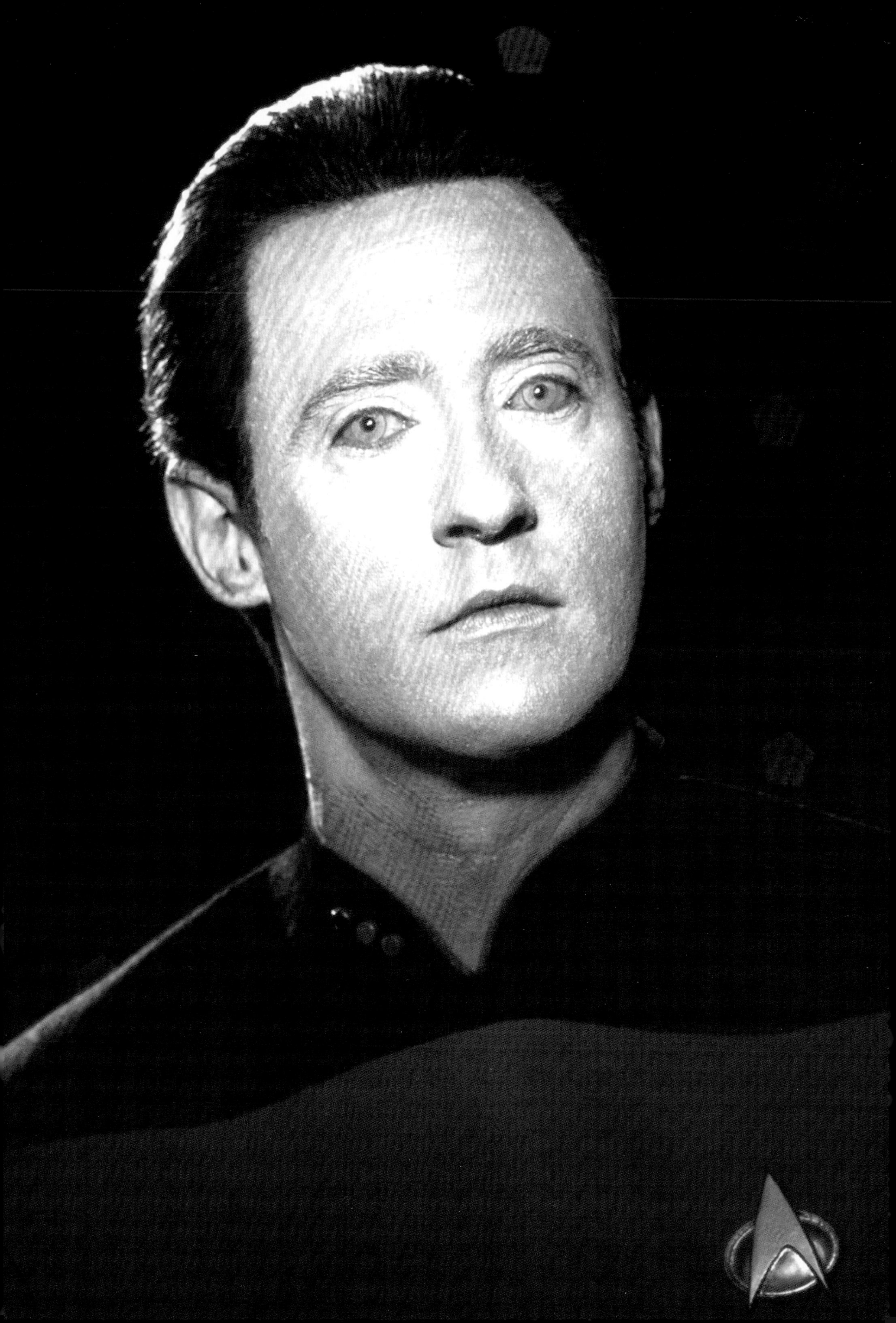

OTHER GREAT TIE-IN COMPANIONS FROM TITAN
ON SALE NOW!

Star Trek: The Movies
ISBN 9781785855924

Fifty Years of Star Trek
ISBN 9781785855931

Star Trek – A Next Generation Companion
ISBN 9781785855948

Star Trek Beyond Souvenir Special
ISBN 9781785860096

Star Trek Discovery Collector's Edition
ISBN 9781785861581

Star Trek Discovery Season One Special
ISBN 9781785861918

Thor Ragnarok Movie Special
ISBN 9781785866371

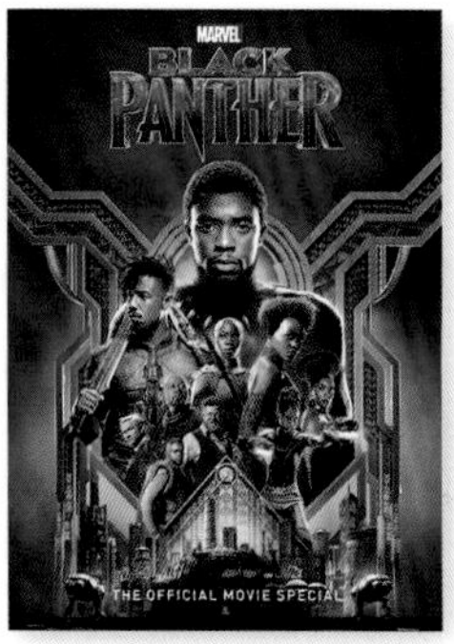

Black Panther Movie Special
ISBN 9781785866531

Ant-Man and the Wasp Movie Special
ISBN 9781785868092

Avengers: Infinity War Movie Special
ISBN 9781785868054

Star Wars: Lords of the Sith
ISBN 9781785851919

Star Wars: Heroes of the Force
ISBN 9781785851926

The Best of Star Wars Insider Volume 1
ISBN 9781785851162

The Best of Star Wars Insider Volume 2
ISBN 9781785851179

The Best of Star Wars Insider Volume 3
ISBN 9781785851896

The Best of Star Wars Insider Volume 4
ISBN 9781785851902

Star Wars: Icons Of The Galaxy
ISBN 9781785851933

Star Wars: The Last Jedi The Official Collector's Edition
ISBN 9781785862113

Star Wars: The Last Jedi The Official Movie Companion
ISBN 9781785863004

Solo: A Star Wars Story The Official Movie Companion
ISBN 9781785863011

TITANCOMICS

For more information visit www.titan-comics.com